Measuring Outcome in the Public Sector

Measuring Outcome in the Public Sector

Edited by
Peter Smith
Reader in Economics, Finance and Accountancy,
University of York

UK Taylor & Francis Ltd, 1 Gunpowder Square, London EC4A 3DE
USA Taylor & Francis Inc., 1900 Frost Road, Suite 101, Bristol, PA 19007

First published 1996

A Catalogue Record for this book is available from the British Library

ISBN 0 7484 0403 1
ISBN 0 7484 0404 X (pbk)

Library of Congress Cataloging-in-Publication Data are available on request

Typeset in 10/12 pt Times
by Solidus (Bristol) Limited

Printed in Great Britain by SRP Ltd., Exeter

Contents

List of Figures and Tables

Preface

Few would deny that the activities of public sector institutions have very profound consequences for individual citizens and for the type of society in which we live. Yet many of those activities are currently undertaken in ignorance of their full, long-term effects. The form – and indeed existence – of many parts of the public sector is more an act of faith than a reasoned response to incontrovertible evidence.

The absence of hard evidence relating to the effects of public sector activity is understandable. Functions are undertaken in the public domain when markets fail. Market failure often occurs when information is poor, or when individuals cannot make informed decisions. The difficulty of identifying and measuring effects is therefore often a reason for an activity being undertaken by the public sector, not a consequence.

There have nevertheless been some notable attempts to remedy the paucity of information on the impact of the public sector, for example, the 'Citizen's Charter' initiative in the United Kingdom, and the 'Service Efforts and Accomplishments' movement in the United States of America. However, the information provided in almost all such performance indicator schemes tends to reflect the activities of the public sector, and not the consequences of those activities.

But, if such performance indicators are supposed to indicate performance, it begs the question: what do we mean by 'performance' in the public sector? In the corporate sector, there is a consensus that performance should ultimately be measured by long-run profits. What, then, is the public sector analogy to the long-run profits sought by the corporate sector? If such an analogy exists, the view of many commentators is that it should be the *outcome* for society of the public sector intervention. In this context, outcome has many dimensions, encompassing the ramifications throughout society of the relevant public sector intervention. It can therefore be interpreted as the value placed by society on the activity. The problem is that, in contrast with the private sector, there is often no consensus as to how such outcome might be evaluated.

In the light of concerns about the vagueness of the notion of outcome, and about how it might be measured, my colleague Alan Williams instigated a series of seminars at the University of York at which researchers at the university described the state of the art relating to outcome in their fields. This book presents the proceedings of that seminar series.

The contributors discuss the notion of outcome in their own area of expertise, and employ a variety of approaches to the topic. However, all were encouraged to take an active part in the entire seminar series, and were therefore aware of the alternative perspectives being pursued. Moreover, in order to give strategic consistency to the project, all contributors were given a framework for analysis, which comprises Chapter 1 of this volume. The hope is therefore that, while reflecting the diversity of research relating to outcome measurement, the various contributions nevertheless offer a coherent approach to the topic. The intention is to offer policy makers, professionals, researchers and other interested parties a view of the state of the art across a wide extent of the public sector, and thereby facilitate progress towards a better understanding of the problems and opportunities associated with outcome measurement.

The book can be considered in four parts:

(a) a conceptual discussion of the notion of outcome (Chapter 1);
(b) outcome in specific programmes (Chapters 2 to 8);
(c) strategic issues relating to outcome (Chapters 9 to 11);
(d) conclusions arising from the book (Chapter 12).

Chapter 1 offers a framework within which a discussion of outcome can be pursued. It first asks three questions which are relevant to any discussion of the topic: what is outcome?; why should it be measured?; and who are the stakeholders who might have an interest in such measurement? The chapter then offers a simple model of the measurement process which suggests that there are three stages involved in any treatment of outcome: first, a measurement stage, in which an attempt is made to capture the relevant notion of outcome; second, an analysis stage, in which the measures are interpreted; and third, an action stage, in which action is taken on the basis of the analysis. The remaining chapters were written within the framework provided by this model.

The next seven chapters describe progress on outcome measurement in some of the most important parts of the public sector. The variety of approaches adopted reflects a historical diversity of research methodologies and preoccupations within the various programmes. The methodologies range from qualitative studies of social security to statistically intricate models of school effectiveness. The preoccupations range from an interest in outcome measurement for the purposes of informing best practice (particularly in health care) to an interest in outcome measurement for the purposes of passing judgment on managerial performance (as, for example, in housing management).

Williams (Chapter 2) describes the state of the art in outcome measurement in health care, research with which he has been intimately associated. In some ways he faces the easiest task in the book, as the prime beneficiaries of a health care system are the patients, a readily identifiable clientele, and there is general agreement that outcome should be measured in terms of changes in the duration and quality of life. However, he shows that outcome in health is nevertheless a remarkably complex concept, and that converting these simple principles into operational measures of effectiveness is surrounded with difficulties.

In contrast, Huby (Chapter 3) examines the concept of outcome in relation to the Social Fund, one of the UK social security instruments, intended to provide lump sums of money for expenses which people living on low incomes cannot be expected to meet from regular social security benefit payments. Here objectives are very far from clear. Indeed there may even be a reluctance on the part of governments to wish to articulate objectives for such programmes. In these circumstances, how can one begin to evaluate outcome? Huby concludes that qualitative issues are always likely to predominate.

Dixon and Suckling (Chapter 4) examine outcome in the university sector. This includes consideration of research, perhaps the most nebulous of all endeavours. How can one evaluate research output when its impact may only become clear in many years' time, and when the complex interactions between distinct research programmes are almost impossible to disentangle?

There has been a long tradition of data collection within the criminal justice system, the topic addressed by Fowles (Chapter 5). This reflects a fairly clear consensus that one of society's ultimate aims is in some sense to minimize criminal activity. However, Fowles discusses the problem of interpreting crime data, in particular the difficulty of identifying to what to attribute variations in crime rates. More fundamentally, he notes that little attention is paid to the quality of justice dispensed by the system, another crucial aspect of outcome.

Nocon and Qureshi (Chapter 6) examine community care, one of the most complex programmes within the modern public sector. What are users, carers and society at large expecting of this massive initiative, which seeks to offer care to those afflicted by problems associated with ageing, mental illness or physical or mental handicap? They note that – in contrast with many other programmes – it may be the *process* of community care that matters most to users, rather than any vague concept of outcome.

Kemp (Chapter 7) examines outcome in the management of social housing. An elaborate system of performance measurement has been put in place in this sector. However, like most performance measurement systems, this considers only issues such as inputs, processes and direct outputs. There has been little effort to establish what might constitute the outcome of housing management, and still less of what might count as a 'good' outcome.

Outcome measurement has reached its most advanced development in the evaluation of schools, discussed by Rico (Chapter 8). There is a readily identified clientele, the pupils; a widely accepted (though admittedly incomplete) indicator of outcome, in the form of examination results; and a well-developed technology for attributing outcome, in the form of multi-level statistical methods. As things stand, the notion of the 'value added' by schools represents the apotheosis of the outcome measurement philosophy.

Having examined the problem of outcome measurement in a variety of sectors, the book then moves on to address some more general issues.

Bradshaw, Bouwknegt and Holmes (Chapter 9) consider one of the most fundamental outcome issues for society as a whole: the prevalence of poverty. They discuss the difficulty of measuring poverty, and construct 12 plausible alternative measures. The coincidence between these measures is then examined, exposing wide variations in the populations identified as 'poor'. This study, then, draws attention to the crucial importance of how an apparently simple concept is converted into an operational measure of outcome.

Much of the impetus behind the new public sector management arises from a conviction that the methods of accounting applied successfully in the corporate sector can be transferred to the public sector. However, Boden and Corden (Chapter 10) show that the analogy between private and public sector is fundamentally compromised by a lack of consensus as to the objectives of the public sector. They therefore commend the approach of 'social audit' as an alternative to conventional accounting techniques, thereby focusing the evaluation on the needs of the various stakeholders. They illustrate the principles with the results of a study of the UK 'family credit' social security payment.

There has for many decades been interest in cross-national comparisons of outcome, and within Europe this interest has been heightened by the growing importance of the European Union. Carr-Hill and Lintott (Chapter 11) summarize progress to date, and document some of the difficulties that will arise in seeking to move towards more comparability between national outcome measurement schemes.

Finally, Chapter 12 draws together some conclusions from the project, and points to the key areas for future work.

The series of seminars on which this book is based was organized by Alan Williams, who is the inspiration behind the project. The seminars were held under the auspices of the Institute for Research in the Social Sciences, an umbrella for the numerous academic departments and research centres in the social sciences at the University of York. Thanks are due to Jonathan Bradshaw, the director, for support. In addition, many of our colleagues attended the seminar series, and we gratefully acknowledge their contributions.

Peter Smith

Chapter 1

A Framework for Analysing the Measurement of Outcome

Peter Smith

1.0 Introduction

The purpose of this chapter is to put forward a framework for evaluating the efficacy of an outcome measurement scheme. After an introduction to the concept of outcome, it discusses the rationale for measuring outcome. It then asks the question: whom is an outcome measurement scheme intended to serve? There follows a description of a simple model of the managerial process underlying the outcome measurement philosophy. It comprises a measurement stage, an analysis stage and an action stage. The chapter concludes with the key issues emerging from the discussion.

1.1 What is Outcome in the Public Sector?

The dictionary definition of outcome is vague. *Chambers* defines it as 'the issue: consequence: result'. Yet in the management of public resources outcome has come to have a very specific connotation, referring to the *impact on society* of a particular public sector activity. The purpose of measuring outcome is then *to assess the valuation placed on the activity*. Of course, how we define 'valuation', and who should be making that judgment, are crucial issues to be discussed at length in the chapters that follow. However, it is important to keep this definition in mind, because once one becomes engulfed in the intricacies of a particular programme it is often easy to lose sight of why outcome measurement is being undertaken.

The reason for this rather specific definition of outcome is the need to distinguish it from the *output* of an activity, which by convention indicates the quantity of the good or service provided, without reference to its broader social impact. Thus, in most circumstances, outputs can be measured without undue difficulty, and there is no shortage of readily available output indicators, such as hospital inpatient episodes per bed or pupils per teacher. However, the measurement of outcome is in principle a different matter entirely, as in principle it entails tracing often intangible ramifications of a programme throughout society. It is a massive move from measuring hospital activity to measuring improvements in the health of the population, or from measuring pupils taught to measuring the intellectual capital produced by schools.

Indeed, it can be argued that – because an assessment of outcome is dependent on the values placed on outputs – it is desirable to distinguish between *output* (which is often reasonably amenable to quantification and objective audit), the *quality* of that output (which may be dependent on individual perceptions) and the *valuation* placed on the output (a matter of individual preference). Such a view implies the existence of an identity of the form:

$$Outcome = Valuation\ (Output \times Quality)$$

That is, outcome is considered as a personal valuation of quality-adjusted output.

In practice, output measures are likely to range from pure measures of process (such as pupils taught), through crude quality-adjusted measures (such as exam success rates), to more refined measures of quality (such as the value added by schools). This latter measure begins to take on the characteristics of an outcome measure. It is therefore a mistake to categorize performance measures as either output or outcome measures. In practice, a continuous spectrum exists between the traditional output measure and the pure outcome measure, and the measures described in later chapters occupy a variety of positions along this spectrum. Most performance measures can be thought of as *intermediate* measures of outcome.

Outcome measurement is closely tied up with the concept of effectiveness: the extent to which an objective of a public sector programme has been met (Tomkins, 1987). The assessment of effectiveness is impossible without satisfactory measures of outcome. Yet, although most public sector auditing bodies pay lip-service to the desirability of addressing effectiveness issues, in practice they have found it difficult to put into practice the principles of outcome measurement. For example, in its own estimation, the Audit Commission for England and Wales has stated that:

> There is still too much concentration in the public sector on inputs and outputs (let alone outcomes), and the Commission has had only modest success in altering that. (Audit Commission, 1991, para 73)

The UK Government sought explicitly to address this problem by requiring the Audit Commission to draw up a list of performance indicators for local government which included measures of effectiveness. Yet when the Commission put its proposals out to consultation, they found that

> ... many [respondents] commented that, in their opinion, the proposals did not adequately address the effectiveness of services in relation to local needs. In particular they perceived a shortage of measures of quality. There was not, however, agreement on how to remedy the defect. (Audit Commission, 1993, p. 6)

This discomfort over the issues of outcome measurement and effectiveness is a common theme in public sector value-for-money audit, and an important purpose of the following chapters is to illustrate why such difficulties arise, and to suggest how they can be overcome.

The growth in interest in outcome measurement is an international phenomenon (Fédération des Experts Comptables Européens, 1991; Harris, 1995). In the United Kingdom it is reflected in the Government's 'Citizen's Charter', which seeks as one of its central objectives to improve the quality of public services. To this end, it has introduced a range of mechanisms which include the increased publication of performance data, and the introduction of incentives for public sector organizations to achieve performance targets (UK Government, 1991). Underlying the Charter is the belief that it is possible to measure outcome in the public sector, and to improve the quality of public services by publishing such measures. The Second Report of the initiative illustrates the extent of its influence over the UK public sector, with 38 Charters for individual services, and hundreds of measures of performance published routinely (UK Government, 1994).

1.2 Why Measure Outcome?

It is not immediately obvious why we should seek to measure outcome. Indeed, for a private good, produced in a competitive market, the question of measuring outcome rarely arises. If one assumes that all the benefits (and costs) of a product accrue to the consumer, then one might assume that the consumer's willingness to pay for the product is a fair indication of the minimum valuation he or she places on it. Thus, because the benefits of the good are entirely private, it is often assumed that a market transaction (the purchase of the good) offers an adequate indication of its impact on society. The major exception to this principle occurs when production or consumption of the good imposes an externality, such as pollution, on some third party. There may then be a need to measure the magnitude of such outcomes, in order to understand the extent to which benefits accruing to consumers are at the expense of other parts of society. The analysis of such environmental impacts has much in common with the measurement of public sector outcome.

A consequence of the market mechanism is that – if a producer fails to produce a product that is useful to society at a price that consumers are willing to pay – then the producer's business will become unviable and production will cease. The threat of bankruptcy is presumed to offer a very tangible sanction against private companies operating in competitive markets. Therefore such a market is said to result in two socially desirable consequences. First, the market provides only goods that are useful to society, at a price consumers are willing to pay. This is allocative efficiency. And second, producers will be forced to maximize the competence with which they convert inputs into those goods. This is managerial (or technical) efficiency.

Almost by definition, however, there is in the public sector no market within which users and other interested parties can express their preferences – indeed, in the case of public goods, such as the police service, it is often difficult to identify who the users are. As a result, the governments who organize public sector services face a difficulty in deciding the size and nature of the public sector. In the absence of markets, the main sources of information about society's preferences are various aspects of the political process, such as elections and lobbying, which are often crude and misleading. Securing allocative efficiency in the public sector is therefore extremely complex. Furthermore, there are no automatic sanctions against providers of services in the public sector analogous to the bankruptcy threat of the corporate sector. As a result, there is no guarantee that services will be provided with maximum managerial efficiency.

The rationale for the Citizen's Charter embodies this view:

> In a free market, competing firms must strive to satisfy their customers, or they will not prosper. Where choice and competition are limited, consumers cannot as easily or effectively make their view count. In many public services, therefore, we need to increase both choice and competition where we can; but we also need to develop other ways of ensuring good standards of service. (UK Government, 1991, p. 4)

The reason for requiring outcome valuations is that public sector policy makers feel the need to exercise *control* over the services for which they are responsible (Anthony and Young, 1984). In particular, they need to make judgments about the past performance of public sector programmes, and about future resource allocation. Thus, in helping to secure control, outcome measurement has both a retrospective and a prospective role.

In its retrospective role, outcome measurement can be used to determine whether the expected benefits of a public sector programme have materialized. This analysis may focus on the quality of a management team. For example, using techniques ranging from the crude (such as 'league tables' of examination results) to the intricate (for example, multilevel modelling techniques) it may become possible to compare the relative performance of schools working towards common goals (Gray *et al.*, 1990). Or the focus may be on the merits of different methods of delivering services. For example, controlled experimentation may offer insights into the social consequences of heart transplantation compared with other forms of managing heart disease (Buxton *et al.*, 1985).

In such circumstances, the economic principles of cost effectiveness and cost–benefit analysis are often valuable (Sugden and Williams, 1978).

In its prospective role, outcome measurement is used to guide public sector resource allocation decisions. The retrospective analysis yields evidence on good practice – whether by competing management teams or alternative modes of service delivery. This evidence can form the basis for setting management teams targets for the future, perhaps by encouraging them to adopt 'best practice'. Or it may help policy makers decide whether a programme is worth implementing, and – if so – which is the best way of delivering the programme.

1.3 Who are the Stakeholders?

The assessment of effectiveness requires the specification of objectives against which outcome can be measured. This begs the question: whose objectives? Depending on the type of public sector programme under consideration, a variety of groups of people have a legitimate interest in its activities. We term these people stakeholders.

The enterprise under examination should be accountable to its stakeholders, and to a greater or lesser extent should take cognisance of their objectives. The need for accountability arises when some principal (such as, say, a parent) delegates authority to some agent (a teacher, say) to undertake a task on their behalf. The notion of accountability has often been found to be elusive, but is generally held to encompass two fundamental principles: first, that the agents should give an account of activities to the principals; and second, that the principals should be able to hold the agents to account if performance is out of line with expectations (Stewart, 1984).

In the corporate sector, it can be argued that there is usually little question as to whose interests should be served by the firm: namely, the firm's owners, and its customers. The owners, or shareholders, require that an adequate return is made on their capital, and if this is not the case they have available the immediate and important sanction of selling their shares. It is noteworthy that – because of their ability to pass judgment on the management of the firm at any time – the shareholders have a powerful incentive to subject the firm's performance to careful scrutiny, or to hire an intermediary to do so on their behalf. The firm's customers are readily identifiable by their willingness to purchase the firm's products, and in competitive markets they have the obvious sanction of taking their custom elsewhere. It must be presumed that the outcome of the firm's efforts is reflected in customer satisfaction.

This argument ignores the difficulties that arise when there are externalities associated with the firm's product, or when the product market is not competitive (perhaps because the firm is a natural monopoly). It also sidesteps the important issue of the wider social responsibility of firms to their employees and society at large, an issue which requires an examination of the outcome of corporate behaviour beyond the narrow purview of shareholders and customers. However, this crude characterization of a firm's stakeholders does explain why the pattern of accountability in the corporate sector is relatively simple.

The notion of accountability in the public sector is far more complex. Indeed, it can be argued that many of the services we shall be considering in later chapters are found in the public sector precisely because for one reason or another they cannot be forced into the narrow straitjacket of accountability adopted in the corporate sector. Thus, for example, police forces are funded by national and local taxpayers. Those taxpayers (whether individuals or corporations) therefore have a legitimate interest in police activity, as do national and local politicians. The 'users' of the police are moreover difficult to identify. They include in different ways victims of crime, potential victims, criminals and suspects, the general public, and society at large. In some way, policy makers in police forces have to reconcile often conflicting pressures from these various constituencies.

It is of course possible to extend the list of stakeholders indefinitely, and it is important to bear in mind that there will often be a variety of views within any one group. Given below are some of the more important groups of stakeholders to be considered in most public sector programmes:

- users (or potential users);
- taxpayers;
- central government;
- local government;
- other statutory organizations;
- employees;
- the general public;
- representatives acting on behalf of the above.

Each of these groups will, to a greater or lesser extent, feel that those services should be accountable to them. The role of outcome measurement is to enable the managers of the services to render an account of their activities to those stakeholders. However, the precise pattern of accountability that exists for a particular service will depend heavily on the structure of the organization seeking to deliver the service (Carter, 1991). This is discussed further below.

It is worth noting that the Citizen's Charter initiative takes a very limited view of stakeholders in the public sector. Thus, John Major claims that 'public services are there for only one reason – to serve the user' (UK Government, 1994, foreword). And the Updated Parent's Charter lists only parents, guardians, grandparents, aunts, uncles and employers as having an interest in children's education (Department for Education, 1994). As the following chapters make clear, this simplistic 'consumer' view of public services is often inadequate.

Finally, in considering the multiplicity of stakeholders, it should be noted that the means whereby they are able to hold managers to account (the second component of accountability) are diverse, and often very crude. For example, users and individual taxpayers may be able to vote for representatives whom they feel will secure outcomes nearest to their own preferences. Other parties, such as corporations or voluntary organizations, may use less formal means. In total, the pressures operating on managers can be thought of as a political process, which is messy, poorly understood, and open to manipulation. Measures of outcome will be used in a variety of ways to inform that process, and not necessarily in the way which the designers of a scheme had in mind (Carter *et al.*, 1992).

Thus, in seeking to implement any outcome measurement scheme, it is imperative to recognize that outcome measurement can never be 'objective', and must always be with regard to some group of stakeholders. That being the case, it is important to make explicit who those stakeholders are, and to acknowledge that the interests of other stakeholders probably cannot be pursued within the context of a single outcome measurement scheme.

1.4 A Simple Model of Outcome Measurement

This section sets out a simple model to explain how outcome measurement is intended to help policy makers secure control of public sector resources. How that control is exercised depends on the structure of the organization being examined. In a bureaucracy such as the UK National Health Service, the main concern is with internal or *managerial* control. In such organizations, the central management wishes to control the periphery, and outcome measures can be used as an instrument for control. For example, in the maternity services, the Chief Executive of the NHS has made it clear that local health authorities that secure unsatisfactory perinatal mortality rates will be given 'a hard time', a threat that illustrates the direct bureaucratic control he exerts over the organization (Committee of Public Accounts, 1990, para. 3206).

An alternative mode of control is *political* control. Here the outcome measures are used to inform persons external to the organization about its performance. Those outsiders may, for example, be electors or their representatives, with the less direct sanctions of votes and political pressure. Of course, if it is effective, the external pressure placed on the organization will have ramifications for its internal management.

A third mode of control of rapidly increasing importance is *contractual* control, whereby the principal is a central purchasing organization (such as a health authority) and the agent is a separate provider organization (such as a hospital trust). Under these arrangements, control is by means of a formal contract, and sanctions include penalty clauses and the threat of termination of the contract. Here outcome measures may form an explicit part of the contract, and can therefore be used to service the contractual relationship between purchaser and provider. The UK 'Next Steps' initiative has resulted in the establishment of 92 agencies, delivering a large proportion of public services (UK Government, 1993).

It is important to understand how outcome measures help to secure these various sorts of control, and in order to do so we introduce the notion of 'cybernetics', the science of control, derived from the Greek word *κυβερνητησ* for a steersman (Beer, 1966). The scientific model of control is illustrated in Figure 1.1. The system to be controlled (perhaps, say, a school) is observed, and some suitable outcome measures obtained, such as examination results. These are analysed, perhaps in the light of local socioeconomic conditions, to gain an understanding of how the system is performing. Resulting from this analysis, a judgment on the school's management can be made, and appropriate action taken, perhaps in the form of setting examination success targets for the future.

This crude model begs the question as to who is to undertake the controlling, and how that control is exercised. For example, as noted above, a number of parties – such as parents, employers and the general public – may feel they have a legitimate interest in influencing the control of the school, and each party may have a different means of influencing the school's behaviour. Thus there is no single straightforward model of control. However, the model shown in Figure 1.1 is helpful because it separates the three stages of control that almost all outcome measures must service: the measurement stage; the analysis stage; and the action stage. We now discuss the problems that arise in each of these stages.

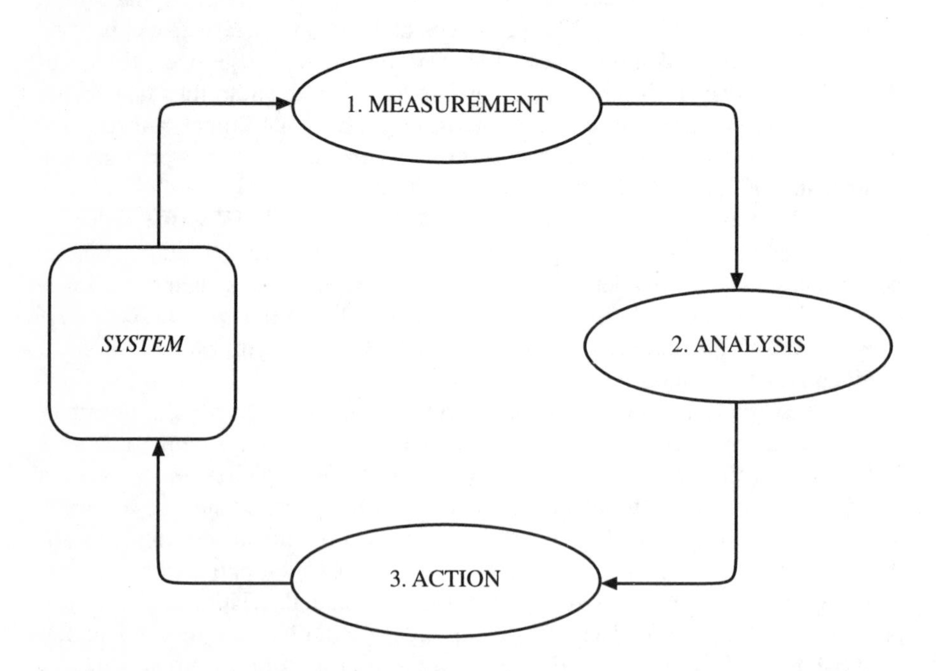

Figure 1.1 The cybernetic model of control

The Measurement Problem

Following the discussion above, the purpose of outcome measurement is to capture the valuation placed by stakeholders on the activities of a public sector programme. This process has four stages:

- identifying stakeholders;
- identifying objectives;
- developing indices of achievement;
- monitoring side-effects.

These are now considered in turn.

One could argue that outcome should be measured by directly seeking the opinions of the various stakeholders, using devices such as questionnaires and market research. This strategy may be appropriate in certain circumstances, for example when different methods of delivering services are being compared in a controlled experiment, and there is a fair degree of consensus as to the objectives of the services. However, in general, such techniques are impractical, because of their high costs, the possibility of serious bias, and the frequent difficulty of identifying and surveying stakeholders. Indeed, many legitimate stakeholders may have no direct experience of the service, and rely on outcome measures to form their judgment on its performance. And even direct users of the service – for example, hospital patients – may have only limited information with which to judge outcome (Carr-Hill, 1992).

The decision to term some phenomenon an 'outcome' represents an implicit judgment that it is of more than trivial consequence to some significant group of stakeholders. That is, in one sense or another, the outcome is related to some *objective* held by the stakeholders. It is rare to find consensus about what constitutes the objectives of a public sector programme. Thus, in making a choice of outcome measures, the outcome measurer is implicitly reflecting the objectives of one group of stakeholders, possibly at the expense of another group. That is, no outcome measurement scheme can be free of values, and any evaluation of outcome must be in respect of a particular set of objectives. This is an important issue which is raised in many of the following chapters. In seeking to measure outcome, therefore, the first decision that needs to be taken concerns the choice of stakeholders whose objectives will underlie the scheme.

However, even a relatively homogeneous group of stakeholders is likely to have a wide range of objectives concerning a particular service, so it will usually be necessary to select only a subset of its objectives for consideration. The second decision therefore concerns the choice of objectives. By way of illustration, Table 1.1 lists some of the groups with an interest in the performance of a school, and an indication of four of the objectives they may hold, with regard to the educational attainment, attendance, behaviour and delinquency of pupils. The importance attached by the various stakeholders to the objectives (indicated

Table 1.1: Some possible objectives and stakeholders for schools

	Parents	Employers	Pupils	Teachers
Attainment				
Attendance				
Behaviour				
Delinquency				

by the cells of the table) may vary considerably, and so a different choice of objectives may emerge, depending on which stakeholders are to be considered. The problem of selecting objectives is a central reason for the difficulties encountered by auditing bodies in addressing effectiveness issues, particularly when they are seeking to be non-partisan.

Having chosen a set of objectives, the next stage is to devise numerical indices which reflect progress towards those objectives. These measurement scales will almost always be proxies for levels of attainment. This might be because an objective – such as pupil behaviour – is resistant to quantification. However, even with concepts which are relatively amenable to quantification – such as educational attainment – the precise form of measure chosen usually cannot embrace the complexity of the underlying objective. Thus, although examination results may be accepted as a reasonable reflection of educational attainment, it is in practice necessary to select a particular index of examination success – such as the number of passes achieved – which is a possibly crude proxy for the underlying phenomenon of attainment.

More generally, it will usually be necessary to use some *indicator* of outcome, which does not directly capture the phenomenon of interest, but which is thought to be correlated with the relevant stakeholders' valuation of outcome. An example might be the use of the time taken to process social security claims as a proxy for the quality of benefit agency performance. In practice, indicators of outcome are often the conventional measures of process which have tended to dominate most performance indicator schemes, and therefore lie towards the output end of the output:outcome spectrum described above. It is rare to find any widely accepted direct measure of outcome.

Indeed, as the following chapters will show, the immediate problem confronting the outcome measurer is very often the prosaic one of seeking *any* means of capturing an objective – such as the improvement of pupil behaviour – in quantitative terms. If the stakeholders of interest are service users, then there may be a role for user satisfaction surveys as a means of identifying which readily measurable phenomena are the most important correlates of user satisfaction. Clearly, it is not feasible always to survey users. But if a small-scale survey can be undertaken in a limited and controlled setting, the results of that survey can be used to help inform which routine data might be collected as proxies for user satisfaction.

However, the complexity of this task should not be underestimated. It might for example be interesting to survey university graduates to identify the key determinants of student satisfaction, and to examine the extent to which they correspond to the data published by the University Funding Council (Johnes, 1992). Yet to do so one would need to decide at what stage after their studies graduates should be surveyed; to formulate a question which elicited a meaningful measure of satisfaction; and to ensure that a representative sample of graduates had been found. And even then, of course, one would probably have to acknowledge that graduates have only a limited insight into the benefits they have derived from their studies, and that – even from the perspective of the graduates themselves – many considerations other than expressed satisfaction should be taken into account when comparing the relative merits of universities.

Finally, it is important to recognize that almost all public sector intervention leads to unanticipated side-effects, not necessarily directly related to the objectives of the programme. Thus, for example, the programme to reduce waiting times for elective surgery in the National Health Service may result in hospitals diverting resources away from non-surgical specialties, such as geriatric medicine (Department of Health, 1991). This side-effect, which is effectively an externality of the waiting time initiative of the Patient's Charter, may have profound implications for patients not directly concerned with surgery. In principle, if an outcome measurement scheme is to be complete, it must monitor such side-effects. Yet, almost by definition, it is often difficult to envisage where externalities may arise. This problem suggests the need for a very broad 'scanning' function, as advocated by Etzioni (1968), as part of the outcome measurement process.

In summary, *pace* the quotation from the Citizen's Charter given earlier, users are sometimes not readily identifiable, and are often not the only important group of stakeholders. The development of outcome measures requires first a statement of objectives of the programme under consideration. It may be difficult to devise measures which are even proxies for some objectives, but to fail to do so may mean relegating such objectives to secondary importance. Most indices of performance are in truth closer to activity or output measures, which may omit important qualitative components. Consideration should therefore be given as to how quality might be incorporated into the measures. Any assessment of outcome then has to make judgments on the valuations of the observed quality-adjusted outputs. There is an intrinsic difficulty in drawing a boundary around any outcome analysis which is being undertaken, because most programmes have unintended side-effects, and so some broad scanning function should be put in place to monitor such side-effects.

The Analysis Problem

The satisfactory measurement of outcome is only the first stage of the control process. Next is required an interpretation of the chosen measures. Of course, much depends on who is to undertake the analysis. If the analysis is to be left to individual citizens, then the emphasis may be on disclosing data, and leaving those citizens to draw their own conclusions using their private analytic frameworks. This model is likely to be pursued mostly when the user has a clear choice as to individual action, and therefore has an incentive to scrutinize the data. An example might be prospective university students.

However, even if outcomes can be measured with some degree of completeness and precision, there are numerous problems involved in interpreting the data. There is, moreover, a problem with encouraging individual citizens to undertake the necessary analysis, because of their lack of power to effect any change. For this reason, governments often set up expert audit bodies, to undertake scrutiny on behalf of stakeholders. In England and Wales, the Audit Commission undertakes this role in local government and the National Health Service, while the National Audit Office examines central government activity. These bodies have access to a great deal of technical expertise, but still have the problem of deciding on whose behalf they are undertaking the analysis, and how to communicate the results of their analysis. Moreover, they are naturally reluctant to become involved in judgments on outcome, recognizing the danger of favouring one set of stakeholders at the expense of another (Audit Commission, 1991).

In order to proceed, the analyst – whether private citizen or expert auditor – needs to develop a model of causality. Given in Figure 1.2 is the conventional model of performance that underlies most discussion of efficiency and effectiveness. The unit to be analysed (which may be a particular mode of delivering services, or a particular management team) consumes various *physical inputs*, such as staff, buildings and materials. The activity being analysed produces *physical outputs*. A valuation is placed on these outputs by the relevant group of stakeholders. The outcome measures are of course proxies for these valuations. Then the ratio of benefits to costs gives an indication of the performance of the unit being analysed.

In the corporate sector, 'benefits' are usually measured in terms of revenues, and it is therefore relatively easy to construct measures of profitability which –

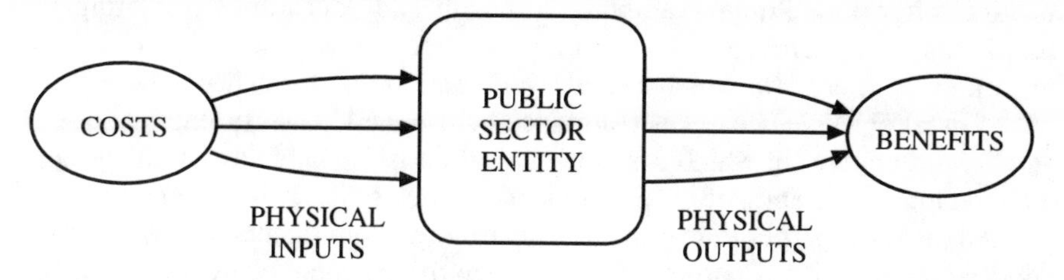

Figure 1.2 A simple model of performance

notwithstanding certain shortcomings – enjoy a broad degree of acceptance. The position in the public sector is much more complex, not least because of the multiplicity of views concerning the valuation to be placed on outputs.

The model set out in Figure 1.2 assumes that the unit under scrutiny is an isolated entity, for which inputs and outputs are readily and unambiguously identified. In practice, several complications arise. These can be summarized as follows:

- the treatment of joint inputs and outputs;
- variations in organizational environments;
- the treatment of long-term issues;
- random variability in outcome measures;
- the incorporation of equity considerations.

In practice, many public sector outcomes are the *joint* result of the efforts of a number of organizations, and to seek to attribute an output (let alone an outcome) to a single programme may be misleading, if not futile. For example, the level of juvenile crime is likely to be the outcome of the joint efforts of (at the very least) personal social services, housing programmes, schools and policing. To identify the contribution of one of these programmes in isolation may be meaningless.

In a similar vein, different management teams operate in different *environments*. Social security benefits offices handle very different mixes of benefit claimants, an environment over which they have little if any control. To compare the performance of offices without taking account of these different environments is clearly misleading, and may lead to serious misjudgments. This concern is central to the resistance of teachers and other stakeholders to the use of crude league tables of school examination results. Rico (Chapter 8) shows how the value-added concept can be used as one means of adjusting for different intakes of pupils.

A fundamental shortcoming of the crude performance model is that it is essentially static in nature, and ignores *long-term* issues. An important reason why certain programmes are usually found in the public sector is that their benefits only accrue over a long time horizon, a situation in which conventional markets often fail. Prime examples are health and education. Evaluating the performance of such programmes is complicated. Either one waits for all the outcomes to emerge (in which case the judgment on performance is hopelessly out of date) or one evaluates performance before the long-term implications of activity are known (in which case the evaluation is incomplete). In either case, over-zealous application of the performance model is clearly inappropriate.

All measures suffer to varying extents from random fluctuations which may signify nothing. This is particularly true when the outcome being measured is a relatively rare event. For example, in the maternity services, the *variability* of the perinatal mortality rate from one year to the next within a local health authority may simply be the result of random statistical fluctuations, and may offer no information on the performance of the health authority. Much of the public sector (in particular, health and personal social services) includes as an important part of its responsibilities the aversion of very serious but relatively rare events. In these circumstances, to judge performance on the incidence of these events may be seriously misleading.

Finally, conventional markets are not concerned with issues of fairness. However, many public sector programmes have some concept of *equity* as a central concern. The UK National Health Service, with its commitment to provide equal access to health care for people in equal need, is a celebrated example of this principle. The equity goal therefore becomes another dimension along which outcome must be measured, often involving the measurement of some concept of client need as a preliminary stage in the analysis.

In summary, then, underlying the outcome measurement philosophy is the belief that a particular unit can be evaluated according to some ratio of outcomes to inputs, along the following lines:

$$P = \frac{V_1Y_1 + V_2Y_2 + \ldots + V_sY_s}{U_1X_1 + U_2X_2 + \ldots + U_mX_m}$$

P is performance. There are m inputs, $X_1, \ldots, X_m$ and s outputs $Y_1, \ldots, Y_s$, which have ideally been adjusted for quality. The weights on the inputs are $U_1, \ldots, U_m$, and can probably reasonably unambiguously be interpreted as the prices of the inputs. However, the weights on the quality-adjusted outputs are $V_1, \ldots, V_s$, and are dependent on the preferences of whoever is commissioning the evaluation. Thus the top line of the expression for P represents the outcome of the unit's activity, as evaluated with regard to a particular set of values $V_1, \ldots, V_s$. Identification of outcomes is complicated by the possibility of joint outputs, the existence of environmental factors amongst the inputs and the measurement of long-term outputs, all of which may be difficult to capture in quantified terms.

There is rarely any ideal level of performance against which to judge a particular programme. Instead, it is necessary to compare outcome secured by a series of similar programmes. The comparison may be between different organizations (such as schools) seeking to deliver the same services. The main problem with this sort of cross-sectional analysis is that of ensuring that all the salient differences between the organizations – such as variations in environmental circumstances and accounting procedures – have been taken into account. Alternatively, the same organization may be compared across different time periods. This time-series approach is often the only feasible method of appraising natural monopolies, such as national defence services. Its principal shortcoming is the need to take account of changes in external factors which may affect performance, such as macroeconomic circumstances and technological progress.

The analyst therefore faces a daunting task in seeking to gain an insight into the performance of management or the efficacy of particular types of service delivery. Ideally, it may be possible to measure all the relevant variables and to assign values to the output weights. In these circumstances the ratio becomes the standard benefit:cost ratio of economic analysis, and the efficient programme is that securing the highest such ratio. This is often very demanding in its data requirements, and requires the analyst to specify a set of values.

At the opposite extreme to the construction of a benefit:cost ratio, one might select just one input and one indicator of outcome and present a league table of performance. Clearly in most circumstances this univariate approach is likely to be inadequate, given the multidimensional nature of the public sector. However, it has the virtue of being clearly understandable, and – apart from the values implicit in the choice of outcome indicator – it does not require the specification of the relative values placed on outputs. Moreover, it is possible to derive more than one such ratio, allowing users to concentrate on the aspects of performance that interest them. This is the approach that has been adopted by the Audit Commission in developing a set of over 200 performance indicators for local government in England and Wales (Audit Commission, 1993).

Thus, in interpreting outcome measures, it is necessary to disentangle the causes of variations in outcome. The difficulty of considering joint outputs, environmental inputs, long-term issues and random variability suggests the need for very careful modelling before drawing any conclusions on the efficacy of a particular management team or programme. In practice, it is almost always impossible to measure all the relevant variables, and it must be accepted that the analysis is both incomplete and partisan, in the sense that a particular set of stakeholders' values are being used. It is important that the limitations of an outcome measurement scheme are made explicit.

The Action Problem

This section briefly examines the actions that may be taken once the analysis of outcome has been completed. The action stage may be trivial. For example, if the problem was one of comparing alternative methods of managing a particular clinical condition, then the action stage may simply be advice or instructions to clinicians to adopt the favoured technique. Similarly, prospective university students will apply to the universities of their choice. However, in many circumstances the choice of action is far less clear cut, and some actions may lead to unintended consequences.

Again, before discussing possible actions that might be taken, it is important to remember the different control mechanisms that exist for securing managerial change. In a bureaucracy, the change can be secured by decree (although – as Kornai [1992] shows in relation to the Soviet experience – it is often difficult to secure the desired changes even when in theory control is by direct command). Where a principal seeks to control the agent contractually, the change can be secured through the terms of the contract (but again, it is often difficult to specify a comprehensive set of quantified targets and constraints which is not open to differences of interpretation). Where control is through the political process, the results of the analysis must first be communicated to stakeholders. They in turn have available a number of indirect mechanisms of control, such as voting pressure, media campaigns and appeal to higher levels of government, which have only indirect influences on management behaviour.

Given the difficulties associated with seeking to dictate directly to management the action they should take, the usual action resulting from an examination of outcome is to set targets in quantitative terms. Process targets (such as the childhood immunization rates set for general practitioners in the UK) have to be used when outcome is difficult or impossible to measure. However, the logic of measuring outcome should be that targets should be set as close as possible to the outcome end of the output:outcome spectrum.

Such targets may be explicit. For example, through the medium of the 1993–4 agreement with the Benefits Agency, the UK Government set benefits offices the target of clearing 67 per cent of child benefit claims within 10 days (Benefits Agency, 1993). In setting explicit targets, many of the considerations set out in the previous section apply, such as the uncontrollable environment in which the unit operates. The first stage is to establish a 'benchmark', which indicates the level of outcome the unit under analysis should be able to secure if it performs at a maximum level of efficiency, given the constraints within which it operates. In practice, a benchmark may be impossible to establish with any certainty. And in any case it is often impossible for a unit to move immediately to a more efficient use of resources – for example, if it entails disposal of assets or retraining of staff. It is therefore usual to set explicit targets which are intermediate between current performance and the benchmark.

It is more frequently the case that targets are implicit. District Health Authorities are not set explicit targets for perinatal mortality. However, because the outcome measure is published and given a high political profile – and because managers will receive praise or opprobrium as a consequence of their local performance – they will inevitably formulate an implicit target concerning this outcome measure. It is for example plausible to argue that managers will not wish to be exposed as an outlier on the chosen outcome measure, and will therefore assume an implicit target of moving towards the typical performance of units with which they might be compared. The implicit targets generated by an outcome measurement scheme will depend on the structure of the organization, the managerial rewards (or penalties) associated with the scheme, and the perceptions of managers.

It is therefore important to recognize that the setting of outcome targets cannot be viewed in isolation from the penalties and rewards offered to those who are accountable. The Chief Executive of the NHS promised to give maternity service managers with poor perinatal mortality rates 'a hard time'. Much will depend on managers' interpretation of what is meant by that threat. If it suggests increased scrutiny of their behaviour, reduced promotion prospects or indeed loss of jobs, then it may have a profound effect on managerial actions, even if there is little that managers can do to improve the outcome for which they are held responsible. However, if the threat is perceived as hollow, then it may have no effect whatsoever.

The early performance indicators for local government (which included few measures of outcome) appeared to have no effect on local government behaviour, probably because – although they were published locally – managers and elected representatives perceived that neither voters nor the central government had effective sanctions with which to punish apparently poor performance (Smith, 1988). More recently initiatives, such as the Citizen's Charter, have sought to introduce concrete sanctions. For example, the Parent's Charter offers parents the right to send their children to the school of their choice, an attempt to introduce the sanctions of the marketplace into education (Department of Education and Science, 1991).

An important consideration associated with the model of control described here arises whenever the same measures are used retrospectively (to measure performance) and prospectively (to set targets). The measures cease to be neutral reporting devices, and instead become important instruments of control. Because the organization being controlled is a human phenomenon, it is able to anticipate the actions of the controller, and individuals may take action to prevent the controller taking action which is unfavourable to them. In short, the use of selected outcome measures as instruments of control may lead to unintended and possibly dysfunctional consequences (Smith, 1995). For example, the emphasis in the NHS on measuring outcome in terms of waiting times for elective surgery may have led to undue emphasis being placed on inpatient surgical services, at the expense of services, such as mental illness, for which no outcome measures have been developed. The Soviet economy was a rich source of experience of dysfunctional consequences, which is summarized elsewhere (Nove, 1980).

Thus, if it is effective, an outcome measurement scheme is likely to induce behavioural responses on the part of managers. However, those responses may not always be those that are intended, and could be dysfunctional. It is therefore important to ensure that the putative benefits of an outcome measurement scheme – manifested in improved control of the organization – outweigh any possible costs, which may include unintended side-effects as well as the direct costs of collecting and analysing data.

1.5 Conclusions

This chapter has sought to examine the components of the concept of outcome, to indicate the rationale for seeking to measure outcome, and to describe the problems that arise when doing so. In spite of the difficulties that have been raised, there is a very respectable rationale for attempting to measure outcome. Without information about the broad impact of public services on society, there is a grave danger that resources are misdirected, and that – in the process – the usefulness of the public sector is discredited. There is therefore every reason for researchers and policy makers to examine the potential for measuring outcome throughout the public sector.

However, the discussion has brought to light a number of problems of both a theoretical and practical nature which impede the implementation of outcome measurement schemes. On the theoretical side, the problems centre on the difficulty of determining the relevant objectives of the programme under consideration. In practical terms, the principal difficulties are those of capturing the phenomenon of interest in quantitative terms, and of analysing the consequent data. There is also the ever present danger of inducing dysfunctional responses on the part of management.

The following chapters describe the search for outcome measures in a variety of public sector programmes. They show how the problems described above impinge on outcome measurement in those programmes, and assess the prospects for future developments.

References

Anthony, R. N. and Young, D. W. (1984) *Management Control in Nonprofit Organizations*, 3rd Edn, Homewood: Richard D. Irwin.

Audit Commission (1991) *How Effective is the Audit Commission? Promoting Value for Money in Local Public Services*, London: HMSO.

Audit Commission (1993) *Citizen's Charter Indicators: Charting a Course*, London: HMSO.

Beer, S. (1966) *Decision and Control*, Chichester: Wiley.

Benefits Agency (1993) *Business Plan, 1993/1994*, London: Department of Social Security.

Buxton, M., Acheson, R., Caine, N., Gibson, S. and O'Brien, B. (1985) *Costs and Benefits of the Heart Transplant Programmes at Harefield and Papworth Hospitals*, London: HMSO.

Carr-Hill, R. A. (1992) 'The measurement of patient satisfaction', *Journal of Public Health Medicine*, **14**, pp. 236–49.

Carter, N. (1991), 'Learning to measure performance: the use of indicators in organizations', *Public Administration*, **69**, pp. 85–101.

Carter, N., Klein, R. E. and Day, P. (1992) *How Organizations Measure Success: the Use of Performance Indicators in Government*, London: Routledge.

Committee of Public Accounts (1990) *Maternity Services, Thirty-fifth Report, Session 1989–90*, London: HMSO.

Department for Education (1994) *The Updated Parent's Charter*, London: DFE.

Department of Education and Science (1991) *The Parent's Charter*, London: DES.

Department of the Environment (1981) *Local Authority Annual Reports*, London: HMSO.

Department of Health (1991) *The Patient's Charter*, London: HMSO.

Etzioni, A. (1968) *The Active Society: a Theory of Societal and Political Processes*, New York: Free Press.

Fédération des Experts Comptables Européens (1991) *Performance Measurement in Public Sector Management*, London: Chartered Institute of Public Finance and Accountancy.

Gray, J., Jesson, D. and Sime, N. (1990) 'Estimating differences in the exam performance of secondary schools in 6 LEAs – a multilevel approach to school effectiveness', *Oxford Review of Education*, **16**, pp. 137–58.

Harris, J. (1995) 'Service efforts and accomplishments: a primer of current practice and an agenda for future research', *International Journal of Public Administration*, **18**, pp. 253–76.

Johnes, G. (1992) 'Performance indicators in higher education – a survey of recent work', *Oxford Review of Economic Policy*, **8**(2), pp. 19–34.

Kornai, J. (1992) *The Socialist System: the Political Economy of Communism*, Oxford: Clarendon Press.

Nove, A. (1980) *The Soviet Economic System*, London: Allen & Unwin.

Smith, P. (1988) 'Assessing competition among local authorities in England and Wales', *Financial Accountability and Management*, **4**, pp. 235–51.

Smith, P. (1993) 'Outcome-related performance indicators and organizational control in the public sector', *British Journal of Management*, **4**, pp. 135–51.

Smith, P. (1995) 'On the unintended consequences of publishing performance data in the public sector', *International Journal of Public Administration*, **18**, pp. 277–310.

Stewart, J. D. (1984) 'The role of information in public accountability' in Hopwood, A. and Tomkins, C. (Eds) *Issues in Public Sector Accounting*, Oxford: Phillip Allan.

Sugden, R. and Williams, A. (1978) *The Principles of Practical Cost–Benefit Analysis*, Oxford: Oxford University Press.

Tomkins, C. (1987) *Achieving Efficiency, Economy and Effectiveness in the Public Sector*, London: Kogan Page.

United Kingdom Government (1991) *The Citizen's Charter*, London: HMSO.

United Kingdom Government (1993) *Next Steps Review 1993*, London: HMSO.

United Kingdom Government (1994) *The Citizen's Charter, Second Report: 1994*, London: HMSO.

Chapter 2

Health and Health Care

Alan Williams

2.0 Introduction

The first problem to be confronted when discussing outcome measurement in the field of health is whether we are to concentrate on health-as-affected-by-health-care, or whether our interests are the broader ones of evaluating *all* public sector activities (and all private sector activities too?) which impinge upon health. The latter is such a broad canvas that I have decided to set it aside in the present context, despite the obvious dangers of so doing. Prime amongst these dangers is that of encouraging people to believe that health care is the most important determinant of health, when probably that role goes to income, with education and smoking status following close behind! So, although I am going to concentrate on the measurement of outcome in a (public) health care system, this should not be taken as implying that I consider the health care system as the most important source of health in society.

In pursuing that remit I shall follow the organizational framework set out in Chapter 1.

2.1 What is Outcome in the Health Care Sector?

Accepting that 'the purpose of measuring outcome is to assess the valuation society places on an activity' (p. 1), and that 'outcome is considered as a personal valuation of quality-adjusted output' (p. 2), such measures have to be contrasted with measures which simply record the amount of work done (patients treated) or the amount of work waiting to be done (waiting lists) or the intensity with which particular resources are used (bed occupancy rates, consultations per doctor). The classic distinctions in the health care field are due to Donabedian (1966) who (in the context of medical audit) identified 'structure', 'process' and 'outcome' as the key categories. *Structure* refers to the facilities available (otherwise known as 'resources' or 'inputs'), *process* refers to what people actually do (alias 'activities' or 'throughputs'), and *outcome* refers to what is achieved ('effectiveness' or 'output'). He noted that some kinds of medical audit consist only of checking that people have the appropriate facilities. Other kinds of audit go on to check whether these facilities (which may include the skills and knowledge of the doctor) are used in an appropriate way (the right tests are requested, the results are properly interpreted, the appropriate treatment is offered, and treatments are carried out competently). Yet other kinds of audit go on to check on outcomes (e.g. peri-operative mortality rates, complication rates).

In the context of medical audit it has (understandably) been clinical biomedical measures which have dominated the scene. If a drug is given to reduce blood pressure, the key clinical question is 'did it actually reduce blood pressure, and if so by how much?'. The answer to this question may be different from the answer to the question 'did the patient feel better after the treatment than before?' (Jachuk *et al.*, 1982). This has led social scientists to argue that we should also be drawing on *lay concepts of health* in order to generate a non-clinical framework for evaluating the outcome of health care, from the perspective of the patient rather than from the perspective of the health care professional (Williams, 1985). One would expect there to be some overlap between the two, of course, since both are concerned with survival prospects and with the avoidance of disability, pain and distress. But it is relatively rare for these latter ('quality-of-life') items to play a central role in clinical trials or medical audit, and the systematic measurement of patients' own overall assessment of the benefits from treatment is even more rare. Hence a perceived need to broaden the range of outcome measures that are used routinely in the health care field.

2.2 Why Measure Outcome?

The public health care system is a classic case where valuing outcome by individuals' willingness and ability to pay through a market has been rejected as ethically inappropriate (Williams, 1992). The favoured alternative principle has been provision according to 'need', which in turn raises a host of further questions requiring clarification (Williams, 1975). How is 'need' related to 'wants' or to 'demand'? Is 'need' an absolute or a relative concept? If needs outstrip the resources available to meet them, how should they be prioritized? And, returning to Donabedian's classification, is 'need' focused on resources (a need for hospital beds) or on activities (a need for more hip replacements) or on outcome (a need for improved health)?

Because outcome measurement is about 'the valuation *society* places on an activity' we have also to confront the issue of how we move from individual notions of need to societal notions of need. This brings to the fore the agency role of doctors. Patients do not demand treatment, they demand better health, and it is the doctor who translates the latter into the former. In so doing the doctor is enjoined to respect the autonomy of the patient: that is, to have regard to the patient's individual objectives and values. But the doctor is also typically given the task of deciding whether the treatment of one patient should have higher priority than the treatment of another patient, because doctors are regarded as the people best placed to determine relative 'need'. In this context, need comes to mean 'capacity to benefit from treatment'. If outcome measurement is to be useful in measuring capacity to benefit from treatment, it has to be capable of being applied in a comparable way to different patients, with different conditions being offered different treatments, at different times, in different settings (e.g., at home, in a general practitioner's surgery, in a hospital). Thus outcome measures in health care need to meet this specification if they are to deal with the fundamental issues of setting priorities and monitoring performance at societal level (Williams and Kind, 1992).

2.3 Who are the Stakeholders?

Taking the list of potential stakeholders in Chapter 1 as a starting point, we can identify patients and their nearest and dearest as the current users, virtually the entire population as potential users, employers as people anxious to minimize sickness-absence, the taxpayers seeking to avoid the wasteful use of their money, the central government (especially the Department of Health and the NHS) exercising political and managerial accountability, local government (especially the social services) as bodies providing complementary activities in the social care field, voluntary bodies engaged in similar activities, a great variety of research sponsoring bodies (public and private), professional bodies such as the Medical and Nursing Royal Colleges, and the general public in a more detached role concerned, for instance, with matters of equity in the provision of health care.

It will be obvious that the motives of each of these stakeholders will be very different, as will their role in any system of accountability. Moreover most people will be playing more than one role, with a potential conflict of interest between them. An individual may react differently as a patient and as a taxpayer. Doctors may have problems balancing the conflicting demands of patients, taxpayers (as mediated by the budget constraints placed upon them by managers), and professional colleagues (through standards set and monitored by medical audit or possibly statutorily). Outcome measures should have a key role in all of these contexts, but their precise nature will vary with context, and how welcome they will be will depend on what message they convey. Doctors are unlikely to welcome measures which indicate that the treatments they customarily offer are not very effective, and it is understandable (though not excusable) that they might wish to keep such information confidential. Similarly, politicians are likely to highlight data which place their policies in a good light, and to suppress (or make it difficult to collect) data which might place their policies in a poor light. Thus outcome measurement in the health field is likely to operate in a rather highly charged environment if it is used not just for self-appraisal but also to assist in holding people accountable (in a very broad sense) to others.

2.4 A Model of Outcome Measurement

In a public health care system such as the UK National Health Service we find all three of the control mechanisms sketched out in the introductory chapter playing a prominent role. *Prima facie* these overlapping control mechanisms should create no difficulties, because in a broad sense all participants are committed to the same objective, namely improving people's health as much as possible, given the resources at our disposal. But you do not need to scratch very deeply beneath the surface of this rhetoric to discover some rather sharp differences of opinion, for instance about whether the NHS has the right level (and distribution) of resources at its disposal, about whether health is being measured in the right way, about whether the patterns of responsibility within the system are conducive to its avowed objectives, and similar fundamental issues concerning the functioning of what has to be a highly decentralized system. But, as noted earlier, it is possible to make some inroads into this territory by separating 'the three stages of control that almost all outcome measures must service: the measurement stage; the analysis stage; and the action stage.' (p. 8). I will therefore proceed by tackling each of these in turn.

The Measurement Problem

The stakeholders who, traditionally, have played the dominant role in measuring outcome in health care have been the doctors. One of the prime purposes of recent work in this field has therefore been to counteract the biases introduced (often unconsciously) by this clinical focus of interest. Thus there has recently been increasing emphasis upon eliciting *patients*' views about their 'personal valuation of quality-adjusted output', and even upon eliciting the views of *the general public* upon that same subject, representing as they do current and future patients, the taxpayers and the electorate simultaneously. It is upon this rather ambitious undertaking that I shall concentrate in what follows.

Because the general public play multiple roles, they will have different objectives according to the role they see themselves in at any particular time. As current patients they want nothing but the best, and quickly. As potential future patients they want the accessibility that can only be ensured by running the system with some spare capacity. But as taxpayers they want costs kept within bounds and people treated according to some society-wide prioritization of relative need. And as an electorate, they may be interested in distributive justice and making the world (or their bit of it) a better place. Thus an ideal outcome measure should enable people to address all of these issues (though obviously they will need other information as well).

The choice of numerical indices which reflect progress (or lack of it) towards these multifarious objectives is probably the single most controversial issue in the measurement of health outcomes. There is no consensus as to what the key dimensions of health actually are, what is the best way of valuing them, or how individual valuations should be aggregated to form a societal view. Although it is widely agreed that people value *both* life expectancy *and* the quality of that life expectancy, there is no consensus as to the rate at which the one should be sacrificed for the sake of the other, and many people still act as if the preservation of life takes *absolute* precedence over the relief of pain etc. (Harris, 1985). Nor, when health has been defined and measured in some way, is there consensus as to what distribution of health (or what distribution of the benefits of health care) would be regarded as 'fair' or 'just' or 'equitable' (Williams, 1994), and there are even differences of opinion amongst the experts as to which measures of inequality are the most appropriate ones to use in this context (Van Doorslaer *et al.*, 1993).

But the existence of controversy does not mean that the task is impossible, merely that it is contentious. Let me sketch out one way through this minefield (Williams, 1995) which will indicate the problems that are encountered, and which have to be overcome (wittingly or unwittingly) no matter what approach is taken.

If the stakeholders are the general public, then one way of reaching them is through eliciting the views of a representative sample of them by interviewing them in their own homes. It should be noted that this approach fails to pick up the views of the currently institutionalized population, and of those who are too ill or infirm to cope with such interviews. But what views should be elicited? Some investigators have asked directly for people's views about what is currently happening in the NHS, or about any recent episodes of care the individual may have received, or about whether there should be more of this and less of that. These approaches do not however touch upon what is fundamental to outcome measurement, namely what value people attach to different health states that they might find themselves in, with or without treatment. Such information can be elicited by presenting people with descriptions of what it is like to be in different health states, and using any one or more of a number of valuation techniques to get these states rated one against another. We might thereby discover the relative importance to people of relieving pain, or reducing anxiety, or improving mobility, or not having to rely on others to wash or dress you, and so on. People can also be asked whether some of these states would be regarded as being so bad that, if they lasted for any great length of time, death would be preferable.

For societal decision making such individual valuations have to be aggregated, of course, by taking average or median values and using these to assess whether a particular change in health status (described in terms of pain, anxiety, mobility, self-care, etc.) is or is not an improvement, as viewed by the general public. Particular *individuals* will, of course, have different views from the average or median view, which will generate tension between what people want as patients and what the electorate considers 'reasonable'. But it may also be that particular *groups* of people have different views from each other (e.g. the old may have different views from the young, or men from women, or people in professional and managerial occupations from people in manual occupations). Such differences can be identified, quantified and highlighted through such outcome measures, and their policy implications explored. And it is but one step further to ask people whether they think that everyone should count equally in the aggregation process (Charny *et al.*, 1989), or whether some people deserve priority over others (such as the parents of young children over their childless contemporaries). It will be obvious from this brief catalogue of issues why the subject is contentious: it is so because the issues it brings to the surface are contentious! This is why some people would prefer them to be left beneath the surface and confronted privately (usually by doctors).

The Analysis Problem

Interpreting the implications of such outcome data for the provision of health care requires us to be able to establish a high probability that activity *A* is responsible for outcome *X*. This problem is essentially a scientific one concerning study design, and it exists independently of the particular success measure used. To go back to an earlier example, the problem of study design exists in establishing whether or not a particular drug lowers blood pressure, and, if so, what is the precise relationship between the dosage and the quantitative effect on blood pressure. It should therefore come as no surprise to discover that it also exists in establishing whether the drug makes people feel better, and if so by how much, and how sensitive these feelings are to different dosages.

The special problem in the health field with the measurement of 'health-related quality-of-life' (HRQOL) is that it is frequently dismissed by doctors and other clinical researchers as a 'soft' measure, to be given little weight alongside 'hard' clinical data (such as blood pressure) or survival rates. Setting aside the fact that many of these supposedly 'hard' data are in fact subject to significant measurement error, there are two issues that need to be separated out in the interests of clarity. One is 'subjectivity' versus 'objectivity', and the other is 'interpersonal variability'.

The reluctance to accept measures simply because they are subjective is, in my view, misplaced. There is nothing intrinsically superior about an 'objective' measure like 'blood pressure' which gives it pride of place over a 'subjective' measure like intensity of pain or level of anxiety. At the end of the day both objective and subjective measures have to be assessed for their (subjective) importance to the people concerned. It is this that should determine which gets pride of place. If people with a particular condition care more about the relief of pain than about long-term survival prospects, then the measurement of pain should take precedence over life expectancy in any clinical trial concerning the treatment of that condition. It is not a matter of 'subjective' versus 'objective', but a matter of 'important' versus 'unimportant'.

Concern about the 'interpersonal variability' of the phenomena under consideration is an altogether different matter, and concentrates our attention on the appropriate use of measures of central tendency (such as means or medians) to summarize aggregate data. It must be stressed that this is just as much a problem with 'objective' data as with 'subjective' data. For instance, how far from the mean level of blood pressure does a person have to be for their blood pressure to be declared 'abnormal' and therefore requiring treatment? Similarly, how big a difference must exist between the mean blood pressure of two different groups of people (e.g. the old versus the young) for this to require some different definition of 'normalcy' for each such group? The mere existence of large interpersonal variability does not invalidate a measure, but it does indicate that we should be cautious about how we interpret the implications of movements in its mean or median value. For instance, if old people value health states differently from the rest of the population, then when evaluating the benefits of geriatric care we may get different answers when using the patients' values from those we get when using the values of the general public (and we may get yet different ones when using the judgments of clinicians). It is not the job of those generating outcome measures to resolve these conflicts (which are essentially political) but it is their job to ensure that their measures do not conceal such conflicts. It would indeed be preferable for such measures actually to identify and highlight the underlying phenomena which cause such conflicts, so that they can be addressed at that fundamental level, and not superficially glossed over. So again there is nothing intrinsically superior about a measure which has minimal interpersonal variability. It will certainly be more convenient to handle, and easier to interpret, but if it is less important than the phenomenon which exhibits wide interpersonal variability, the latter should have the greater weight.

A somewhat different interpretive issue arises in the health care field with the measurement of HRQOL, namely how far to go in condensing the information that goes into the outcome measure. HRQOL is a multidimensional concept, typically ranging over a gamut of physical, psychological, social and sometimes even spiritual elements. But for analytical purposes such data have to be condensed. At the very least they get reduced to a 'profile' in which some 5 to 15 dimensions are distinguished, with a single summary rating made on each one. For clinical monitoring or diagnostic purposes, covering a small number of people, a profile may well be appropriate and manageable, but where judgments of overall change have to be made (and especially where the numbers of affected people are large) profiles will not do. A typical response is then to take the average score across all dimensions (perhaps by first standardizing each to a 0 to 100 scale). Although convenient, this is quite arbitrary, in the sense that there is no guarantee that such a set of 'weights' actually reflects the relative values attached by patients (or anyone else for that matter) to moving between one profile-described state to another profile-described state. It would be better if such valuation weights were derived by offering the profile-described states to people to value directly, one against another, as suggested above. With such a set of value-weights, each profile can be reduced to a single index number reflecting the overall value of the state in HRQOL terms. There will remain the problem of integrating this HRQOL index with mortality data where health care activities affect both (which they usually will). To integrate quality of life with quantity of life, in some such measure as the Quality Adjusted Life Year, a further step is required, namely valuing HRQOL in such a way that being dead = 0 (so that states rated worse than dead have negative scores). This happens automatically with some methods for eliciting values (e.g. time-trade-off, or standard-gamble).

The other issue about aggregation concerns the weight to be given to each individual in the aggregation process (Williams, 1993a). In clinical trials using conventional measures such as survival rates at some specific point in time (e.g. 6 months after treatment, or 2 years after treatment) what is counted is simply the number of deaths and the number of survivals. In other words each person counts equally, which implies that, from a societal viewpoint, all survivals are of equal value and all deaths are of equal value. It makes no difference if the deaths are of the young or of the old, or men or women, or rich or poor, or good or evil, or beautiful or ugly, or black or white, or Catholic or Protestant or whatever. Usually this will be entirely appropriate, but sometimes it won't be. We may, for instance, want to know whether death rates are higher amongst one group or another, since this may have both clinical and political implications. If so we may wish such data to be disaggregated and presented separately for each group.

Precisely these same considerations apply when looking at more complex outcome measures such as Quality-Adjusted-Life-Years (QALYs). It may turn out that certain treatments yield more QALYs for some groups than others, and it may be important to document this. As in the previous example, this may have both clinical and political implications, for instance concerning equity (if it is felt that certain groups should be given priority over other groups by attaching a higher value to any health gains they get compared with those got by others). Some people think that it is not the job of the outcome measurers to elicit such weights and incorporate them into their measures, since this is essentially a political judgment. But if the views of the general public are to inform that political judgment, we shall need the kind of data that the outcome measurers could generate through their value elicitation procedures with the general public. If they do not do it, there will be a strong possibility that such data will not be elicited at all, or will be generated in such a way that they cannot be used systematically with the outcome measures that have been developed. Such studies as have been done indicate that most people would give priority to the young over the old (and the old think this too!), to people with young children over those without, and (less strongly) to those who have cared for their own health over those who have not.

The Action Problem

I have assumed that it is the health gains from different health care activities that are our focus of interest in the kind of outcome measurement I have been describing. The size and nature of such gains are matters of immediate concern to patients and their nearest and dearest, to the health care professionals who are treating them, to potential future patients who may one day face the same problems, to researchers looking for success criteria which match the values of current and future patients, to professional bodies setting standards of performance to be monitored through clinical audit, to health care managers trying to decide which treatments are most beneficial in relation to their costs, to public health specialists trying to estimate the extent of unmet need (i.e. benefits which could be provided but which currently are not), to politicians trying to decide whether their policies are working or not (in terms of delivering better health to the population at large), to the government trying to decide whether to put more or less resources into health care (as opposed to other health-affecting activities), and to the general public trying to judge whether they are getting a good deal out of their health care system (Williams, 1993b).

The agenda for action here is obviously enormous. Working through the foregoing list of interested parties one by one, I will simply indicate a few key issues that each would be able to address better if appropriate outcome measures of the kind I have been describing were available to them. Current patients and their nearest and dearest would be able to make better informed choices about the therapeutic alternatives open to them (including opting for no treatment). Their health care professionals would themselves be better informed about the likely consequences for patients' quality of life of the clinical alternatives under consideration, which might lead them to change their clinical policies. Future patients would have more realistic expectations about what medical care can and cannot do, and possibly change both their health-care-seeking behaviour and their general lifestyle as a consequence. Researchers could adopt HRQOL measures alongside conventional clinical measures in clinical trials and other evaluative studies, thereby generating information that will be of direct value to patients as well as to the clinicians who advise them. Instead of focusing on structure and process measures, the conduct of clinical audit could focus on patient outcome in HRQOL terms (as well as on the rather crude, and often uninformative, mortality rates), so as to test and improve the performance of clinicians and bring it up to the level achieved by the best. With this information also available to health care managers, they would be better placed to decide which activities to expand or contract, and which innovations had now reached the stage where they should be included in the therapies that were worth offering routinely to people. The measurement of unmet need (where need means 'capacity to benefit') implies using outcome measures in surveys of population health, by which means, if linked to the prevalence of effectively treatable conditions, it would be possible to estimate the magnitude of undelivered health gains in the population at large (which would be a rather more meaningful statistic than the number of people waiting for treatment!). Following the trend over time in such a statistic would also provide some indication of how well policies are working at the aggregate level – data which are typically lacking even with quite major health care reforms. And if such data enabled us to establish rather more clearly what extra health benefits we were getting from extra resources put into health care (compared with extra resources put into other health-affecting activities, such as alleviating poverty or reducing cigarette smoking), we might get some better idea than we have at present about whether or not health care is 'underfunded'. Better information on all of these issues, as well as on the distribution of health and health care within the society, would be a boon also to the electorate when they are trying periodically to weigh up the conflicting claims of the different parties about whether things are getting better or worse, and in what respects.

But the problem of incentives remains. One reason why a comprehensive reappraisal of outcome measurement in health care, from the perspective of the general public, has been so surprisingly neglected in the past is that no one has had any strong incentive to do it. Doctors have not been effectively accountable to anyone except their professional colleagues, and many of them still feel strongly that this is the way things should stay. Although we hear a great deal about responsibility to patients, this has in fact been mediated by norms set up by their colleagues (and not, for instance, by patient groups, although the latter are coming to play a more prominent role in some circumstances) (Williams, 1991). The courts in Britain do not see it as their role to second-guess clinical judgment, and it is a sufficient defence to demonstrate that there is *some* responsible body of medical opinion which would support whatever is being objected to. Clinical audit is jealously guarded as a wholly professional domain, participation in which is not even compulsory, its conduct being usually quite unsystematic, and its results not even disclosed (as a general rule) to the managers of the hospitals in which it is practised. In such a protective environment only the most dedicated and public-spirited and research-minded practitioners are likely to break out of the mould, their possible reward being research grants, publications and distinction awards. The rest remain defensive and uncooperative, and sometimes even mildly paranoid!

The ultimate horror in this scenario is, of course, 'performance-related pay'. Unfortunately the rate of progress with outcome measurement has been so slow that such performance measures are likely to operate predominantly at the process level. The dangers inherent in this approach can be graphically illustrated with regard to that persistent performance measure, the waiting list. Let us start with the mythology (Williams, 1990). It runs like this: once people have been seen by a doctor and declared to need treatment they should be treated immediately. The only reason they are *not* treated immediately is because the NHS is short of resources. *Therefore*, if you give the NHS more resources and insist that they are directed to those activities for which the waiting lists (or times) are longest, then there will be no more waiting. What is the reality? Most medical conditions are not just 'there' or 'not there'. Criteria are established by doctors to decide whether a condition is severe enough to warrant treatment at all, and, if so, what intensity of treatment is appropriate, and how soon it should be started. A condition may be so severe, and/or likely to deteriorate so rapidly in the absence of treatment, that urgent action is required if there is an effective treatment available. No such patient should be on a waiting list, and I suspect that no such patient normally is. On the other hand, many conditions are chronic and very slow moving, and the judgment as to the best stage at which to treat them varies greatly from doctor to doctor, from place to place, from time to time and from patient to patient. There is a large 'grey zone' in which doctors operate by conventional rules of thumb, and if capacity is short they get a bit more selective, and if capacity expands they get a bit less selective, but always within the large 'grey zone'. So the doctor's declaration that someone 'needs' treatment, and should therefore be put on a waiting list, is *not* a statement that that person needs treatment so urgently that under no circumstances should treatment be delayed.

So what is a 'reasonable' length of time to wait? From an individual patient's viewpoint, this may be whatever length of time is required to make the arrangements necessary to minimize the disruptive effect of the treatment itself. For this purpose, predictability of the actual dates when treatment will take place may be far more important than the wait itself, and in the management of waiting lists more attention might be devoted to eliciting patients' preferences in this respect. Clearly the balance of advantage will depend on how bad the patient's current health state is, how disruptive treatment is, and how much the patient's health is likely to improve as a result of the treatment.

But when we look at all this from the supply side, the efficient scheduling of work within the system is greatly facilitated by knowing that you have a small 'stock' of 'work' waiting to be done, which can be fitted in amongst the more urgent work as the opportunity arises. But why does this entirely reasonable 'small stock of work' grow to such monstrous proportions? To understand this we must peer into the darker corners of the waiting list phenomenon. First of all, many NHS doctors supplement their incomes by engaging in private practice. Private practice flourishes in specialities and in places where NHS waiting times are long. So it greatly helps the profitability of private practice if the 'grey zone' is drawn upon to keep NHS waiting lists longer than is desirable simply for efficient management of the NHS work flow.

The second important consideration is that people have noticed that every now and again, a Good Fairy comes along and distributes goodies to those who have exceptionally long waiting lists (or times). These 'goodies' consist of extra staff or other facilities which have hitherto been denied, and you don't have to be a genius to work out that you are more likely to get goodies the longer is your waiting list. So the 'grey zone' is tapped once more to strengthen your case for being classed amongst those people who deserve goodies. And since this is an ongoing system, if the receipt of goodies enables you to step up the work rate and make incursions into your list, you had better fill it up again as soon as possible by ensuring that the local general practitioners keep you well supplied with 'grey zone' cases, otherwise private practice and/or future eligibility for goodies will suffer. The incentives are perverse!

If we used outcome measures instead of process measures we could get out of this trap (Gudex *et al.*, 1990). The key information we need is the difference between a patient's current health state and their health state after treatment. A waiting list is really a pile of health benefits waiting to be delivered to the customers. Some of these benefits are quite substantial (e.g. turning a pensioner crippled with a painful deformed hip into someone who can move about freely without pain), others are quite small (e.g. removing minor blemishes). Suppose patients on any particular waiting list were arranged in order of the size of the benefit they were being denied, and priority were to be given to those who stood to benefit most. We might well find that the longer the waiting list the more minor were the benefits to be gained by those who were on it. Indeed, if my 'grey zone' model is correct, that is exactly what I would expect. With information on the benefits that are being foregone, we could also operate more equitable rules, such as that people being denied large benefits should move forward in the queue faster than those waiting for only small ones. Performance-related pay then focuses on health gains delivered. No credit is given for health gains *not* delivered, which is what rewarding long waiting lists does!

2.5 Conclusions

Outcome measurement in health care enjoys the great advantage that it operates in a field in which there has been a strong tradition of evaluative research, built up over many decades by clinical researchers. Social scientists have been recent 'invaders' of this territory, and their attempts to colonize it have not (and do not) meet with the wholehearted approval and support either of the previous colonizers (the clinical researchers) or of the indigenous population (the health care professionals). But health care has become such a sizeable consumer of the nation's resources (and, as the experience of the USA demonstrates, it could swallow up a lot more if let loose), that people rightly expect a new kind of accountability from those practising it. They want explanations cast in terms they can understand about what is being achieved by this vast and complex apparatus, and they want to assure themselves that the values that pervade it are those held by those who pay for it and those who need it. This, by and large, has been the pitch adopted by the social science community in the outcome measurement field in health care, and it will be interesting to see whether, over the next decade, their ideas can move forward from the stage of being accepted in principle (which, by 1995, I think they now are) to being made operational and influential in practice (which at present they only are sporadically and in a few situations). Despite the problems I have identified, I am hopeful that more progress will be made with outcome measurement in the health care field than elsewhere, because, despite the professional and political defensiveness it engenders, the *scientific* culture within health care favours it, and this culture still enjoys high prestige. We must make sure we do not tarnish its image!

References

Charny M. C. *et al.* (1989) 'Choosing who shall not be treated in the NHS', *Social Science and Medicine*, **28**, (12), pp. 1331–8.

Donabedian, A. (1966) 'Evaluating the quality of medical care', *Milbank Memorial Fund Quarterly*, **4**, pp. 166–206.

Gudex, C. *et al.* (1990) 'Prioritising waiting lists', *Health Trends*, **22** (3), pp. 103–8.

Harris, J. (1985) *The Value of Life*, London: Routledge & Kegan Paul.

Jachuk, S. J., Brierley, H., Jachuk, S. and Willcox, P. M. (1982) 'The effect of hypotensive drugs on the quality of life', *Journal of the Royal College of General Practitioners*, **32**, pp. 103–5.

Van Doorslaer, E., Wagstaff, A. and Rutten, F. (Eds) (1993) *Equity in the Finance and Delivery of Health Care: an International Perspective*, CEC Health Services Research 8, Oxford: Oxford University Press.

Williams, A. H. (1975) 'Need as a demand concept' in Culyer, A. J. (Ed.) *Economic Policies and Social Goals*, London: Martin Robertson.

Williams, A. H. (1985) 'The nature, meaning and measurement of health and illness: an economic viewpoint', *Social Science and Medicine*, **20** (10), pp. 1023–7.

Williams, A. H. (1990) 'Escape the trap', *Health Service Journal*, **100** (5188), pp. 242–3.

Williams, A. H. (1991) 'Incentives, ethics and clinical freedom' in Lopez-Casasnovas, G. (Ed.) *Incentives in Health Systems*, pp. 24–30, Berlin: Springer.

Williams, A. H. (1992) 'Priority setting in a needs-based system' in Gelijns, A. C. (Ed.) *Technology and Health Care in an Era of Limits*, Washington DC: National Academy Press.

Williams, A. H. (1993a) 'Some methodological issues in the use of cost–benefit analysis in health care' in El-Agraa, A. M. (Ed.) *Public and International Economics*, pp. 33–41, London: St Martin's Press.

Williams, A. H. (1993b) 'Quality assurance from the perspective of health economics', *Proceedings of the Royal Society of Edinburgh*, **101B**, pp. 105–14.

Williams, A. H. (1994) *Economics, QALYs and Medical Ethics: a Health Economist's Perspective*, Discussion Paper 121, York: Centre for Health Economics.

Williams, A. H. (1995) *The Measurement and Valuation of Health: a Chronicle*,

Discussion Paper 136, York, Centre for Health Economics.
Williams, A. H. and Kind, P. (1992) 'The present state of play about QALYs' in Hopkins, A. (Ed.) *Measures of the Quality of Life and the Uses to Which Such Measures May be Put*, pp. 21–34, London: Royal College of Physicians of London.

Chapter 3

Outcome Measures for Social Security

Meg Huby

3.0 Introduction

In the face of limited resources and potentially limitless demands there is growing pressure to justify government spending on particular policy interventions rather than others. The expansion of the managerial culture into the social policy arena has led to demands for government programmes to be examined in terms of their effectiveness, efficiency and economy – the three Es of 'management-speak'. Few would argue that these are not desirable attributes of any spending programme but the question of how to measure them is far from clear-cut. The effectiveness of a programme in achieving its objectives, its efficiency in terms of producing a defined outcome with the lowest possible input and its achievement of that outcome at minimum cost to the Treasury all rely for their measurement on clear outcome objectives and mechanisms through which outcomes can be measured.

In the case of social welfare programmes the problem of measuring outcomes is particularly marked. One difficulty lies in the fact that not only policy outcomes but also the original policy objectives can look very different to different interest groups so that the search for a small number of simple indicators is likely to be a fruitless exercise. The very concept of 'welfare' introduces a further problem. Government policies may produce outputs such as social security cash benefits but the objective of these policies cannot be seen merely to provide people with fixed amounts of cash. Rather the intention is to provide cash to help people to improve the quality of their lives, enabling them to play a productive role in society. This objective is made explicit by the Department of Social Security (DSS) in its statement of strategy, aims and objectives in the 1993 Departmental Report:

> The Government's strategic priorities are to:
> - focus benefits on the most needy;
> - minimize disincentive effects within the benefits structure;

- simplify the benefits system wherever possible;
- ensure that the system adapts to the differing needs of people it is intended to benefit, not force people to adapt to a complex system;
- bear down on fraud and abuse;
- encourage personal responsibility. (Cm 2213, 1993)

It is relatively easy to measure social security outputs in terms of benefit expenditure, numbers of benefit recipients, or resulting income levels for different types of families or households. Major problems arise, however, when we attempt to assess outcomes in terms of the impact of benefit payments on the lives of recipients. Yet without adequate measures of outcome it remains impossible to evaluate not only the effectiveness with which a welfare programme meets its social objectives, but also the extent to which it is efficient and economical.

This chapter exemplifies some of the problems inherent in outcome measurement using the case of the Department of Social Security's Social Fund. The analysis is conducted within the framework of a study undertaken by the Social Policy Research Unit at the University of York for the Department of Social Security. It raises general questions about the use of 'hard' quantitative and 'soft' qualitative measures of outcome, about the value-systems underlying interpretation of these measures and about the relative merits of resource allocation based on transparent outcome measures which are known to be inadequate and allocation based on opaque decision-making mechanisms which incorporate a high degree of chance.

3.1 The Social Fund

The Social Fund is intended to provide lump sums of money for expenses which people living on low incomes cannot be expected to meet from regular social security benefit payments. It was introduced in 1988 as part of the social security reforms stemming from the Fowler Reviews (Cmnd 9518, 1985; Cmnd 9691, 1985) and replaced the previous system of single payments. Single payments constituted a regulated system under which lump sum grants were paid to anyone satisfying the conditions of entitlement.

The Social Fund differs from the previous scheme in a number of respects, three of which are of particular importance to the arguments presented in this chapter:

(i) The community care grant, budgeting loan and crisis loan schemes which account for the bulk of Social Fund expenditure are based on discretion rather than entitlement. Social Fund Officers make decisions about applications on a discretionary basis in the context of legislation and guidelines.

(ii) The majority of Social Fund awards are made as loans rather than non-repayable grants.
(iii) The fund is cash-limited and each district office must work the scheme within a fixed annual local budget.

The operation of discretion within a fixed budget demands that Social Fund Officers must attempt to prioritize applications so that the fund targets assistance on areas of 'greatest need'. There is a vast literature on the concept of need, preoccupied with how needs should be measured and also whether they are subjective and relative or whether there are common basic needs (Doyal and Gough, 1991). In the context of the Social Fund we are concerned with needs for goods and services required to maintain a certain standard of living. Fundamentally, the need for such items is relative and depends for its legitimacy on the prevailing standard of living in a society, the state of the economy, the norms of living, the prevailing idea of what is fair and just, and how these ideas are interpreted in policy and legislation. Even when a number of parties are agreed that a particular need exists, there remains the question of what the satisfaction of that need entails. In the case of the Social Fund, the award of money might be seen as supplying an applicant with the *means* to meet a need by purchasing an item or service. Yet actual satisfaction of the need may depend on less tangible factors – the quality of item or service purchased, for example, or the costs and benefits perceived by the applicant in resorting to a Social Fund loan. It is these elusive aspects of satisfying need which call for measures of outcome going beyond simple counts of numbers of awards or amounts of money spent by the fund.

From its inception the Social Fund was criticized from many quarters as being likely to lead to a reduction rather than an increase in welfare for many people living on low incomes (Becker and Silburn, 1990; Bennett, 1989; Berthoud, 1986; Smith, 1990; SSAC, 1990). Early research findings from Citizens Advice Bureaux, Probation Services, The Children's Society, numerous other charities and larger projects by the Benefits Research Unit and the Social Security Consortium suggested that the fears of the critics were well founded (SSRC, 1991; Stewart and Stewart, 1991). The commissioning of a large-scale independent evaluation of the scheme in 1989 may have been at least partly a response from the Department of Social Security to growing public concern. Investment in research acted as a demonstration that the Department was taking action to address the problems highlighted by critics and at the same time bought time during which the high media profile of the Social Fund was reduced (Hansard, 21 January 1992, Col. 181; Hansard, 8 June 1992, Cols 6–8). Previous findings were being dismissed by the DSS as 'anecdotal evidence', the subject had become politically sensitive and there was huge pressure to ensure that methods used in the evaluation were unimpeachable.

A major goal of the research was to assess the extent to which the Social Fund was achieving its objective of 'targeting help on the areas of greatest need'.

If we see the fund as an output of the social security system, then the extent to which it meets need can be viewed as an outcome of the policy, an outcome which might look very different to different stakeholders in the policy environment (Jenkins, 1993).

3.2 The Stakeholders in the Social Fund

It is not unusual to find a specific policy arena in which tensions arise between different objectives (Minogue, 1993). The public funding of the social security system gives many groups of people a legitimate interest in the scheme and each of these groups may have a rather different way of looking at its objectives.

The Poor

People currently using the scheme are by definition at the lowest end of the income distribution. But people's situations are not fixed in time and any member of society might in principle become a potential user following a change in circumstances. Although this clearly gives everyone an interest in ensuring that the fund works effectively, differing ideas about the probability of ever needing to use it result in a spectrum of interest, from those who are currently in need to those who are unable to envisage ever being a Social Fund applicant. The position of any individual on this spectrum may vary with time and consequently this group of stakeholders might be regarded as being the general population.

The Department of Social Security and the Benefits Agency

For this group, the effectiveness of the Social Fund has repercussions on the extent to which wider objectives of social security, such as the relief of poverty, can be achieved. In addition to this is the requirement of civil servants to satisfy their line managers and ultimately to provide government ministers with the means to meet their political objectives.

Other Professional Agencies

The interest of agencies such as Social Services, Welfare Rights organizations and Probation Services in the Social Fund lies in the way in which its successful operation enables them to achieve their own objectives in improving the welfare of their clients.

The Minister and Government

The high profile of the Social Fund, at least in its first years, had made it politically sensitive and the government was anxious to ensure that it could be legitimized. Ideally it would be seen to meet the needs of the poorest people in society without prejudicing broader government aims to reduce 'the number of people becoming dependent on benefits' (Cm 2213, 1993), maintain the 'work ethic' and reduce public expenditure.

Very few of these stakeholders have direct experience of using the Social Fund. Yet because of their interests they must form some kind of judgment about its effectiveness. Such judgments must be based on measures of how the scheme is working. However, variations in interest mean that different groups will seek different measures and it will be impossible to define any single indicator of performance which will provide sufficient information to meet the requirements of all groups.

The extent to which the Social Fund meets need results in external costs and benefits to society which go beyond the impact on individual applicants. The success of the Fund could increase wider social well-being, since most members of society feel better about themselves if they are secure in the knowledge that other people are not suffering from poverty or deprivation. There is also utility in knowing that the state is running an effective and efficient social security system over which it exercises clear control.

On the other hand, some stakeholders may gain benefit from knowing that the system does not provide too much to help the poor but rather works to support the idea of a work ethic by maintaining work incentives within the system. In a more abstract sense there may be some implicit political gain and perceived benefits to the 'taxpayer' in keeping a sector of the population essentially excluded from pursuing what most people regard as a normal lifestyle, both to act as a deterrent to others and to make others feel relatively better off.

The results of research to examine the extent to which the Social Fund meets need are therefore likely to mean very different things to different interest groups. In carrying out the study it was important to maintain good relationships with people in all of these groups, to ensure access was allowed to official records, to ensure access to survey and in-depth interview respondents, but most of all to maintain the academic integrity which would be necessary if the work were to be accepted as credible and independent of particular interest group influence.

3.3 Dimensions of Outcome

It was essential to explore the issue of 'meeting need' from a number of different perspectives, a process which clarified research questions and led to the choice of particular research methods. Figure 3.1 shows the conceptual model on which the research design was based.

The Social Fund aims to meet some of the needs of people living on low incomes. These needs are *felt* by people in their own social and physical contexts and are *expressed* when applications are made to the fund. Applicants may be clients of, or have contacts with, other agencies. Social workers, probation officers and welfare rights officers, for example, operating within their own professional capacities, may have their own perceptions of their clients' needs and, following the taxonomy of Bradshaw (1972) we can refer to these perceptions of need as *normative*.

Decisions about Social Fund applications are made by Social Fund Officers, each with his or her own personal ideology which will influence the way in which officers use professional judgment and discretion. Decisions are also

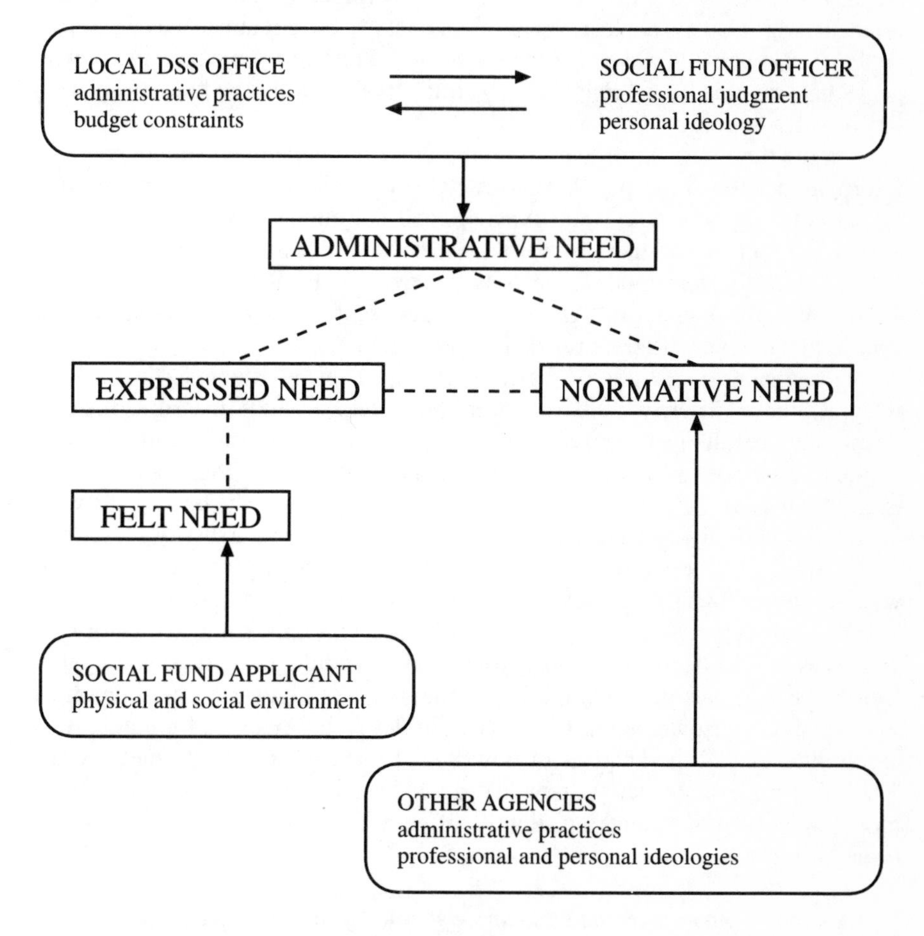

Figure 3.1 A conceptual model of perceptions of need

influenced by the working context of local Benefits Agency offices, each with its own administrative ethos and practices and its own budget constraints. Social Fund Officers see the needs of applicants in what we have termed an *administrative* sense.

In the case of a single Social Fund application, all of these perceptions refer to the same 'need'. Yet the actors do not necessarily see the need in the same way and in order to address the research questions it was important to try to understand some of the tensions and contradictions which could arise between different views of need and consequently between different views of outcome. This required the use of a wide range of research methods and measures.

Quantitative information was required about the range and type of things which people living on low incomes said they needed. It was possible to distinguish needs identified in the course of research interviews from those which respondents said they had expressed when making Social Fund applications. It was also possible to quantify some of the circumstances in which applications were given awards or were refused. This gave some measure of who gets what from the Social Fund but says little about how far the fund meets need in a broader sense.

Taking the research further required the use of qualitative methods to glean information about how people construct their needs, why they approach the Social Fund for help with some expenses and not others, how they see awards as meeting their needs and how partial awards, loans or refusals impact on their lives. These different kinds of information were collected for four groups of applicants – those given full grants, those given loans, those given only partial awards and people who were refused help altogether.

In reporting the results of the research, however, no attempt was made to integrate these different kinds of information into a single measure. Instead, quantitative results were presented but were elaborated on and qualified, using qualitative work to provide a more comprehensive picture. Table 3.1 gives an example of how the perceived benefits of receiving a Social Fund award were analysed quantitatively using data obtained from an open-ended survey question.

A similar survey question elicited information about problems associated with receiving Social Fund awards, some of which appeared to contradict the beneficial aspects which people had mentioned. It was impossible to quantify the way in which the benefits accruing from an award could be conditional on other factors; or the ways in which the immediate benefits of awards could be offset by attendant disadvantages. Qualitative in-depth interview information was required to extend the analysis of how Social Fund awards might meet needs. The following example shows how in order to best meet a real need, Social Fund money was spent on something slightly different from the items for which it had been awarded.

> Another woman carer said that she was told by her local office that she could apply once every six months for a grant to care for her son who

Table 3.1 Benefits of receiving a Social Fund award (Question: How did getting this money from the Social Fund improve things for you (and your household)?)

Benefit	*% grant recipients*	*% loan recipients*	*Total*
Home now warmer/cleaner/more pleasant to live in	39.3	45.6	43.9
Less worry, more peace of mind	26.1	19.6	21.3
Improved health	15.1	14.0	14.3
Feel happier/children happier	11.5	9.1	9.8
Home safer	2.0	4.5	3.8
Feel more self-respect	1.5	3.5	3.0
Obvious benefits of purchasing items	27.0	25.0	25.5
Total (unweighted) cases	114	328	445

Source: Huby and Dix, 1992.

suffers from incontinence. This had been 'a big boost' to her and she described how the money was used:

> I get the grant for him and I get, I usually get, a grant for a bed, bedding which is three single sheets, three single blankets. But I buy a quilt because they're easier to wash than keep washing blankets. (Huby and Dix, 1992: 101)

Other interviews revealed how the initial benefits of receiving an award could be short-lived, especially when partial awards meant that goods must be bought second-hand:

> Yes, I did have a washing machine, the original washing machine that I got with the loan, I'd had that two weeks and that broke. It was a second-hand one. I couldn't get a new one. Because I didn't have enough money to get a new one. Two weeks and that broke down. I had to wash everything up in the bath. (Huby and Dix, 1992: 103)

These examples demonstrate how figures about the number of Social Fund awards that are made and the amount of money that is spent on the scheme are at best inadequate measures of how far the fund meets need. Annual reports from the Secretary of State for Social Security focus solely on such quantitative measures of output but say nothing about whether this output results in outcomes which increase or reduce welfare or well-being.

It was difficult at first to convince policy makers in the DSS of the crucial importance of the qualitative elements of the research. Although they did agree to fund this part of the exercise, in the end their responses to the report tended to focus on some of the more sophisticated statistical work in which a variety of multivariate techniques were applied to a set of 50 possible indicators of need. These techniques failed to reveal any significant patterns to suggest that people who received Social Fund awards could be said to be in any greater need than others who were refused.

The report met with a favourable response from all quarters and attracted a high level of media attention, perhaps because of the full picture it gave, addressing many different dimensions of outcome. Professional agencies welcomed its findings as validating their own experiences of the Social Fund and the Minister for Social Security publicly acknowledged the integrity and thoroughness of the study (BBC2 *Newsnight*, 8 July 1992). Publication of the research report did not, however, result in any discernible change in policy – the Social Fund and the poor are still firmly in place. Nor do the methods used really resolve the problem of deriving any comprehensive outcome measure which could be put to use simply and practically in future policy evaluation. What the research does do is exemplify some general problems of outcome measurement which are applicable to most areas of social policy and welfare.

3.4 Allocation of the Social Fund Budget

We have seen so far that simple quantitative measures of spending are inadequate to describe the outcomes of Social Fund policy in the sense of evaluating the extent to which the fund is meeting need. Furthermore it is clear that wider measures of outcome suggest that the fund is not achieving its objective of targeting help on areas of greatest need.

Budget limitations on the fund, however, do affect its capacity to meet need. So if outcomes are to be improved it is essential that resources are allocated efficiently. Yet, through a curious circularity of logic, current mechanisms for resource allocation to local offices are partly based on demand defined by the number of awards already made. This system would tend to target resources where need was greatest only if numbers of awards reflected satisfactory outcomes in terms of increasing the welfare of those most in need. We have discussed above the inadequacy of using simple quantitative methods to measure outcome in terms of satisfaction of need. Thus, while a more holistic approach points to the desirability of improving outcomes, attempts to do this through adjustments in resource allocation based on the same inadequate measures of outcome may obfuscate, perpetuate or even accentuate the problem.

Attempts have been made to establish a rational underpinning for allocating Social Fund budgets to local DSS offices. The size of the pot is fixed during negotiations between the Department and the Treasury, but local budgets are adjusted annually to reflect the numbers of awards made from the fund in the previous year. Thus an office with low numbers of applications and awards is unlikely to increase its budget share.

This system equates the easily measurable number and cost of awards with the more difficult measure of level of need in a local office area and a lower award rate is interpreted as the existence of less need. There is no evidence, however, to suggest that any such relationship exists. On the contrary, the Social Fund has been described as a lottery (Craig, 1988), a description borne out by Huby and Dix (1992). Given the absence of any pattern in the way awards are made, it becomes impossible logically to use a quantitative count of cost of awards as an indicator of local needs for the purpose of resource allocation.

Furthermore, as suggested by Huby (1992), numbers of awards may even be inversely related to levels of local need. In a particularly poor area the combination of high application rates and a fixed budget will lead to high numbers of refusals. Qualitative work (Huby and Dix, 1992) shows how people tailor their expressed needs, at least to some extent, according to their perceptions of the likelihood of receiving help. Experiences of the Social Fund have lowered expectations among income support claimants and in areas where refusal rates are perceived to be high many people with very real needs may not apply to the fund simply because they are aware of the high probability of refusal and 'it's not worth the effort'.

This situation raises the question of whether it is better to allocate resources using a transparent allocation formula even though the rationality underlying it is flawed. Or is it better to accept that allocation unavoidably involves some element of discretion, chance or political judgment? In the first case we have shown how 'hard' quantitative measures, if accepted unquestioningly, can lead to distortions in resource allocation. Even if the inadequacies of quantitative measures are recognized at first, it becomes all too easy to forget about them as the system becomes entrenched. In the second case, it could be argued that, if the pretence of rationality were dropped, people faced with the known 'lottery' of the Social Fund could make their own informed decisions about whether or not to try an application.

3.5 Effectiveness and Efficiency

The issue of transparency is also important when considering the cost-effectiveness and efficiency of the scheme. Ideally cost-effectiveness measures require some estimate of utility gain for each unit cost. But whose utility? In simple spending terms, the Social Fund with a net grants budget of £60 million in 1988–9 replaced 1987–8 expenditure on single payment grants of £205 million. This cut in spending was justified with reference to the 'targeting' element of the new scheme, implying that although the budget was reduced the money spent would be carefully directed to those people *most in need* and so would result in little loss of welfare. This target group was not, however, defined.

If target groups are not explicitly identified then there are no means of assessing the cost-effectiveness of the system, at least in terms of the utility of the end-users. Similarly, since it is impossible to identify desired outcomes in terms of target groups, it is not possible to measure efficiency in terms of least cost outcome.

But identifying target groups for Social Fund help involves making judgments about who the fund *should* be helping and by implication who it should not. There are clearly political risks involved in making these judgments explicit. It might, for example, be regarded as a safe move to identify disabled people over the age of 75 as targets for high-priority help. However, it is more risky thereby explicitly to exclude from the system lone parents or young people with drug or alcohol problems. The political benefits of shrouding target group identification in the cloak of discretion are therefore offset by the consequent problems this raises for measuring outcomes to determine effectiveness and efficiency.

3.6 Conclusions

We have discussed the way in which lack of adequate measures of outcome in social security can place limitations on options for allocating resources and have seen how failure to identify target groups within which to measure outcomes can prevent the development of measures for assessing effectiveness and efficiency in resource expenditure. At the root of both of these problems lies the difficulty of combining 'hard' quantitative and 'soft' qualitative aspects of outcome into a single measure.

We have seen also that policy outcomes may look different to different stakeholders and that an effective measure of outcome needs to be approached from a number of different angles. Policies which are capable of acting as vehicles for real change to improve social welfare must be informed by adequate evaluations of outcome, by consideration, that is, using both 'hard' and 'soft' measures. It is questionable, however, whether government objectives for the Social Fund encompass a desire for real change in the living standards of the poor. If we assume instead that they are dominated by an implicit aim to save money, then the inadequacy of current outcome measures has political advantages. The reduced budget (compared with single payments expenditure) and the language of 'targeting' are used to imply that the system has been made more efficient, rather than that lower spending levels have been achieved through lower levels of provision. In the absence of good outcome measures and without a clear definition of target groups it is as difficult for critics to provide evidence to refute this claim as it is for policy makers to substantiate it. The result is that the Social Fund remains in place, its cash limits ensuring that spending is kept firmly under the control of the Department of Social Security and the Treasury.

Whether evaluating policies in either health or broader social welfare, it is becoming accepted that attention must be paid to the quality of life as well as to its duration. Even definitions of poverty are now moving on to encompass aspects of well-being and social participation as well as income levels (Bradshaw and Holmes, 1989; Bradshaw and Parker, 1993). Any attempt to capture this elusive measure will necessarily involve both description and valuation. But whose values count? In many organizations the search for simple indicators of performance has resulted in measures which merely reflect and reinforce the values of the power elite. But even if we could develop new indicators to combine the interests of different stakeholders we would still be left with the task of integrating some measures which are quantitative with others which are qualitative. Perhaps it is time to abandon the search for this 'holy grail' and to recognize instead the need to see the limitations of purely quantitative measures of outcome. Rather than trying to reduce life to simple numbers we could then put numbers to good use by clothing their interpretation in thought and compassion.

References

Becker, S. and Silburn, R. (1990) *The New Poor Clients*, Nottingham: Community Care/ Benefits Research Unit.

Bennett, F. (1989) 'The Social Fund in context', in Craig, G. (Ed.) *Your Flexible Friend*, London: Social Security Research Consortium.

Berthoud, R. (1986) 'The Social Fund – will it work?' *Policy Studies*, **8** (1), pp. 8–26.

Bradshaw, J. (1972) 'A taxonomy of social need', in McClachan, G. (Ed.) *Problems and Progress in Medical Care,* Oxford: Oxford University Press.

Bradshaw, J. and Holmes, H. (1989) *Living on the Edge: a Study of Living Standards on Benefit in Tyne and Wear*, London: CPAG.

Bradshaw, J. and Parker, H. (1993) *Budget Standards for the United Kingdom*, London: Avebury Gower.

Craig, G. (1988) 'The nightmare lottery of the Social Fund', *Social Work Today*, **24** (November), pp. 15–17.

Cmnd 9518 (1985) *Reform of Social Security: Programme for Change*, London: HMSO.

Cmnd 9691 (1985) *Reform of Social Security: Programme for Action*, London: HMSO.

Cm 2213 (1993) *Social Security Departmental Report. The Government's Expenditure Plans 1993–94 to 1995–96*, London: HMSO.

Doyal, L. and Gough, I. (1991) *A Theory of Human Need*, London: Macmillan.

Huby, M. (1992) 'The Social Fund: managing budgets, meeting needs?', in Corden, A., Robertson, E. & Tolley, K. (Eds) *Meeting Needs in an Affluent Society*, pp. 209–19, London: Avebury.

Huby, M. and Dix, G. (1992) *Evaluating the Social Fund*, Department of Social Security Research Report No. 8, London: HMSO.

Jenkins, B. (1993) 'Policy analysis: models and approaches', in Hill, M. (Ed.) *The Policy Process: A Reader*, pp. 34–47, London: Harvester Wheatsheaf.

Minogue, M. (1993) 'Theory and practice in public policy and administration', in Hill, M. (Ed.) *The Policy Process: a Reader*, pp. 10–34, London: Harvester Wheatsheaf.

Smith, R. (1990) *Under the Breadline*, London: The Children's Society.
SSAC (1990) *Social Security Advisory Committee Seventh Report, 1990*, London: HMSO.
Social Security Research Consortium (1991) *Cash Limited – Limited Cash*, London: Association of Metropolitan Authorities.
Stewart, G. and Stewart, J. (1991) *Relieving Poverty*, London: Association of Metropolitan Authorities.

Chapter 4

Outcome Measures in Higher Education

Huw Dixon and John Suckling

4.0 Introduction

The university sector is differentiated from the other types of educational institutions in that it is involved in the joint production of research and teaching. Whilst there are some university institutions that are almost entirely devoted to research, and some almost entirely to teaching, most involve a mix of activities. Clearly, the dividing line between research and teaching is blurred: for example, is the supervision of doctoral students and postgraduates in general counted as primarily one of teaching or of research? However, we follow most authors in viewing the dichotomy as useful. Joint production poses particular problems for outcome measurement: there is both the issue of how you measure the two types of outcome individually, and then how you combine these measures if some notion of overall efficiency is required. This chapter is intended as a non-technical introduction to the topic of outcome measures in higher education. More comprehensive and detailed economic analyses of higher educuation can be found in Johnes and Taylor (1990) and Johnes (1993).

4.1 The Economic Approach to Education[1]

The economic rationale for performance indicators in the university sector lies in the nature of education and research. Provision of education and basic research through private supply and demand will result in a suboptimal provision for two reasons. Education itself is seen as having positive externalities attached to it: that is, the benefits to society exceed the benefits to the individual. Private demand would depend on the latter and be less than society's demand. Second, research findings are 'public goods', in the sense that they are non-excludable (research findings are available in academic journals) and non-rival (my use of a research finding does not reduce its availability to you, unlike for example an apple). Private provision of education is sub-optimal because demand is less than it should be, and private provision of research is sub-optimal because no private supplier will supply a good which users have free access to. In such circumstances (e.g. defence, sanitation, street lighting) governments step in to make the appropriate decision. Also free market provision of education would depend on the willingness and ability to pay of (usually) parents or family. Where parents are unwilling or unable to pay the state may treat education as a 'merit good', that is a good that people should have irrespective of their ability to pay.

4.2 The Government as Resource Provider

The need for performance indicators arises when universities are funded by governments. Governments do not provide education and research, academics in universities do. What governments do is decide how much to spend on inputs to teaching and research. From the government's perspective the problem is fourfold: (a) does it know what it wants?; (b) is it getting what it wants?; (c) is it getting value for money?; and (d) is it spending the right amount? Question (a) requires the government to formulate some idea of how the outputs of university feed in to its own view of 'social welfare'. Question (b) ideally needs measures of outcome which reflect the normative objectives in (a). Question (c) focuses on efficiency, or the relation between *inputs* and *outputs*. Question (d) depends on how the government trades off university expenditure against other areas of government spending.

How, then, can governments get universities to produce what the government wants in education and research – aim (b) – and efficiency – aim (c)? The problem lies in the 'principal–agent' relationship between government and universities. The 'principal' here is the government which funds demand for university output and the 'agent' is the university system suppliers. Where the agent but not the principal has the knowledge and ability to provide what the principal wants, how does the principal get what the principal wants? Universities (academics, bureaucrats, support staff, students) may have different objectives (such as a quiet life, higher pay, more chalk, more test-tubes, existing subject mix) from those of the government (such as lower costs, higher quality, more control, different subject mix). The issue is further complicated in Britain where the government has delegated its 'principal' role to the Higher Education Funding Council (HEFC). The Department of Education gives a budget and a set of objectives to the HEFC which then translates these into policies to guide and control universities. In addition British universities are independent institutions with a large degree of autonomy.

The role of performance indicators (PIs) here is to measure outputs, which in turn are intended to reflect some concept of outcome. Whilst inputs can be valued in money terms, outputs cannot be. However, by relating appropriate output PIs to payments, the funding principal (the HEFC) can provide economic incentives to influence the agents' behaviour (the universities).

4.3 Performance Indicators and Universities

What sort of PIs are needed? They must (a) reflect the multidimensional nature of university outcomes and inputs, (b) allow input and outcome comparisons across universities, (c) be aggregatable and dis-aggregatable, (d) be robust: that is, the data providers – the universities – should not be able to distort indices in their favour, and (e) where appropriate be capable of relating funding to performance. Given that satisfactory output measures can be developed as proxies for outcomes, the main problems lie in areas (b) – universities are not identical with respect to outputs or inputs; (c) – it is not clear how education and research PIs can be combined; and (d) – can universities manipulate PIs in their favour?

Consider performance indicators which measure the outcome of education: for example the average degree class of students, or the percentage obtaining results above a certain level. There are two problems here. First, since universities classify their own degrees they can manipulate the results by awarding higher grades. In the period 1976–8 the percentage of firsts/upper seconds awarded has risen from 35 per cent to 45 per cent, despite the proportion of 18–21-year-olds in higher education rising significantly in the same period.[2] Second, universities are not identical with respect to the quality of student input. So degree results should be adjusted to allow for this. One suggestion, in line with the methods discussed in Chapter 8, is the 'value added' approach – that performance be measured by the increase in educational attainment of each student. Unlike in schools the university intake is relatively homogenous and most entrants can be compared on the basis of standard A-level/GCSE entrant scores. Measuring value added would require the estimation of the probability of obtaining a given degree class or above conditional on the entrant score. A university would be deemed to generate more value added if the probability was higher for the same entrant score.

In the UK for 1979–88 Johnes and Taylor (1990) found a 98 per cent correlation between A-level scores and degree class. This aggregate hides a lot of variation: in particular subject area matters, with the proportion of graduates who obtained an upper second or first in 1987–8 varying from 16.3 per cent in medicine and dentistry to nearly 57 per cent in languages (Johnes and Taylor, 1990, Table 7.3). Johnes and Taylor (1987) constructed a crude model to predict the degree results of individual universities: the only significant explanatory variables were: A levels, the percentage of students living at home, the 'Scottish' dummy and the proportion of expenditure going on library facilities. Student–staff ratios were found to be insignificant. The predicted versus the actual degree outcome can then be compared to see whether a university is doing better or worse than expected. Over the period 1983–6 some universities consistently performed better than predicted (Cambridge, Nottingham, York) and hence have possibly higher value added, whilst others (Newcastle, Durham, Exeter) did consistently worse (see Johnes and Taylor, 1990, Table 7.4). Whilst this sort of exercise is possible, it has yet to be done in anything but a crude way.

University current inputs can be measured using their monetary value. But there are difficulties in valuing capital inputs: for example, how do you value buildings that have not been on the market for many years, or may be restricted to a particular use? Cost data can be combined with output data to get a measure of efficiency and relative performance. For example, what is the average cost of educating students to degree level at university A as opposed to university B, or an equivalent measure in terms of value added? This has to be done carefully, to make sure that like is compared with like: different subjects have different costs associated with them (organic chemistry costs more than history).

Outcome measurement is further complicated by the joint product nature of university output: teaching and research. Whilst the teaching and research outcomes might be amenable to measurement, cost allocation between teaching and research is to some extent arbitrary and not obvious. For example university A might have higher staffing costs because it includes many more distinguished researchers than university B, and so more senior staff who are paid more; and how are the largely fixed costs of libraries, laboratories, computer centres etc. allocated between their teaching and research functions?

An implicit assumption in the above discussion is that the various output measures are uniform between universities and subjects. Thus a first-class degree from university A is the equivalent of a first-class degree from university B, a second-class degree in discipline X is the equivalent of a second-class degree in discipline Y within and between universities. Similarly a publication is a publication is a publication, whatever the journal or subject.

The market for graduates may sort out degree quality by subject and university by seeing how quickly and with what conditions of employment graduates find work. But there is no equivalent to the national examinations and standards as in the UK school system. Inter-university comparability of results is audited by the system of external examiners, in which an academic from the same subject area but from a different university confirms the standards of marking of constituent papers and the subsequent class of degree awarded. A particular external examiner will only hold that appointment for usually three years, before being replaced by someone from a different university. Also each university is free to set its own standards and rules on undergraduate degree classification so that the same set of marks may achieve a different degree classification at different universities. Postgraduate taught and research degree quality is confirmed in a similar way. There is thus a degree of comparability of output quality across universities.

The quality of research output is also measured by peer review on perhaps a stronger basis than for teaching. First, research activity is in general a more competitive arena than teaching for achieving higher salaries and academic prestige. Second, more and more research funding is determined by competition. Third, there is intense competition to publish research output in prestige journals. The process might well be labelled academic Darwinism – the weak go to the wall, the strong survive. The analogy goes further. The citation index which picks up how many times a particular idea and its carrier (the chapter or journal article) is cited in subsequent publications identifies those ideas which run and run and those which die quickly.

Several measures of research output have been suggested. First, subjective peer review in which academics in a particular discipline rank their fellow departments by order of research quality. There are problems: who should do the ranking, all members in a particular discipline, a committee, an individual; and how are the arbiter(s) selected? And how is quality measured?

Second, it is possible to measure research output and quality by looking at the publications by members of a department. A first measure is the total number of publications divided by the number of department academic staff. This gives the average number of publications per head, thus adjusting for size of department. To adjust for quality, publications must be ranked qualitatively and/or quantitatively, again by peer review, different weights being attached to different kinds of publications, for example prestige journals versus textbook chapters, refereed versus non-refereed journals. The choice of weights can be critical. Is a publication in a core journal worth two times or ten times as much as a publication in a non-core journal? Or if for example there are 20 acceptable journals ranked from 1 to 20, does a publication in the top journal get a weight of 20, a publication in the next-best journal a weight of 19 and so on? Per capita departmental research output in each of these schemes would thus be the sum of the journal-weighted number of publications divided by the number of academics. Such a measure can be manipulated by a department by reducing the number of academics in the divisor thus raising the average. Care is needed.

Third is the citations index. Here the number of times a particular publication is cited in the bibliographies of subsequent publications is taken as a measure of quality. This is nearer to an outcome measure than most of the performance indicators discussed in this chapter, as it captures – albeit imperfectly – the impact of research activity on the wider academic community. However, the weighting problem is still evident in the way in which the number of citations for departmental publications is aggregated. Do we just add up the number of citations? What does the frequency distribution of citations look like? So of three articles published by members of a department, if one article is cited 400 times, the next four times and the third once, is the appropriate index $405 = 400 + 4 + 1$, or should the three numbers be combined in a way that diminishes the effect of the 400? A department with the above kind of distribution might well prefer a straight aggregation of the basic numbers, but a department with say a 20:10:4 distribution might prefer a weighting system that allowed 1 point for 0–5 citations, 2 points for 6–10 citations, and 3 points for 11+ citations. The straight adding-up scheme favours the first department (a score of 405 vs 35) the second scheme favours the second department (5 vs 7). Weighting schemes are not necessarily neutral. The appropriate measure of output is then average citations per head.

An additional problem with the above two measures is that they are person particular. Publications move with their author so if an author moves department so the research ranking of the departments involved may change.

Lastly, the amount of research money attracted by a department can be construed as a measure of research output and quality. Research income can come under two headings: funds for basic research distributed by research councils, themselves the recipients of block research grants from government; and contract research from outside bodies. The former are largely determined by peer review, research council committees ranking research proposals by their view of what is important. The latter are more market driven: a customer wants some research done and puts out a contract to that end. To the extent that these funds are competed for, they may indeed reflect the quality of the department and its members. There is potential bias in that small departments may find it difficult to launch big-money proposals, and there may be funder bias in favour of big-money proposals. Small departments and small proposals are squeezed out with a detrimental impact on their rankings.

So where does that leave us? Exact measures exist for teaching output, for example we can count the number of students each year, or the proportion of graduates getting an upper second or better. Some of these measures, such as the number of students, can be used to compare institutions; others, such as the number of graduates getting at least an upper second, may be less good in this respect. On the research side there may be more arguments about what is a measure of good research, but whatever measure is selected allows direct comparison between institutions. However, moving beyond measures of output towards measures of outcome may be more problematic.

4.4 Measuring Efficiency

The principal reason for seeking to measure outcome is to derive measures of efficiency. Technical efficiency relates to output, however defined, per unit of input, however defined. The higher the ratio, other things being equal, the better. Economic or 'allocative' efficiency is rather different. Where money values can be attached to outcomes and inputs this requires that an activity be pursued to the point where the marginal gain in outcome value be just equal to the marginal increase in input cost.

Where outcome cannot be measured in money terms – as for universities – the rule is different, so long as outcome can nevertheless be captured by some output proxy. Here allocative efficiency is reached when for a single output PI and a money measure of inputs, the marginal increase in the PI divided by the marginal increase in the input measure is the same for all universities. This is not straightforward. The university is a multi-product, multi-input institution. An aggregate output measure requires performance indicators for teaching and research, and also a way of combining these to form a single index. The calculation is straightforward, the final index is a weighted sum of the constituent indices. The problem is, what value should the weights take? That is, what proportionate value should be attached to research versus teaching? The aggregation of the various inputs in principle poses the same problem, but this can be bypassed by using the money value of inputs.

In practice, for the 'old' universities in the UK, comparisons have been made using the following indicators (Johnes and Taylor, 1990, Tables 1.4, 1.5):

(i) unit costs = expenditure on academic departments per full-time-equivalent student;
(ii) percentage of students not completing their degree course;
(iii) percentage of graduates with a first- or upper-second class degree result;
(iv) percentage of graduates unemployed or in short-term job;
(v) research grants (£UK) per full-time academic;
(vi) research rating of university.

Each university was then ranked from best (=1) to worst (=45) for each of the above attributes. The resulting rankings for each university were then added and divided by six to get an overall average. This average (the lower the average the better the university) then produced a ranking of universities. Oxford was best, Ulster the worst. The drawbacks of this method exemplify the above problems. Aggregation hides the performance of individual departments within each university; each of the above attributes is deemed of equal weight; and there is no attempt to correct for the different quality of student intake.

Johnes and Taylor (1990) are critical of all of these measures:

(i) Subject-mix and staff–student ratio account for 80 per cent of university unit cost differences. The proper comparison is subject-based unit cost comparisons.
(ii) Most of the variation in non-completion rates was explained by three factors: new entrants' average A-level score, proportion of students taking business studies/language studies and the proportion of students in university residences.
(iii) Some 80 per cent of the variation in degree results between universities is explained by student intake quality as measured by their A-level score plus some minor variables, e.g. type of university.
(iv) About 90 per cent of the variation in the proportion of graduates in full-time employment within six months of graduating is explained by the proportion of vocational degree students in the university degree mix, whether graduate

employers visit the university and whether the university is in an area of high unemployment.

(vi) Research output varied significantly with the staff–student ratio, research resources, geographical position and university type.

Thus again PI choice is not unambiguous.

4.5 Interaction of Performance Indicators, Funding and Behaviour

Clearly, academic life is of its nature very competitive: individuals compete in exams, and as academics go on to compete with each other to publish research and acquire fame and prestige amongst their fellow academics. Furthermore, they compete for promotion and for plum jobs at the best departments. However, in Britain at the university level, it was only in 1992–3 that the Higher Education Funding Council first introduced a system directly relating funding to an indicator of research performance. The indicator used was a peer review of the research output of universities, done on a subject-by-subject (i.e. departmental) basis, using information on research output (e.g. publications, research grants). Each department was given a quality rating akin to the star rating for hotels. A 5-star department is the best, with an international reputation in most areas, down to a 1-star department which shows little evidence of good research.

The following mechanism operated. The HEFC allocates a total amount available for research at the national level. This is then allocated by the HEFC between subject groups. The peer-group review then serves to allocate this between departments. The details of this need not concern us here, but this leads to a great divergence of funding between departments. Thus if we take biology as an example using the actual 1992 figures, a 5-star biology department received about £26000 per member of staff (or equivalent), whilst a 2-star department received only £6600, and a 1-star in any subject received nothing.

There are thus big financial incentives for universities to raise their research rating, and there is a clear interaction between the performance indicator, funding mechanism and behaviour. The actual sum received by university departments under this scheme was the product of two variables: a 'volume' measure, which measured the department in terms of full-time staff equivalents, and the 'quality' measure (the star rating minus one). There is a big incentive for universities to raise the research rating of large departments. For example, a biology department of 45 staff equivalents would earn £300000 more if it had an extra star under the 1992 rules. However, there is also a big incentive to appoint more members of staff to highly rated departments, since they bring with them (eventually) more money from the volume side.

One can see universities and departments jockeying for position in the next research round in 1996 at the time of writing. Clearly, however, all departments cannot be winners, since there will be a zero-sum game within each subject. Thus the linking of research funding to research performance in this way has turned out to be very effective in terms of generating competition between universities for the fixed cake. Indeed, the whole culture of research has changed, at least in our own perception. There were in fact pervious research selectivity exercises in 1986 and 1989, and even though these did not have direct financial rewards, the lust for prestige caused a great shift of emphasis towards research activity in British universities.

Now, suppose that HEFC stuck to this same allocation mechanism as a method of allocating research funds. What would happen in the long run? There are two factors at work here. First, there is the fact that the cost of an additional member of staff will be lower in a 5-star department than a 1-star department: thus one would expect universities to hire more people in higher rated departments than in lower rated departments. This would lead to a shift of resources from poor research departments to good research departments. However, there is the second force, which pulls in the other way: new appointments that raise the research rating of a department will have a large value, since they will raise the research funds of all the other members of the department as well. There are limits to both of these processes: there is a distribution of abilities, and a fixed proportion of 5-star researchers. If it turns out to be hard to shift departments between different grades, then the 'volume' effect will dominate: the lower marginal cost of staff to highly rated departments will dominate, and these will expand whilst lower rated departments will either have to seek alternative funding or shrink. On the other hand, if the top departments expand too much, then the average quality will eventually decline, leading to a drop in research rating. However, whilst the exact long-run equilibrium is difficult to predict, the most obvious effect is to raise the salaries of the most able researchers. Since they are in the short run in a fixed supply, the competition of different universities for the same pool of people will bid up their salaries. There is clear evidence of this at the moment, in terms of the greater ease of promotion in many subjects, and also in the rise in professorial pay (the evidence here is anecdotal, but we are certain the figures will bear this out).

When funding is linked to performance indicators, the effects are not necessarily beneficial. The current system in the UK has certainly raised the rewards to individual academics from developing a successful research record, and has thus raised the 'productivity' of researchers in the UK in terms of publications per head of all types. However, when we look at the university level, the picture is not so clear. There are two ways of raising the quality of research: one is 'poaching' good researchers from other institutions, the other is working hard to improve the research environment of existing staff. Now, from an individual university, both of these are equally valid. From society's perspective, however, the former has little or no aggregate benefit (poaching is just a redistribution of talent, and the negative effect on the poached university will offset to some extent the gains to the poacher). The latter is, however, more unambiguously beneficial.

4.6 Conclusion

In this brief chapter, we have tried to introduce some of the basic issues involved in the measurement of performance in universities, illustrating this in the UK context. Whilst we have not covered several areas (the measurement of efficiency, financial indicators *inter alia*) in any depth, we hope to have shown the various methodological issues involved. We have shown that – while outputs are relatively easy to measure – there are great difficulties involved in deriving even crude measures of outcome. From an economist's perspective, the most interesting aspects of attempts to measure performance are the interaction of performance measures with funding mechanisms. When indicators are used to allocate funds, then behaviour changes: more effort is put into improving the indicator in order to increase funding. As our example of research funding illustrates, the 'rent seeking' behaviour engendered by this link needs to be thought through by policy makers. Whilst some consequences are socially useful, others may be wasteful. In the current environment of competition in British universities, there is often more to be gained from grade inflation and 'poaching' researchers from rival institutions than attending to improving the actual process of teaching or research within institutions.

Notes

1. For an explanation of the economic concepts used in this paper, see Gravelle and Rees (1992).
2. The statistics for British universities can be found in the CVCP management statistics (CVCP, 1989 onwards).

References

Committee of Vice-Chancellors and Principals (1989) *University Management Statistics and Performance Indicators, UK Universities*, Cheltenham: CVCP.

Gravelle, H. and Rees, R. (1992) *Micro-economics*, 2nd Edn, London: Longman, Ch. 22.

Jarrat Report (1985) *Report of the Steering Committee for Efficiency Studies in Universities*, London: Committee of Vice-Chancellors and Principals.

Johnes, G. (1993) *Economics of Education*, London: Macmillan.

Johnes, J. and Taylor, J. (1987) 'Degree quality: an investigation into differences between UK universities', *Higher Education*, **16**, pp. 581–602.

Johnes, J. and Taylor, J. (1990), *Performance Indicators in Higher Education*, SRHE/ Open University Press.

Chapter 5

Outcome Measurement in the Criminal Justice System

A. J. Fowles

5.0 Introduction

Crime will fall: watch this space (*Independent*, 29 September 1994)

Fall in crime a myth as police chiefs massage the figures (*Sunday Times*, 16 October 1994)

These two headlines which appeared in the broadsheet press some three weeks apart in the autumn of 1994 are a good indication of the cynicism with which the Press greet the publication of crime statistics. On 27 September 1994 the Home Office published their Statistical Bulletin 'Notifiable Offences England and Wales, July 1993 to June 1994' (Home Office, 1994a). The Home Office announced that 5.4 million notifiable offences were recorded by the police in the 12 months to June 1994, a fall of 5.5 per cent compared with the previous 12-month period. This was the first fall in notifiable offences in many years and reversed the apparent trend in which crime figures doubled during the period in office since 1979 of the Conservative Party, the party of law and order. The Home Office allegedly published the Bulletin a week earlier than would normally have been the case to provide some good news for the Home Secretary to take to the Conservative Party annual conference. In the absence of this good news, the Home Secretary would have had to report that the 27-point plan to reduce crime announced at the 1993 conference had not materialized, as it was then being savaged by the House of Lords. On the same day the Home Office published the results of the latest British Crime Survey, but to much less media attention. The Survey is an alternative method of measuring the amount of crime, and has consistently shown much higher levels of crime than those shown by the statistics produced by the police.

The *Sunday Times* story provided one of the most sustained attacks on police data-collection methods seen in the mass media, although it was only publicizing what criminologists, Home Office statisticians, officials and ministers (and journalists) have known for a long time. Home Office officials and ministers state that they recognize the problems of the crime statistics but still treat them as real when they show a decline. The *Sunday Times* report stated that 'hundreds of thousands of serious crimes have been quietly dropped from police records as senior officers massage their statistics to meet new Home Office efficiency targets'. The report continued by saying that about 220000 crimes had been left out of the figures as a result of police manipulation of the figures. The police, it was alleged, had refused to accept reports of some offences as being insufficiently serious to merit recording. Some offences were recorded as less serious than they otherwise might have been. The move towards performance-related pay and short-term contracts for police officers was blamed for the pressures on senior officers to 'massage' the figures.

This chapter will look at some of the problems relating to measuring outcomes in the criminal justice system, some of which stem in part from the problem of defining this system. First, therefore, the criminal justice system is described. It is complex and its boundaries are increasingly imprecise. There are many individuals and organizations with a stake in the justice system, and often their interests conflict. As a result, the discussion shows that the objectives of the criminal justice system can be stated at a number of levels, ranging from abstract ideals of justice, equal protection of the laws and respect for rights, to a desire for a system which produces cheap and speedy results. There is then a discussion of some of the issues relating to crime figures which have been recognized by Home Office statisticians and others for some time, together with the implications of the British Crime Surveys which have been carried out in the last decade. The argument then moves on to the evaluation of penal sanctions and their methodological problems. Researchers in criminal justice have treated outcomes quite differently from the preoccupations suggested by routine crime figures. Relevant material has to be collected as a special exercise and is given virtually no publicity in the news media when it is published. The chapter ends with some conclusions for future prospects.

The news stories mentioned above highlight a number of points about the criminal justice system which this chapter will seek to explore. There is a huge interest in the figures relating to the first stages of the criminal justice system, as measured by the quantity of crime recorded by the police each year. Virtually no public attention is paid to other measures of the criminal justice system. It is impossible to find a headline, in recent years, on the reconviction rates of people leaving prison. The system does not collect data systematically on the quality of justice it provides. Official measures concentrate on the efficiency of the criminal justice system rather than its effectiveness. We have no real way of measuring the quality of justice, although we know that many people plead guilty in court to speed up the whole process, and that guilty pleas in Crown Court are given discounts in terms of sentences handed down. If everyone appearing in court exercised their right to trial, the courts would grind to a halt and the prison system would fill to bursting point in months.

5.1 Structure of the Criminal Justice System

We talk about the criminal justice system, although it is not really a system in the sense of being a set of interconnected parts. However, this should not prevent us from recognizing that it may be perceived as a system by those on the receiving end of its ministrations. The system comprises a mixture of bodies such as:

- central government, in the form of the Home Office and the Lord Chancellor's Department;
- the police forces, which are mainly local (although there are non-Home Office national police forces such as the British Transport Police, Ministry of Defence and UK Atomic Energy Authority);
- magistrates' courts, which are staffed locally, and magistrates, who are appointed locally (although there is a growing trend towards centralization now that the magistrates' courts are responsible to the Lord Chancellor's Department);
- the Crown Court, which is part of the new executive agency 'The Courts Service' but is based in local centres;
- the Crown Prosecution Service, which is a national organization but which is based locally with a remit to operate locally;
- the probation services, which are locally based and organized;
- the Prison Service Agency, which is nationally managed but is becoming increasingly localized as financial and managerial control is delegated downwards to prison governors;
- the Legal Aid Board, which is the national body responsible for the administration of legal aid in England and Wales.

At this point it is worth pointing out that this list does not include the private sector, the activities of which have a profound impact on outcomes. For example:

- There are now (and have been for some time) more private security employees than public sector police: the figures are thought to be 250000 and 150000 respectively according to George and Watson (1993) although it is difficult to be precise as the private security industry is virtually unregulated.
- The involvement of the private sector is growing: it has considerable control over access to and surveillance of social spaces such as shopping precincts, shopping malls and the interiors of many shops, as well as in public buildings such as local councils and magistrates' courts.
- The private sector is increasingly involved in the penal system: the Prison Service Agency is planning to have 10 per cent of the prison system privately financed or managed in the near future to provide a stimulus of competition to the state-run sector (Prison Service Agency, 1993).

- The Home Office plans to expand the contracting out of the prison escort service (the delivery of prisoners on remand to courts for trial and/or sentence) to all 14 areas of the Prison Service Agency in England and Wales: this process will involve displacement of police and prison service personnel (Prison Service Agency, 1995, para. 208).
- Detention facilities for the Immigration and Nationality Service have been run privately for many years (Green, 1989).
- There is provision in the Criminal Justice and Public Order Act 1994 for the private sector to run secure training centres for young offenders.
- There has been steady growth in private sector crime prevention companies and schemes.

The division of criminal justice into local and central organizations has always been a significant part of the British system, as central government has been regarded as untrustworthy when it comes to issues of individual rights and freedoms. However, the past 10 or so years have seen increasing centralization of locally organized services. As costs have increased, there have been attempts to bring about greater coordination of the disparate parts of the system. Ministers have used the language of efficiency and effectiveness to justify this process.

5.2 Stakeholders in the Criminal Justice System

Although the criminal justice system is usually seen as the responsibility of professionals working within the system, it has also become or been made into one of the most significant political issues of the age. The level of crime has become an important indicator of the effectiveness of government, as party politicians have struggled to gain electoral advantage. However, the relationships between the different actors are not unproblematic, and there is no unity of interest between many of those involved in the system. Ministers and officials, the police, the judiciary, the prison service and the probation services may be thought of as acting in a concerted way. But one consequence of the criminal justice system being made up of this disparate patchwork of ancient and modern components is that there is no single body responsible for the workings of the criminal justice system. Consequently there is no single measure of its effectiveness, its efficiency, or even its annual expenditure.

Over the years, all of the bodies involved have gone their own ways, pursuing their own objectives whether these were local or national. This changed a little as a result of the Criminal Justice Act 1991, which established a national Criminal Justice Consultative Committee made up of national representatives of the different statutory bodies involved in the criminal justice system. The Legal Affairs Correspondent of the BBC suggested that this body could only have come into existence with the appointment of the present Lord Chief Justice (the most senior criminal trial judge in England and Wales). His predecessor would have left the room if a civil servant were to enter, so strong were his views about judicial independence from the executive. It remains to be seen what the Consultative Committee will do, as at present its main function seems to be to inform the different actors in the system about the financial implications of their decisions. (For example, judges sentencing someone to prison now know that it will cost the Prison Service Agency between £14015 and £34377 per annum depending on the level of security they are thought to need (Prison Service Agency, 1995, p. 46).) There are also local area consultative committees which are supposed to provide a similar forum at a county level.

One of the other important innovations of the Criminal Justice Act 1991 is the requirement in section 95 for the Home Secretary to inform himself about ethnicity issues in the areas of activity for which he has responsibility. This came about as a response to the finding that about 18 per cent of the prison population come from ethnic minorities, compared with their representation in the general population of about 6 per cent (Walmsley *et al.*, 1992). However, it is not yet clear what is going to be done with any relevant information that the Home Secretary collects, especially as he has little influence over areas such as magisterial and judicial training.

One of the main planks of Conservative Party policy since 1979 has been to provide greater resources for the police. The incoming government in 1979 was committed to increasing police pay in relation to other workers and to increasing the number of police officers. But the relationship between government and police has not been a happy one, as the number of offences recorded did not decline in response to the increase in the number of officers. The local organization and accountability of the police has meant that local priorities could legitimately be pursued, and these did not always coincide with those of ministers and voters. Ministers might have preferred action against demonstrators, strikers or football hooligans; householders want their streets patrolled by officers in uniform. The Police and Magistrates' Court Act 1994 is designed to allow the Home Office to impose centrally determined aims and objectives on police forces and to use inspections to enforce their application.

The discussion so far has been about the system and – as is usually the case – victims have not been mentioned. As a generalization, victims have had the lowest and least consideration in the criminal justice system, although the development of victim support schemes and the National Association of Victim Support Schemes has gone a little way towards remedying this defect. There is ample evidence to suggest that victims are often not informed of the progress of their case, and that some victims only discover by chance what has happened by reading about their offender in the local or national newspapers (Victim Support, 1995). Victims are now being asked for their views when their offender is being considered for temporary release from prison, but as yet no one has really grasped the nettle of involving victims in the sentencing process. Thus, although proposals by the Home Secretary to reduce payments to victims of violence through the Criminal Injuries Compensation scheme were held to be unlawful by the Court of Appeal, official commitment to victims seems to be secondary to official commitment to control of public expenditure (*Guardian*, 10 November 1994).

5.3 Objectives of the Criminal Justice System

By setting out the conflicts of interest between the various stakeholders in criminal justice, it has been implied that there is no consensus over what the criminal justice system should be doing. So far in this discussion the criminal justice system has been described rather than defined. Yet it is essential to provide a definition and statement of objectives before any evaluation can be attempted. In doing so, at one level appeals can be made to cultural values of justice – although in practice when dealing with individual criminal acts we are often more concerned with the wrongness of the behaviour. Justice tends to mean fairness when we consider the treatment of individuals accused of wrong acts by the police and the courts. There is a tendency to believe that fairness of procedure leads to fairness of outcome. When individuals have been processed by the courts, punishments are usually justified in terms of ideas of retribution, deterrence, rehabilitation, incapacitation or reform. Some court sentences can satisfy several of these justifications simultaneously.

In practice evaluations of the criminal justice system are much more limited. The Royal Commission on Criminal Justice, which published its report in 1993, limited its enquiry to:

> . . . the stage at which the police are investigating an alleged or reported criminal offence right through to the stage at which a defendant who has been found guilty of such an offence has exhausted his or her rights of appeal. (1993, para. 5)

The Royal Commission went on to note that they were excluding consideration of the causes of crime, sentencing, the legal definition of criminal offences, police powers of both arrest and stop and search, and the granting of bail by the courts.

This might seem to be a considerable retreat from the values mentioned earlier, but statements by government departments of objectives of criminal justice are even more prosaic. Each year the Home Office makes a statement of its aims and the 1995 version states that:

> The principal aims of the Home Office are to secure individuals' rights and freedoms under the law and to provide for the protection and security of the public. (1995b, para. 1.1)

The Annual Report explains the main functions of the Home Office in pursuing these aims in the following terms:

- to promote effective and efficient policing;
- to ensure that the courts have suitable sentencing powers and that they can be given effect;
- to promote effective ways of preventing crime and supporting victims;
- to keep in custody those committed by the courts;
- to maintain and review as necessary the constitutional arrangements, the criminal law and the procedures of the criminal justice system; and
- to regulate a wide range of matters (including gambling and liquor licensing). (para. 1.2)

By contrast the Lord Chancellor's Department states its fundamental aim as 'to ensure the efficient, effective and affordable administration of justice' (1995, para. 2). The Lord Chancellor's Annual Report goes on to state that:

> In support of the Government's objective of controlling public expenditure, the Department has made it a *strategic priority* to control legal aid costs and contain expenditure on court services, while maintaining proper standards of service by means consistent with this priority.
>
> The *guiding principles* which will inform all the Department's work are to:
>
> protect and advance the rule of law;
> ensure a fair and efficient system of justice;
> safeguard the independence of the judiciary and the judicial process;
> provide service to all citizens using or involved in the processes of law;
> ensure openness, subject only to exceptions necessary to protect individuals and the public interest; and
> promote equal opportunities. (paras 3 and 4, emphasis in original)

Both of these official statements demonstrate clearly the contrasting levels of aims and objectives. The second is particularly significant in the way that it raises 'controlling public expenditure' to a strategic priority while a 'fair system of justice' is a guiding principle. The implication seems to be that when efficiency and fairness conflict, efficiency will have priority. Openness and the protection of individuals provide a further possibility for conflict; the identity of the arbiter of 'the public interest' is not mentioned.

5.4 Accounting for Crime

The single most comprehensive source of information about criminal justice in England and Wales is the annual *Criminal Statistics* and the discussion will now turn to look at the main crime figures. In doing so, it is important to draw a distinction between the information about crime which is routinely collected for the administration of justice and related issues of accountability, and that collected for research purposes. The *Criminal Statistics* include information about the throughput of cases recorded by the police as well the clear-up rate, which is treated as a measure of police effectiveness. There has long been recognition of the problems of interpreting longer term trends in crime, as counting and reporting changes may affect comparability from one police force to another, or from one year to the next. This section also considers the British Crime Survey, which provides an alternative way of collecting information about the incidence of crime. The section will conclude with a discussion of evaluative information, which tends to be collected on a 'one-off' basis.

The Home Office has been responsible for the collection and publication of statistics relating to crime in England and Wales since the early nineteenth century and has published annual *Criminal Statistics England and Wales* since the 1850s. Despite changes in the law, these figures have been published in a more or less consistent form over that time. They always contain material on the total number of 'notifiable offences' known to the police. Notifiable offences are the more serious offences, ranging from murder through sexual and other offences against the person to crimes against property such as burglary, theft, forgery and fraud, criminal damage and arson. Counts of notifiable offences represent all the offences recorded by the 43 Home Office police forces. Since 1989 the most important of the non-Home Office police forces (British Transport Police, Ministry of Defence Police and UK Atomic Energy Authority) have also provided crime figures, but these are not included in the national statistics unless the offence has also been recorded by a local Home Office force (Home Office, 1995a, p. 222).

The other major item of information presented by the police forces in the *Criminal Statistics for England and Wales* is the 'clear-up rate', which is often regarded as the main measure of police effectiveness in solving crime. Officially an offence is regarded as 'cleared up' if a person has been charged, summonsed or cautioned for the offence; if the offence has been admitted and is taken into consideration by the court; if the victim is unable or unwilling to give evidence; and – in some cases – if there is sufficient evidence to charge a person but the case is not proceeded with, perhaps because the offender is under the age of criminal responsibility, is already serving a long prison sentence or is mentally ill. Also, it may be the case that no further police action is taken, even if there is sufficient evidence to charge that person. For example, a case may not be proceeded with when information is obtained through a prison interview with a person already serving a custodial sentence for another offence. Moreover, none of this implies that a person charged with an offence is convicted, let alone sentenced.

Clear-up rates have declined over the years. The rate for England and Wales was 45 per cent in 1970 but after rising to 47 per cent in 1973 it fell steadily, and in 1993 it was only 25 per cent. In 1993, 1.3 million notifiable offences were cleared up. In many recent years the rise in recorded crime has outweighed an absolute increase in the number of offences cleared up. The pattern is consistent across the country, with, for example, the majority of police forces showing a fall in clear-up rate in 1993.

There are considerable problems in knowing what clear-up rates mean. They may simply be a reflection of the strategies pursued in the particular forces, and may not be an indication of investigative performance. Chris Mullin, MP, has argued that some police officers persuade inmates to confess to crimes they have not committed as a way of boosting detection rates. He used official figures to show that 44 per cent of all crimes in Merseyside were 'solved' as a result of interviews with prisoners. By contrast, the Metropolitan Police clear up just 1 per cent of offences through such interviews. Other forces which seem to rely heavily on this practice are: West Midlands – 34 per cent, Greater Manchester – 33 per cent, Cheshire – 25 per cent, North Yorkshire – 23 per cent, and South Yorkshire – 22 per cent (*Independent*, 25 May 1992). Two further points need to be made about clear-up rates:

- Home Office research conducted in 1977 looked at the clear-up rates of the police forces in England and Wales. The study involved looking at the statistical association between clear-up and other indicators, such as the proportion of the police budget spent on CID officers and expenditure on the police. But what seemed to be most important was the rate at which crime was reported. The public are responsible for reporting about 70 per cent of crime in the first place, and the police themselves are responsible for observing and/or detecting the rest (Steer, 1980).
- The 'crime mix' is a crucial determinant of clear-up success. Areas with high proportions of certain crimes – such as violence against the person, sexual offences, forgery and fraud, and shoplifting – tend to have high clear-up rates because of the face-to-face contact involved. Indeed shoplifting in one sense does not exist unless someone is observed in the act. These considerations have been found to be more important than virtually all of the indicators which relate to police organization and activity, except for the number of police per head of population in the area being policed (Burrows and Tarling, 1982).

Crime statistics are often presented as if there were no difficulties at all in their collection and presentation, although – as noted above – it is fair to say that the police and the Home Office statisticians will admit to problems associated with the data. I discuss some of these now.

The police cannot be everywhere at the same time, and most crime is reported by ordinary citizens. But there are several reasons why not all incidents of law-breaking are reported:

- there may be no police around to whom the offence can be notified;
- the individual may not recognize him/herself as a victim, as the behaviour

is regarded as 'normal' in their locality;
- it may be not done to 'grass' (inform) in the neighbourhood (as some of the graffiti naming people as 'grasses' on the highway signs on the A19 outside Middlesbrough testify);
- the victim may not want the police to take any interest in their affairs;
- there may be no specific victim (e.g. vagrancy);
- the offence may be consensual when there is an illicit service being given (e.g. sale of drugs, prostitution, illegal abortion).

The Home Office knows a great deal more about why people do not report offences since the introduction of the British Crime Surveys in the 1980s. The British Crime Survey (BCS) has been carried out five times in England and Wales (1982, 1984, 1988, 1992 and 1994), with each survey examining crime in the previous year. Until 1994, a representative sample of about 10000 people aged 16 and over was interviewed. In 1994, the sample was increased to 14500. It is recognized that the Survey does not provide a complete count of crime, as crimes against businesses and drugs offences cannot be covered in a household survey. There are also problems of error associated with representativeness, the problems of peoples' memories, their unwillingness to talk about their experiences as victims, and their failure to realize that an incident is relevant to the survey (Mayhew *et al.*, 1994).

There are important differences between the police methods of recording crime and those used by the BCS. Mayhew and her colleagues suggest that the Survey applies what can be called a 'nominal' definition of crime, without a threshold of severity, and therefore includes any incident which is technically a crime. The police on the other hand use a more 'operational' definition:

> They count incidents reported by victims which are seen as crimes as (i) defined by the criminal law (i.e. which *could* be punished by a court); (ii) which *should* merit the attention of the criminal justice system; and, (iii) which meet organizational demands for reasonable evidence. (Mayhew *et al.*, 1989, p. 4)

The police may decide because the evidence is weak that an incident should be treated as 'no crime', and consequently it will not be recorded in the *Criminal Statistics*. The recording and counting of crime therefore reflects judgments made by both the police and the public. The 1984 Survey showed that, while the majority of unreported incidents were not judged serious or amenable to effective police action, a good number were rated as serious. On the other hand, many incidents that *were* reported were thought to be relatively trivial and not the type of offence to merit much police attention (Pease, 1988).

The key points which come out of the most recent BCS (Mayhew *et al.*, 1994, p. 1) are:

- The BCS estimated a total of 18 million crimes in 1993 against individuals and their property. For those BCS offences which can be compared directly with police statistics problems of incomplete reporting and recording mean that only just over a quarter are estimated to end up in police records.

- Between 1981 and 1993, for those offences which can be compared, the number of crimes recorded by the police increased by 111 per cent; the BCS showed a lower rise of 77 per cent. The divergence in the figures is due to a smaller increase in vandalism and violence according to the BCS. Acquisitive crime has risen by much the same extent on both measures.
- Recorded crime shows a larger increase than the BCS mainly because a greater proportion of crimes are now reported to the police than in 1981. In the case of vandalism and violence, more reported crime may have also been recorded by the police.
- From the most recent figures – 1991 to 1993 – for those crime types which can be compared, recorded crime figures have risen by 7 per cent, whereas BCS figures rose by 18 per cent, reversing the previous pattern. The greater rise in BCS offences was apparent across most offence categories.
- Police figures of crime since 1991 may have risen less steeply than the BCS because the proportion of crimes reported to the police has fallen.

The Home Office itself recognized that the method of collecting statistics ought to be investigated in the early 1960s. A Departmental Committee was set up, which reported in 1967. Their report provides the basis for the current system. The Committee wanted to standardize practices across England and Wales (which was important in 1967 because there were then some 112 police forces at that time – just before the great amalgamation of 1968) (Home Office, 1967).

The Home Office Departmental Committee also recognized that there were problems to do with the recording of offences. For example, what should be done if someone is charged with one type of offence and is eventually convicted of another less serious alternative? The counting rules adopted in 1980 were designed to provide a comprehensive and detailed guidance for the counting of each type of offence. The rules specify that, in most circumstances, only the most serious offence is counted where several offences are committed in one incident. Violence and sexual offences are treated as exceptions when – for instance – there is more than one victim. While central guidance is issued, many decisions have to be taken locally about the recording, classification and counting of crime incidents, and collectively the Home Office statisticians realize that these decisions have an effect on the comparability of statistics for different areas. A broken window might variously be interpreted and recorded as an accident, criminal damage (vandalism) or an attempted burglary.

Fluctuations are extremely difficult to understand and interpret. Does an increase in an offence mean that people are committing more offences? Or does it mean that people are being more honest and reporting offences more quickly? Does the fact that more property is insured mean that thefts are reported only when insurance claims are being made? Are offences being reported because public/individual awareness has increased? For example, are more sexual offences being reported because victims think they will now be treated more sympathetically, or at least be believed?

The *Criminal Statistics for England and Wales* contain large sections on the sentences handed down by the courts, but traditionally have had nothing to say about what happens to offenders after sentence. Bottomley and Pease (1986, p. 162) suggest that there has been less information published about further offending in the postwar than the interwar period. They attribute this change to penal pessimism, and a concern with the criminal justice system as an efficient rather than an effective system. This is not to say that this sort of work has not been done and published. However, it has had a research focus rather than the performance focus of statistics routinely collected and published in the *Criminal Statistics*. Since the 1960s a very large proportion of the research effort in British criminology has been devoted to the evaluation of penal sanctions, in the shape either of studies of the effectiveness of sentencing, or of how sentencing options have been developed and used. The Home Office Research and Planning Unit (and its predecessor Home Office Research Unit) is the largest single concentration of criminologists in Britain, and for much of its existence it has devoted its energies to research of this type, to the virtual exclusion of other topics.

Some information has been collected in a systematic way on all people given particular sentences or sanctions. However, these have not been published in any one place, and an interested reader would have to trace several official publications. The Prison Service has traditionally published information on the reconviction rates of those sentenced to imprisonment, and this information is published in *Prison Statistics England and Wales*. The Parole Board for England and Wales publishes an *Annual Report* which includes information on those recalled from early release on licence. Reasons for recall include breaches of the conditions of licence as well as commission of further offences. When the Home Office publishes information relating to further offending on parole the figure is usually low (less than 10 per cent), but it relates only to those who commit another offence and are convicted during the licence period. Those who offend on licence but are subsequently convicted after the licence has expired would count as a 'success'.

In the 1960s the idea that the courts could sentence offenders 'scientifically' in the sense that they could obtain information about the social criminal background of the offender and then match the sentence or order to the needs of the offender was an explicit part of Home Office policy (Home Office, 1962). Research was conducted to provide sentencers with information about the effectiveness of the various sentencing options then available to the courts in the shape of *The Sentence of the Court: a Handbook for Courts on the Treatment of Offenders* (Home Office, 1964). The subtitle is especially significant, as this publication provided comparisons of the sentencing options based on characteristics of offenders that were thought to be associated with differentials in reconviction rates. Home Office staff identified factors such as the gender of the offender, their age at first conviction, the number of previous convictions, and the nature of the current offence. On the basis of this information it was possible to calculate *expected* and *actual* rates of reconviction for the different sentencing disposals. The sort of conclusion drawn was that fines were followed by the fewest reconvictions (compared with the expected numbers) for both first offenders and recidivists of all ages, probation produced relatively better results when used for offenders with previous convictions, and imprisonment results were better for offenders with previous convictions (Home Office, 1964, para. 161).

Criminologists across the world have spent large amounts of time and effort evaluating penal sanctions and comparing the effectiveness of a wider variety of innovatory schemes. This research has been subjected to meta-analysis, of which the most important was produced by Lipton and his colleagues for the New York State Senate (Lipton *et al.*, 1975). They produced a sophisticated review of evaluation studies written in English since 1945 which met various reliability criteria. The review established that some penal measures did work when applied to specific categories of offenders. However, publication of the full study was preceded by the appearance of an article by one of the authors of the review, Martinson, who broke away and wrote an article entitled 'What works? Questions and answers about prison reform'. This concluded that very little – if anything – worked in the sense of reducing reconviction rates below those expected (Martinson, 1974). This version of the review gained international prominence, and there developed a widespread 'penal nihilism' which influenced many practitioners in the criminal justice system. It led to the idea that nothing worked, and to a general downgrading of what was thought possible in the penal system. This 'nihilism' is still present, but has not completely stopped researchers looking for differential effects in penal sanctions.

The study of reconviction rates by Phillpotts and Lancucki (1979) is somewhat in the tradition of *The Sentence of the Court*, in that it examined the pattern of reconviction of a sample of 5000 offenders sentenced during January 1971. They found that 50 per cent of the males and 22 per cent of the females were reconvicted within a six-year follow-up period. The authors concluded that males given custodial sentences had higher reconviction rates than males given suspended sentences or probation orders or supervision orders, and that these in turn had higher reconviction rates than males given fines or absolute or conditional discharges.

More recently the Home Office has been studying the criminal careers of people involved with the criminal justice system. Just over 35 per cent of males born in 1953 have been convicted of a standard list (almost the same as a notifiable offence) by the age of 35, compared with 8 per cent of females born in that year. Of those males born in 1953, 7 per cent had received a custodial sentence before the age of 36, compared with just under half of 1 per cent of the females (Home Office, 1995a, p. 198).

The Home Office has recently published what it describes as 'the first major comparative study of reconviction rates in this country for 15 years' (Lloyd *et al.*, 1995, p. vii). This research compares the two-year reconviction rates for community service orders, probation orders with and without various requirements (e.g. attendance at a probation day activity centre), and imprisonment. The authors report that past offending is one of the best predictors of reconviction and that there was no firm indication that community penalties outperformed custody or vice versa in preventing re-offending. The study also shows that those committing serious crimes were no more likely to be reconvicted than others – many of the most serious categories of crime had low reconviction rates.

5.5 Conclusions

The nature of the criminal justice system seems to preclude the possibility of measuring what the system is actually doing. It is too complex to be the subject of one measurement device, and the multiplicity of measures that are provided in official statistics simply do not describe the totality of the system. Criminal justice in England and Wales has been divided into separate organizations for historical reasons, and this fragmentation conflicts with the official aim of efficiency which is coming to predominate. Numerous appeals are made to abstract ideals of justice, but the operating instructions for those working in the system on a daily basis are much more mundane and often relate to costs. In the 1960s, the American legal philosopher Herbert Packer identified two models of criminal justice, which he termed the 'crime control' model and the 'due process' model. He suggested that the crime control model is concerned with the routine processing of cases, while the due process model stresses the rights of individual accused persons. The crime control model is an assembly line, while the due process model is an obstacle course. Despite using the rhetoric of the due process model, the criminal justice system operates on crime control principles.

Official statistics reflect this by concentrating on the front of the system – its early stages, as manifested in police activity – and have tended to ignore everything else. It is not possible to isolate the costs of the police statistics which are routinely collected. Yet more evaluative work has to be conducted on a one-off basis, and a case has to be made for the expenditure involved. Police officers, criminologists, Home Office statisticians and officials, and even Home Office ministers know that the figure of 'notifiable offences known to the police' has to be treated with great caution, and they exercise that caution on some occasions. But they all also treat the same figures as real indicators of the state of the nation and forget, at least temporarily, what they know about the processes which lie behind the figures. Since the collection and analysis of the first British Crime Survey there has been a great deal of additional information available as to why some people report offences and others do not. Moreover, Home Office Research Studies are statements of official Home Office policy. Unlike research reports from many other government departments, these reports do not carry any disclaimers, and the assumption can be made that their contents will have been reported to ministers.

The diversity of organizations involved in the criminal justice system means that we know a great deal about its component parts, but very little about how it all hangs together. Each of the component parts of the system is given narrow objectives which can be measured in the form of simple data, and the assumption is made that this will allow greater accountability. But the data are collected and presented in a series of snapshots, so that it is impossible to follow one case or one person through the system from arrest, through decision making by the Crown Prosecution Service, to the courts and then into the penal system. The unit of account is different in successive stages in the process, beginning with offences, then changing to offenders and finally becoming prison receptions. For example, the same person can be received into prison several times in the same year depending on the sentence length. One consequence of this is that it is difficult to give a figure for the number of individuals who come into contact with the criminal justice system each year, and as a result there are heated debates about how widespread criminal activity really is.

Moreover, we have very little information about the 'justice' of the criminal justice system and its effects on society as a whole. Traditionally the assumption has been made that the police are fair, that our legal processes are fair and therefore the outcomes of these processes will be fair. Research is beginning to show that the criminal justice system operates against the interests of some groups in society, and that they are subjected to special surveillance as a result of police stereotyping. Stevens and Willis (1979) have shown how young Afro-Caribbeans are more likely to be stopped, searched and arrested than their white counterparts. Other Home Office research has shown that the unemployed are more likely to be given custodial sentences than those in employment (8 per cent compared with 1 per cent) and more likely to be sentenced to probation (14 per cent of unemployed offenders compared with 5 per cent of those in employment) (Home Office, 1994b).

The institutions of the criminal justice system have been undergoing a period of radical change in their form and structure. Their remits have been progressively reduced in scope and their activities scrutinized to discover how efficiently they process their caseloads. The reasons why people commit crime in the first place or continue after contacts with the criminal justice system are increasingly seen to lie outside their scope. Instead, crime has become seen as a matter of individual responsibility, to be suppressed as quickly and cheaply as possible. As a result, the opportunities for rectifying errors have been reduced as access to legal advice is seen as a disproportionate cost. The new financial regimes put a premium on meeting performance targets, as expressed in a limited and partial set of measures. If this is accomplished at the expense of some other parts of the system, that merely reflects the existing preoccupations of those with power within the system.

References

Bottomley, K. and Pease, K. (1986) *Crime and Punishment: Interpreting the Data*, Milton Keynes: Open University Press.

Burrows, J. and Tarling, R. (1982) *Clearing Up Crime*, London: HMSO.

George, B. and Watson, T. (1993) 'Regulation of the private security industry', *Public Money and Management* (1, January–March), pp. 55–7.

Green, P. (1989) *Private Sector Involvement in the Immigration Detention Centres*, London: Howard League for Penal Reform.

Home Office (1962) *Report of the Departmental Committee on the Probation Service*, Cmnd 1650, London: HMSO.

Home Office (1964) *The Sentence of the Court: a Handbook for the Treatment of Offenders*, London: HMSO.

Home Office (1967) *Report of the Departmental Committee on Criminal Statistics* (Chairman: W. Perks), Cmnd 3448, London: HMSO.

Home Office (1994a) *Notifiable Offences England and Wales, July 1993 to June 1994*, Home Office Statistical Bulletin Issue 24/94, London: Home Office Research and Statistics Department.

Home Office (1994b) *Monitoring the Criminal Justice Acts 1991 and 1993 – Results from a Special Data Collection Exercise*, Issue 20/94, London: Home Office Research and Statistics Department.

Home Office (1995a) *Criminal Statistics for England and Wales 1993*, Cm 2680, London: HMSO.

Home Office (1995b) *Annual Report 1995: the Government's Expenditure Plans 1995–96 to 1997–98 for the Home Office and the Charity Commission*, Cm 2808, London: HMSO.

Lipton, D. *et al.* (1975) *The Effectiveness of Correctional Treatment – a Survey of Treatment Studies*, New York: Praeger.

Lloyd, C., Mair, G. and Hough, M. (1995) *Explaining Reconviction Rates: a Critical Analysis*, London: HMSO.

Lord Chancellor's Department (1995) *Departmental Report of the Lord Chancellor's and Law Officers' Departments – the Government's Expenditure Plans 1995–96 to 1997–98*, Cm 2809, London: HMSO.

Martinson, R. (1974) 'What works? Questions and answers about prison reform', *Public Interest*, **35**, pp. 22–54.

Mayhew, P., Elliott, D. and Dowds, L. (1989) *The 1988 British Crime Survey*, London: HMSO.

Mayhew, P., Mirrlees-Black; C. and Maung , N. A. (1994) *Trends in Crime: Findings from the 1994 British Crime Survey*, Research Findings No. 14, London: Home Office Research and Statistics Department.

Packer, H. L. (1968) *The Limits of the Criminal Sanction*, Stanford, CA: Stanford University Press.

Pease, K. (1988) *Judgements of Crime Seriousness: Evidence from the 1984 British Crime Survey*, Home Office Research and Planning Unit Paper No. 44, London: Home Office.

Phillpotts, G. J. O. and Lancucki, L. B. (1979) *Previous Convictions, Sentence and Reconviction: a Statistical Study of a Sample of 5,000 Offenders Convicted*

in January 1971, London: HMSO.
Prison Service Agency (1993) *Corporate Plan 1993–96*, London: Prison Service.
Prison Service Agency (1995) *Prison Service Annual Report and Accounts April 1993 – March 1994*, HC185, London: HMSO.
Royal Commission on Criminal Justice (1993) *Report*, Cm 2263, London: HMSO.
Steer, D. (1980) *Uncovering Crime: the Police Role*, London: HMSO.
Stevens, P. and Willis, C. (1979) *Race, Crime and Arrests*, London: HMSO.
Victim Support (1995) *The Rights of Victims of Crime – A Policy Paper*, London: Victim Support.
Walmsley, R., Howard, L. and White, S. (1992) *The National Prison Survey 1991: Main Findings*, London: HMSO.

Chapter 6

Outcome Measures in Community Care

Andrew Nocon and Hazel Qureshi

6.0 Introduction

The term 'community care' has a range of meanings. The focus in this chapter is on those policies and services which aim to provide help and support to disabled or older people to assist them to achieve a normal life in their own homes or in a 'homely environment'. Users of such services include older people, younger disabled people with physical or sensory impairments, people with a learning disability and people with mental health problems. The main public sector services which provide community care are local authority social services and community health services. The NHS and Community Care Act 1990 made it clear that local authorities are the lead agencies in ensuring the provision of community care. As in other areas of public sector provision, financial and organizational structures were introduced which were designed to ensure an injection of market principles into service provision. These financial arrangements give incentives for authorities to shift from bureaucratic control over their own services towards a greater degree of agency control through contracting-out services to the private and voluntary sectors.

It must be acknowledged that the boundaries of what constitutes community care are often considered to extend beyond this narrow service or agency-linked focus. User groups emphasize that their quality of life in the community is often dependent on many services other than those provided or purchased by the NHS or by social services authorities. For example, policies in relation to income maintenance, employment, transport and housing may all have substantial effects on their capacity to achieve a normal life (Qureshi *et al.*, 1994). In addition, the majority of care which supports disabled and older people is not provided by formal agencies at all, but by family members and, less commonly, by neighbours and friends. This range of relevant influences on life in the community may not affect the ways in which outcomes for individuals should be defined or measured, but, as will be seen, it certainly brings into prominence many of the difficulties of analysis and interpretation which were outlined in Chapter 1.

The White Paper *Caring for People* (Department of Health *et al.*, 1989) which preceded the legislation outlined a number of broad objectives for individuals which should underpin community care. The changes were intended to:

- enable people to live as normal a life as possible in their own homes or in a homely environment in the local community;
- provide the right amount of care and support to help people achieve maximum possible independence and, by acquiring or re-acquiring basic living skills, help them to achieve their full potential;
- give people a greater individual say in how they live their lives and the services they need to help them to do so. (para. 1.8)

The White Paper stressed that the promotion of choice and independence underpinned the government's proposals. In addition, community care services should:

- respond flexibly and sensitively to the needs of individuals and their carers;
- allow a range of options for consumers;
- intervene no more than is necessary to foster independence;
- concentrate on those with the greatest needs. (para. 1.10)

These objectives were widely accepted, though there remains much debate about the most appropriate means of achieving them. There are as yet no agreed ways of measuring achievement of these objectives in operational practice with individual service users. In routine practice, the measurement of the outcomes of community care for individuals is rare, and is usually confined to destinational outcome: that is, either being, or not being, in some form of residential care. The measurement of inputs, such as the number of hours per week of home care, is more common than the measurement of final outcomes in the form of impacts upon individuals. Immediately following the implementation of the NHS and Community Care Act, monitoring and evaluation from the centre concentrated on outcomes largely in terms of organizational structure and process – for example the implementation of systems for assessment and care management. Subsequently, however, there has been some movement towards an acknowledgement of the importance of measuring outcomes for individuals (SSI/NHS Executive, 1994).

Some work on measuring community care outcomes has been carried out by researchers. However, the measures that have been used are often more detailed and more time-consuming to implement than would be practicable in routine operational situations. In addition, research has tended to reflect different policy concerns in relation to different user groups, rather than to address issues that are common to all users of community care services. While many of the questions investigated by researchers would be relevant to outcome measurement in routine practice, there is a need for existing measures to be translated into a form that could be more widely and easily used.

This chapter concentrates on outcomes for service users and their carers, and the extent to which these are, or might be, measured by social services authorities in routine practice. It is in three sections. We first examine the current organizational context for the provision of community care services, the different objectives those services are expected to meet, and some of the issues that need to be addressed in the measurement, analysis and interpretation of outcomes – as outlined in the cybernetic model in Chapter 1. The second section considers work that is currently being undertaken by social services authorities to monitor whether objectives are being met: we will indicate the extent to which such work takes account of outcomes for individuals. Finally, we examine the potential of existing research-based measures to be incorporated into, or to inform, routine outcome measurement. This section will also suggest ways of developing such measurement, while taking account of operational difficulties that may arise.

6.1 Outcomes in the New Context

As outlined above, social services authorities are expected to separate their commissioning and providing functions and to introduce a contracting system for the purchase of community care services. The commissioning role entails the introduction of care management arrangements, including formal assessment procedures, and the specification of the way needs are to be met. Other organizational changes include the requirement to produce annual community care plans, the introduction of formal complaints procedures and the creation of inspection units. These changes were phased in between 1991 and 1993. The intention is that provision should be needs-led rather than service-led.

An integral part of the changes was the transfer from the Department of Social Security to social services authorities of the responsibility for funding placements in residential and nursing homes. It was argued that access to public funding for such placements should be based on needs assessment rather than merely individual choices to enter residential care (Audit Commission, 1986). Under the previous system, residential care of some kind was often the only choice available to people who needed considerable assistance. One of the reasons given for the change in the 1989 White Paper was that it would make possible an extension of community-based alternatives to residential care, and hence should lead to more acceptable outcomes for service users. At the same time, the measure represented a restriction in individual choice in the sense that some people who previously would have had access to public funding for residential care may no longer be eligible to receive it. Undoubtedly the soaring cost of funding residential care placements through the social security system was a major influence on the decision to introduce the community care changes.

The need for outcome measurement has been heightened by the new arrangements. Purchasers need information about service effectiveness if appropriate contracts are to be agreed. Judgments about the extent to which needs are being met through the new care management arrangements depend on information being available from both initial assessments and subsequent reviews. Effective inspection procedures should focus not just on structures and processes but also on the achievement of specific service objectives. More generally, as will be discussed below, concerns and criticisms have been increasingly voiced by users, carers and the general public about the nature and quality of community care services. If shortcomings are to be fully identified and rectified, information is needed about the outcomes of the services provided.

Although the conventional model of organizational performance (as outlined in Chapter 1) aims to draw a clear distinction between process and outcome, this poses some particular difficulties in relation to community care. Gaster (1991) points out that objectives such as 'responding when users need a service' or 'meeting users' wishes' are aspects of both process and outcome. Equally, 'non-technical' aspects of a service, such as listening, giving time, empathizing, thinking through and looking for underlying problems, giving information and allowing users to make choices, all highlight the difficulty of establishing where process ends and outcomes begin. Users and carers often emphasize process when commenting on the quality of the community care services provided. Evidence to the House of Commons Health Committee (1993) about users' and carers' concerns included statements about unacceptable staff attitudes, buck-passing between agencies and a failure to plan ahead. While it is accepted that aspects of process seem to be important contributors to user and carer satisfaction or dissatisfaction with services, there remain strong arguments for considering direct outcomes for individuals: for example, short delivery times for equipment or adaptations are obviously desirable, but it is pointless to achieve fast delivery of equipment which is not used, or which does not achieve its intention of increasing the independence of the user.

In keeping with the definition in Chapter 1, we understand an outcome for an individual to be the impact, effect or consequence of a service or policy. A number of steps are necessary before it is possible to measure in practice the degree to which service objectives have been achieved for individuals. Decisions taken at each step are rarely straightforward and frequently open to argument. First, it is necessary to understand what aspects of the person's state or situation are intended to be affected: is it their psychological well-being, their opportunity for social activities, or their everyday functioning? Second, once the appropriate domains are selected, it is necessary to decide how to measure these areas so that the changes it is hoped to achieve will be detectable. Finally, the changes which are observed must be interpreted, particularly in relation to whether it is possible to attribute them to the actions of service providers rather than some other cause.

What is to be Measured?

The specific domains to be included in outcome measurement will depend on broad policy objectives, the aims of particular services and the needs of individual users and carers. Those services for different user groups which have been subject to research evaluation have had different underlying objectives. In the case of people with learning disabilities, for example, the focus of community care evaluations has typically been on deinstitutionalization and integration into the community. Mental health services have included community provision for former long-term hospital residents, as well as support for those already living in the community. The emphasis in evaluation of services for physically disabled people has been on rehabilitation and support in community living, while the most common aim in community care evaluation in relation to older people has been the prevention of institutionalization.

These different objectives and emphases have served to define the outcomes that are considered appropriate and hence the specific type of outcome measures that have been developed in evaluative research. For older people, for instance, the focus has typically been on the performance of activities of daily living, warmth, finances and morale – reflecting a policy focus on living at home and the prevention of admission to institutions. For people with learning disabilities, there has been an emphasis on community participation, a homely environment and opportunities to mix with non-disabled people – issues that reflect a reaction to the worst observed characteristics of institutions and a policy concern with deinstitutionalization.

Different Stakeholders

Such issues and concerns, however, tend to reflect policy makers' and professionals' own interests. While there has always been a recognition of different views within those groups, there is now an increasing awareness of the legitimate rights of other stakeholders in determining both the nature of the services to be provided and the definition of desirable outcomes. Those stakeholders include not only central government, social services authorities, the staff involved in service provision, and other statutory and voluntary organizations, but also users, carers and the general public. Even where there is apparent agreement on a broad objective, it does not follow that there will be consensus about how that objective should be measured in practice. For people with a physical impairment, for example, there has been a focus on the measurement of independence in terms of physical functioning and mobility. However, the disability movement has increasingly argued for the importance of autonomy, choice and control as reflections of the concept of independence. Some of the objectives of different stakeholders will now be considered.

The objectives of central government

As was mentioned earlier, the White Paper *Caring for People* indicated that the new arrangements should enable people to 'live as normal a life as possible', 'achieve maximum possible independence', 'give people a greater individual say in how they live their lives', and 'respond flexibly and sensitively' to users' and carers' needs. Such objectives pose a formidable challenge to those involved in evaluating the outcomes of the new arrangements. Broad principles need to be translated into more specific variables that can be measured and words such as 'normal' have to be defined more precisely – all without distorting the specified objectives. In addition, the difficulties of considering the timescale within which effects may be expected to appear will figure prominently in relation to situations of long-term care in which there may be no easily defined end point to intervention.

Users' and carers' views

The importance of users' and carers' views is a central feature of the new arrangements, whether in defining needs and services (as emphasized in *Caring for People*), or in identifying the criteria by which services are to be evaluated (House of Commons, 1993). Users and carers have themselves highlighted many changes and improvements that they wish to see in community care services. Underpinning those services are principles such as: respect, autonomy, being treated as an individual, a recognition of the totality of individual needs, a normal pattern of life within the community, additional help to develop maximum potential, choice, a recognition of the work and needs of carers, and partnership in service planning (Beeforth *et al.*, 1990; CPA, 1990; Henwood, 1993; King's Fund, 1989; Morris, 1993). The specific services required will vary according to the needs of the individuals or groups concerned, ranging across many aspects of practical and emotional support, the built environment, information, prompt service provision and affordable costs. Many users' and carers' definitions of community care encompass far more than just the services provided by social services authorities: the lack of other services can have a major impact on their lives. Some older people have noted that, unless their basic needs for warmth, good health care and an adequate income are met, 'putting in help with meals, with shopping, with cleaning or with getting dressed etc. makes a mockery of care' (Robertson, 1993, p. 17).

The views of users and carers will not always coincide. Conflict could arise, for instance, if a disabled person wished to live independently but carers considered that the risks involved were unacceptable. Some carers, on the other hand, may feel that the personal costs of caring are too high and they may wish to give up caring: for them, improved support in their caring role will not lead to the outcome they desire.

The scope of outcome measurement

Without even specifying the interests of other potential stakeholders, it is clear that the array of issues, needs and aspects of service provision that could potentially be included in outcome measurement is extremely broad. The question that then arises is whether all these issues can be addressed in the course of routine measurement. If not, is it possible to identify some key features that would adequately reflect the broader range of issues? Or would it be necessary to detail specific outcomes in relation to individual needs? It is crucial that, whatever approach is adopted, the emphasis should be on measuring the impact or effectiveness of a service in meeting the desired objectives, and not on those aspects that happen to be easily measurable. Outcome measurement should also provide some way to take account of unanticipated events or developments that have an impact on the desired outcomes.

Analysis and Interpretation

As indicated, there will be a range of inputs contributing towards, or hindering, the achievement of a normal life: disentangling their separate effects may be problematic. In addition, people with similar levels of impairment will vary considerably in the extent to which they have access to, or are willing to use, the range of potential resources which might assist them. Thus we cannot expect a straightforward relationship between the level of public services received and an outcome for an individual such as, for example, continuing residence in the community, or quality of life. In evaluative research such difficulties of analysis are tackled by the use of control groups for comparison, within various forms of experimental or quasi-experimental design. In routine practice, other ways have to be found for deciding on the significance of changes which are observed. Comparison may be with some minimum or ideal standards which might be derived from research or from professional knowledge or aspirations in relation to the particular user group (Wilkin *et al*., 1992).

Alternatively, comparison may be between districts or teams within an authority. In interpreting such data, some effort has to be made to take account of known differences in the likely characteristics of service users and levels of need within these subgroups, before any questions are raised about possible differences in practice influencing outcomes. In addition, since the relationship between service inputs and outcomes is of concern, it is important to ensure that service inputs have been clearly and consistently defined. Terms such as care management, referral or counselling have a notoriously wide range of meanings within services and there is a history of sets of inconclusive or apparently contradictory findings about the effectiveness of particular forms of intervention which reflect this looseness of definition (Smith, 1987).

One further way to approach the question of attribution in individual cases is to ask people directly. In a study which compared information derived from a structured measure of health status (the SF-36) with that obtained in qualitative interviews, Hill *et al.* (1994) argued that the effects of certain interventions, in relation to continence promotion and mental health, were not detectable with the structured measure. In interview, however, service users and carers were enthusiastic about the differences that services had made. These effects were masked by overall deterioration due to other conditions, or by a reduction in depression leading to an increased awareness of other difficulties. In another paper, Hill and Harries (1993) identified some of the technical and methodological problems in using the SF-36 as an outcome-assessment instrument with older people. Whilst they acknowledged that there is a role for structured outcome measures, they concluded that it may be more appropriate to begin by listening to what patients have to say without the constraint of structured questionnaires which have been developed by 'experts', for 'experts'. Together these papers suggest a considerable role for qualitative methods in determining the relevant dimensions of outcome from the user's point of view, and in providing evidence for attribution in situations where there is no control group for comparison.

6.2 Outcome-related Work in Social Services Authorities

A concern with outcomes is implicit in much of social services authorities' work. This section will examine some of the organizational procedures and methods that are designed, variously, to provide a mechanism for specifying the objectives to be achieved, indicate whether authorities are achieving their objectives, improve authorities' ability to meet users' and carers' needs, and obtain feedback about services. These procedures include: performance measurement, inspection arrangements, the contracting process, care management reviews, quality initiatives and satisfaction surveys. Some of these procedures offer a potential basis for more systematically specifying and measuring outcomes.

Performance Measurement

Social services authorities are required to submit management information about their work to the Department of Health and the Chartered Institute of Public Finance and Accountancy. Such information focuses largely on service inputs (such as numbers of staff or expenditure on particular services) or outputs (numbers of residential placements or meals on wheels). In addition, some authorities have collected information about the community care arrangements introduced in 1993, including the number of comprehensive assessments completed, placements in different types of home and the time that elapses before a placement is made: such indicators are seen as a means of monitoring departmental performance (Warburton, 1993). While indicating some destinational outcomes, such information is essentially activity and process orientated.

Since 1993, social services authorities have also had to collect information for the Audit Commission in relation to the Citizen's Charter indicators for local authority services (Audit Commission, 1992). The aim of these indicators is to provide information for the general public about local services, and to enable comparisons to be made between authorities. Given the costs of data collection, the indicators that have been selected are largely based on information already available. In 1994–5 they included: basic demographic information, percentages of particular groups of people (such as older people) receiving specified services, process outcomes (e.g., the broad results of assessments), and net expenditure per head of population on social services.

While the Citizen's Charter indicators have been welcomed as a basis for greater public accountability, criticism has been levelled at their proposed aim of comparing the services provided by different local authorities. Many factors can underpin different levels of provision in different localities: the extent of deprivation, availability of services from non-statutory agencies, existence of community support networks, efficiency with which services are used, and, not least, different definitions and nature of the services provided. The indicators themselves focus mainly on information that is easily obtainable, rather than seeking to identify the issues that are most important. Gathering data on the indicators none the less calls for the commitment of a large proportion of the time and resources available within social services research and information units. Although research was commissioned by the Audit Commission to ascertain which aspects of local authority services were considered most important by the general public, social services were excluded because of 'difficulties of confidentiality in interviewing social services clients' (personal communication). As they stand, the social services indicators do not include any assessment of outcomes for users or carers, nor any evaluation by users or carers of the quality or effectiveness of services.

Inspection

Social services inspection units were established primarily to evaluate the quality of care and quality of life in residential care homes. In addition to this statutory responsibility, optional functions include the development of quality assurance programmes and the inspection of other services such as domiciliary care (Department of Health, 1990). While inspection is not in itself the same as outcome measurement, it may offer some opportunities to measure outcomes.

A handbook produced by the Social Services Inspectorate on the inspection of home support services (SSI, 1993) specifies the key values that should underpin such services: autonomy, independence of decision making, choice of lifestyle, respect for the intrinsic dignity of each person and privacy from unnecessary intrusion. In order to be effectively monitored, such values need to be translated into service principles to be included in service specifications and quality standards. Specific principles include user control, being able to choose from different service options and making decisions about daily routines and lifestyles. More detailed criteria include: whether users can choose what to wear, how to prepare food, whether tasks are performed at times that suit users, respect for personal choice (e.g. in relation to having a bath or shower), respect for users' wishes to carry out certain tasks themselves and the right of users to refuse help.

While such criteria reflect the principles set out in *Caring for People*, they again relate primarily to the process of service provision. The actual success of the services, according to the handbook, is to be judged through the regular collection of data about user satisfaction and expressed needs and preferences. Individual assessments and reviews also provide a basis for monitoring the extent to which previously identified needs and objectives have been met. Satisfaction surveys and the review process thus represent a means of measuring outcomes for users and carers – though reservations about both the principles and practice underpinning these methods will be discussed below. The main focus of the inspection process itself is on evaluating the quality of service provision rather than monitoring 'final' outcomes for individual users. This would only be an effective approach to measuring outcomes if relationships were clearly established between the characteristics of service provision and consequent outcomes for service users. Alternatively, inspection might involve the more direct measurement of outcomes. In this case, however, a standardized approach would have to be used. One study of inspection practices found that inspectors' judgments of the same service can differ considerably (Gibbs and Sinclair, 1992): this suggests that inspectors' personal judgment is likely to be an insufficient basis for the objective measurement of outcomes for users.

Contracting

The contracting process offers an opportunity to specify the nature and quantity of the services to be provided. Given that the ultimate objective of services is to meet users' needs, the clearest way of ensuring that this objective is achieved would be to incorporate outcome measurement within the contract-monitoring process.

A study of social services contracts found, however, that most contracts focus on service inputs and on descriptions of the services to be provided (Smith and Thomas, 1993). Some do specify outputs, such as the number of users to be served. However, outcomes themselves are typically expressed in very general terms, leading to a lack of clarity about the way contract success might be monitored. How, for example, would it be possible to establish compliance with the statement that 'users will have dignity respected in every possible way at all times'? Some contracts do include more detailed statements about the way that broad aims might be translated into everyday practice: residents of elderly people's homes, for instance, would be encouraged 'to do as much as possible for themselves and others, including carrying out simple daily tasks'. Ultimately, though, measurable objectives would have to take account of the specific needs of individual residents or users, details of which cannot be included within broader service contracts.

Although the majority of contracts examined by Smith and Thomas refer to some form of monitoring, this generally relates not to outcomes for individual users but to compliance with the overall terms of the contract. Some contracts mention user feedback, and there are also references to surveys, interviews and user forums. However, it is unclear who would be responsible for obtaining such feedback: the authors note that appropriate monitoring systems have yet to be developed. The contracts indicate that it is easier to define the activities that have developed over the years and that together constitute 'community care', than to define community care itself or its precise objectives – let alone to design a methodology for measuring in a routine but reliable way whether those objectives are being met in practice.

Care Management

Individual needs assessment and the production of care plans to meet those needs constitute the essence of care management. Once services have been provided, periodic reviews should take place to establish how effectively needs are being met, identify any changes in needs and monitor the quality of services provided, including the gathering of users' and carers' views (Department of Health, 1990).

The extent to which the initial assessment offers a baseline for measuring outcomes depends, however, on the assessment format used and the amount of detail recorded. The repeated use of a validated and reliable instrument with the same individuals, for instance, offers the possibility of identifying changes in the level of need following the input of services. In practice, though, agencies have often constructed assessment formats on the basis of practitioners' knowledge of relevant issues, but without necessarily adopting tested measures. This means that the assessment may include a range of appropriate categories and variables to be examined, but the information recorded may be limited to the existence of a need in a particular area, without specifying the exact nature or level of the need. A report from the Social Services Inspectorate (SSI) and NHS Executive (1993) noted that assessors frequently sought to define traditional service responses to individual needs, rather than making a more holistic analysis and identifying the specific outcomes that users want. In some cases, the threat of legal action if an authority failed to meet identified needs could result in minimal information being recorded about needs. If longer term objectives were specified at all, this was often only in broad terms such as 'supporting a person at home'.

All these factors mean that the subsequent review of needs may, at best, indicate in a general way whether the provision of a service has succeeded in 'meeting need', without specifying its precise impact on an individual user's or carer's well-being, quality of life or ability to maintain an independent lifestyle. It could be argued that a general statement about the ability of a service to assist a user or carer is a sufficient means of monitoring the service's effectiveness. However, it remains subjective: it is unclear how the initial assessment was made, what precise objectives the service is meant to achieve, on what basis a judgment is made that needs have or have not been met, or the specific type of need that a replication of the service could be expected to meet.

The use of validated and reliable measures would go a long way towards improving the quality of initial assessments and offer a practical way of measuring outcomes. The SSI/NHS Executive report did not specifically examine the potential for using such measures, although it identified many problems in the existing assessment formats that were being used: an emphasis on more measurable elements rather than factors such as user attitudes or carer commitment; a lack of attention to cultural requirements; staff feeling deskilled by the completion of tick-boxes; and users and carers feeling disabled by the length and complexity of many forms. The report also noted a movement away from generic assessment formats to more specialist documentation that was more orientated towards specific purposes, settings or user groups – and which could thus identify individuals' needs more accurately and avoid aspects which had little or no relevance. Nevertheless, questions might be asked about: the reasons why existing, validated measures are not being used in practice; the implications of narrowing the focus of assessment to specific aspects (rather than carrying out comprehensive assessments); and the appropriateness of using formal measures at all, if the aim is to allow staff to use their professional skills to explore areas of need or, as is the case in some localities, to enable users to define needs themselves – which might more closely reflect the intentions of *Caring for People*. While such questions appear to relate mainly to technical issues (concerning the design of assessment formats) or the issue of appropriateness (in relation to individual users' needs), a further consideration might concern the potential political embarrassment related to unambiguous measures of need if high levels of unmet need were identified.

The SSI/NHS Executive report also noted that there were difficulties in carrying out subsequent reviews, largely because of the time these required and the work pressures arising out of the new community care arrangements. As a result, reviews were sometimes carried out by telephone or by questionnaire – although the report did not specify the specific form of such reviews. Questionnaires we have obtained from social services authorities show that some authorities have used satisfaction surveys to focus on the effectiveness of the assessment process, rather than formally collating data about outcomes from reviews themselves. The reason for their choice is a suspicion that care managers might be likely to bias the results if they were to carry out evaluations of their own work. Such a consideration would certainly be valid where the evaluation uses an open-ended format, is concerned with the quality of the assessment process itself, allows the evaluator to judge the effectiveness of the service provided, and – above all – does not involve the use of instruments with a proven record of reliability. However, the questionnaires that have been used have provided only a limited amount of information about outcomes. In one case, the relevant question asks 'Do you now get the help from Social Services that you need?', with space for further comments. A draft interview schedule produced by another Social Services Department asks 'Has your life changed as a result of the new services' and 'If yes, how?'. It has to be acknowledged, though, that the primary purpose of such surveys is to obtain users' views about the quality of the services provided, rather than to assess outcomes as such.

Quality Initiatives

While a concern with quality now imbues the work of most social services authorities, the nature of quality initiatives varies considerably, depending on the specific issue in question. Initiatives may involve the setting of standards, audit of individual units, development of quality systems, or training (Leckie, 1994; McMillan, 1993). The focus can be on management issues, such as the assessment of team performance, or the integration of evaluation and professional practice (Kearney and Miller, 1994). Alternatively, service provision may be examined, using a wide variety of methods: semi-structured interviews, surveys, checklists and observation (James *et al.*, 1992). In some places, users and carers are involved in this work. The focus of initiatives is sometimes on users' and carers' own views of services, the extent of their involvement in service planning or their quality of life.

The main concern of many quality initiatives is with process and outputs rather than outcomes. It is certainly easier to set standards, establish whether work has been carried out, monitor whether specifications have been adhered to, identify defects and quantify products or activities than to determine service effectiveness or outcomes. Nevertheless, there is no reason why quality initiatives should not focus on desired outcomes, how to achieve them, and how to monitor whether they are being achieved. Two of Maxwell's (1984) dimensions of quality are the relevance of services to need (at a community level) and the effectiveness of services for individuals – the other dimensions being access to services, equity, social acceptability, efficiency and economy. Pfeffer and Coote (1991) offer a framework for quality based on commonly agreed goals and meeting individual needs. Their definition encompasses fitness for purpose (linked to definitions set by experts), responsiveness (as indicated by users' evaluation of the service) and empowerment (whereby users control the decisions that are made).

Quality initiatives usually examine specific services in detail. While they may not be suited to routine outcome monitoring, they would be an appropriate means of measuring outcomes where aspects of process are known to be suitable proxies for desired outcomes. Alternatively, they offer an opportunity to investigate outcomes where no measures yet exist. In this case, they offer an opportunity to explore stakeholders' views of the desired outcomes of individual services and to develop ways of measuring those outcomes.

Satisfaction Surveys

One approach to service evaluation currently being adopted by some social services authorities is the use of satisfaction surveys. In principle, this represents a welcome attempt to incorporate a user and carer dimension into service evaluation. However, both the design and interpretation of such surveys are fraught with difficulties.

General questions, for instance, can lead to general or perfunctory responses. Respondents may be satisfied with one aspect of a service but dissatisfied with others. While a primary distinction needs to be made between process and outcome, the specific aspects of each have to be made clear. Cheetham *et al.* (1992) note that satisfaction with specific aspects of, say, residential care does not mean that users are satisfied with residential care as a way of life. Where changes occur in satisfaction levels, there is a need for clarity as to whether these refer to one or several component aspects of a service (Carr-Hill, 1992). In some cases, respondents may express overall satisfaction even though they receive no benefit from services; in other cases, they may benefit but none the less express dissatisfaction.

Users' responses may be determined by a range of factors. Some people may be unwilling to criticize 'free' services; they may fear that complaints could lead to service withdrawal; their judgments may be influenced by their views about individual staff; dissatisfaction with process could be forgotten once a desired service is provided; and some will seek to provide responses that are designed to please the questioner (Allen *et al.*, 1992; Barnes, 1992; Huxley and Mohamad, 1991; Judge and Solomon, 1993; Wilson, 1993). Individuals' expectations, which form a basis for subsequent satisfaction, will themselves vary. Some users will have no clear prior views. Others' expectations may be determined by prior experiences or the experiences of others, but also by individual definitions of what is an acceptable level of service and a subjective sense of what they deserve (Wilkin *et al.*, 1992). A distinction is often made between a preferred, ideal service and the lower expectation of what may be reasonably expected in reality (Locker and Dunt, 1978): satisfaction may then relate just to the achievement of a minimum standard and, indeed, dissatisfaction may only be expressed if there is a gross discrepancy between that expected standard and actual experience (Wilkin *et al.*, 1992). Moreover, expectations can change over time. Changes resulting from contact with a service make retrospective evaluation difficult; a prospective approach risks influencing expectations (Huxley and Mohamad, 1991).

Overall, therefore, satisfaction surveys may seem to offer a relatively direct and effortless way of obtaining users' and carers' views about service outcomes. For the information they provide to be of value, though, it is essential that the issues they address should have been clearly identified and that the questions be shown to produce valid and reliable answers. Despite their apparent attractiveness, they do not offer a short cut to outcome measurement.

6.3 Alternative Approaches

Existing Measures

The currently available measures of community care outcomes have generally been developed either for research purposes or for use in related settings such as health care. Of course, community care embodies aspects of both health and social care. However, although there is a substantial literature on health outcomes, such measures are most fully developed in relation to acute care, and many of the practical and conceptual difficulties of looking at community care outcomes are common to health and social care. These include the difficulties of assessing the impact of long-term continuing care which may have no particular end point, and the impact of preventive services, where effects may be long term and there may be considerable problems in attributing effects to services. As has been indicated, there are measures developed for evaluative research studies, for instance, into the impact of policies such as the relocation of residents from long-stay hospitals, or services such as care management, respite or day care for specific groups of users or carers. Work is also being carried out on the measurement of social life and integration, though adequate measures have still to be produced. Generally, though, the instruments used in research contexts are longer or more complex than would be practicable in routine operational practice. In some cases, operationalizing the principles that are intended to underpin outcome measurement can be problematic. This has been the case, for instance, with the 'five accomplishments' (community presence, choice, competence, respect and community participation) that were identified by O'Brien and Lyle (1987) as a framework for examining the quality of life of people with learning disability (Henwood, 1993).

Of the measures developed within the health care field, some may be applicable to community care: they may include measures of quality of life, morale, stress, distress, and the ability to carry out activities of daily living (as reviewed by Qureshi *et al.*, 1994). However, such measures would not address users' and carers' own varied and wide-ranging expectations of community care, or the government's specific objectives, outlined in *Caring for People*, such as promoting independent living, a choice of services and greater user involvement in individual care planning. While work has been carried out on the framework of issues that constitute user empowerment in community care (Taylor *et al.*, 1992), that framework has yet to be translated into workable measures. Barnes (in Cormie and Crichton, 1994) has developed a questionnaire to assess whether membership of user panels leads to increased empowerment for older people. However, it is too early to say how useful the approach will be.

Directions for Further Development

Although work within social services authorities does not systematically address the question of community care outcomes, existing processes – whether in the form of quality initiatives, inspection programmes or care management – provide a potentially useful setting for developmental work. Rather than attempting to encompass the whole of community care, such work might begin by identifying a particular service about which outcome information is required in relation to current policy or practice issues: examples might include the shift from residential care to more intensive domiciliary support, or service areas about which users have expressed high levels of dissatisfaction.

There is, then, a need to fully explore users' and carers' own views about the objectives and desired outcomes of the service in question. Both services and outcome measures have been almost entirely professionally or organizationally defined in the past, yet the new community care arrangements emphasize the central importance of users and carers in all aspects of service planning and evaluation. Professionals, users and carers can potentially learn from each other, and the likely existence of a variety of criteria for determining outcomes means that discussion and, ideally, consensus are required: it remains to be seen whether such consensus can be achieved in practice.

Once objectives have been identified, the next step is to draw on the existing knowledge base, including research about service effectiveness and the availability of existing measures, in order to develop and test measures to address those objectives – in a form that can be used in the course of routine practice. The measures should include both subjective and objective elements: while it is essential that users should receive services that they value, agencies are responsible for ensuring a degree of equity in the way they allocate resources among people with similar needs. Measures must also be able to identify any unintended consequences, whether positive or negative, of a particular service. Not least, account needs to be taken of other inputs, such as informal support or services from other agencies, and of users' and carers' changing needs over time. Unless such factors are identified, it will not be possible to gauge the impact of particular services.

In some cases, the focus may be on processes rather than final outcomes. This could be appropriate where users and carers perceive aspects of process as important elements of the outcome of services – especially given the grey area between process and outcomes, as discussed earlier. Second, a focus on process may be legitimate where there is a well-established causal relationship between process and outcomes, and where measures of process can be used as proxies for outcomes.

Implementation Issues

Having measures is of little use, though, if staff are not prepared to use them. Historically the major profession involved, social work, has been seen as having a culture antithetical to hard measurement, convinced of the importance of the unmeasurable and the intangible (Cheetham *et al.*, 1992), and resistant to evidence about the relative effectiveness of different forms of intervention, even where such evidence exists (MacDonald *et al.*, 1992). Professional resistance to further data collection is often strong, especially if this is expected to become part of everyday practice. Previous experiences of data collection not leading to changes in practice or service provision may be combined with other workload pressures or scepticism about the feasibility of encapsulating the potential breadth and complexity of community care outcomes within a single measurement instrument (Cheetham *et al.*, 1992; Priest and McCarthy, 1993). While staff have more positive attitudes towards monitoring systems that they have been involved in developing, this, too, is costly in terms of the extra work required; in addition, staff would still have to be persuaded of the value of such work. Despite such problems, there are examples of developmental work involving frontline practitioners within both health care (e.g. Higginson, 1994; Philp *et al.*, 1994; Roberts *et al.*, 1994) and social care (e.g. Goldberg and Warburton, 1979; Priest and McCarthy, 1993).

A further prerequisite is for management information systems and human resources to process and analyse outcome data. Many social services authorities' IT systems are limited in their scope, and would be unable to handle the routine collection of outcome data on all the services being purchased or provided. Nor would it be easy for existing research and information staff to allocate the additional time needed to monitor or collate outcome data – let alone to carry out either regular or occasional surveys themselves.

6.4 Conclusions

The importance of outcome measurement in community care is being increasingly recognized: it can help agencies to evaluate the services that have been provided and to plan future provision; it offers practitioners a means of measuring the impact and effectiveness of their work and of informing their professional practice; and it offers a means of monitoring the extent to which government objectives are being achieved.

Despite widespread interest, though, community care outcomes are not being routinely or systematically measured – with the exception of destinational outcomes such as admissions to residential care, which only relate to one small aspect of the work of social services authorities and of which the precise meaning and usefulness are questionable anyway. Certainly, there is no currently available package of outcome measures for use by social services authorities. Work is needed in a variety of contexts in order to provide a comprehensive picture of the outcomes to be measured as well as to develop and test techniques for carrying this out. The task may be complex, but it is a necessary task if information is to be obtained about service effectiveness and if the needs of service users are to be appropriately met.

References

Allen, I., Hogg, D. and Peace, S. (1992) *Elderly People: Choice, Participation and Satisfaction*, London: Policy Studies Institute.

Audit Commission (1986) *Making a Reality of Community Care*, London: HMSO.

Audit Commission (1992) *Charting a Course*, London: HMSO.

Barnes, M. (1992) 'Beyond satisfaction surveys: involving people in research', *Generations Review*, **2** (4), pp. 15–17.

Beeforth, M., Conlan, E., Field, V., Hoser, B. and Sayce, L. (Eds) (1990) *Whose Service is it Anyway? Users' Views on Co-ordinating Community Care*, London: Research and Development for Psychiatry.

Carr-Hill, R. (1992) 'The measurement of patient satisfaction', *Journal of Public Health Medicine*, **14** (3): 236–49.

Cheetham, J., Fuller, R., McIvor, G. and Petch, A. (1992) *Evaluating Social Work Effectiveness*, Buckingham: Open University Press.

Cormie, J. and Crichton, M. (1994) *Fife User Panels Project: New Ways of Working*, Edinburgh: Age Concern Scotland.

CPA (1990) *Community Life: a Code of Practice for Community Care*, London: Centre for Policy on Ageing.

Department of Health (1990) *Community Care in the Next Decade and Beyond: Policy Guidance*, London: HMSO.

Department of Health, Department of Social Security, Scottish Office and Welsh Office (1989) *Caring for People*, Cm 849, London: HMSO.

Gaster, L. (1991) *Quality at the Front Line*, Bristol: School of Advanced Urban Studies, University of Bristol.

Gibbs, I. and Sinclair, I. (1992) 'Consistency: a pre-requisite for inspecting old people's homes?', *British Journal of Social Work*, **22** (5), pp. 535–50.

Goldberg, E.M. and Warburton, R.W. (1979) *Ends and Means in Social Work: the Development and Outcome of a Case Review System for Social Workers*, Social Services Library No. 35, London: National Institute for Social Work.

Henwood, M. (1993) *Measuring up to the Strategy? Learning Difficulties, Quality and the All Wales Strategy*, joint review conducted by the Social Services Inspectorate

(Wales) and the Audit Commission, Cardiff: Welsh Office.

Higginson, I. (1994) 'Clinical teams, general practice, audit and outcomes', workshop at BMA conference on 'Outcomes into Clinical Practice', June, London.

Hill, S. and Harries, U. (1993) 'The outcomes process: some reflections from research with people in their 60s and 70s', *Critical Public Health*, **4** (4), pp. 21–8.

Hill, S., Harries, U. and Popay, J. (1994) 'Assessing the outcomes of community based health services for older people: the Short Form 36's responsiveness to change', Draft manuscript, Salford: Public Health Research and Resource Centre.

House of Commons (1993) *Community Care: The Way Forward*, 6th Report of the Health Committee, HC 482-I, London: HMSO.

Huxley, P. and Mohamad, H. (1991) 'The development of a general satisfaction questionnaire for use in programme evaluation', *Social Work and Social Sciences Review*, **3** (1), pp. 63–74.

James, A., Brooks, T. and Towell, D. (1992) *Committed to Quality: Quality Assurance in Social Services Departments*, London: HMSO.

Judge, K. and Solomon, M. (1993) 'Public opinion and the National Health Service: patterns and perspectives in consumer satisfaction', *Journal of Social Policy*, **22** (3), pp. 299–327.

Kearney, P. and Miller, D. (1994) 'The numbers game', *Community Care* (13 January), pp. 22–3.

King's Fund (1989) *Carers' Needs: a Ten Point Plan for Carers*, London: King's Fund Centre.

Leckie, T. (1994) 'Quality assurance in social work', in Connor, A. and Black, S. (Eds) *Performance Review and Quality in Social Care*, London: Jessica Kingsley.

Locker, D. and Dunt, D. (1978) 'Theoretical and methodological issues in sociological studies of consumer satisfaction with medical care', *Social Science and Medicine*, **12**, pp. 283–92.

MacDonald, G. and Sheldon, B. with Gillespie, J. (1992) 'Contemporary studies of the effectiveness of social work', *British Journal of Social Work*, **22** (6), pp. 615–43.

Maxwell, R. J. (1984) 'Quality assessment in health', *British Medical Journal*, **288**, pp. 1470–2.

McMillan, I. (1993) 'An integral force', *Community Care* Supplement, 27 May, p. vi.

Morris, J. (1993) *Independent Lives? Community Care and Disabled People*, Basingstoke: Macmillan.

O'Brien, J. and Lyle, C. (1987) *Framework for Accomplishment*, Atlanta, GA: Responsive Systems Associates.

Pfeffer, N. and Coote, A. (1991) *Is Quality Good for You?*, Social Policy Paper No. 5, London: Institute for Public Policy Research.

Philp, I., Goddard, A., Connell, C., Metcalfe, A., Tse, V. and Bray, J. (1994) 'Development and evaluation of an information system for quality assurance', *Age and Ageing*, **23**: pp. 150–3.

Priest, P. and McCarthy, M. (1993) 'Developing a measure of client needs and outcomes by a community team for people with learning disabilities', *Health and Social Care*, **1** (3), pp. 181–5.

Qureshi, H., Nocon, A. and Thompson, C. (1994) *Measuring Outcomes of Community Care for Users and Carers: a Review*, Social Policy Research Unit Working Paper DH 1203, York: Social Policy Research Unit, University of York.

Roberts, H., Khee, T.S. and Philp, I. (1994) 'Setting priorities for measurement of

performance for geriatric medical services', *Age and Ageing*, **23**, pp. 154–7.
Robertson, S. (1993) *Fed and Watered: the Views of Older People on Need Assessment and Care Management*, Edinburgh: Age Concern Scotland.
Smith, D. (1987) 'The limits of positivism in social work research', *British Journal of Social Work*, **17**, pp. 401–16.
Smith, P. and Thomas, N. (1993) 'Contracts and competition in public services', paper presented at ADSS Research Conference, Bristol.
SSI (1993) *Developing Quality Standards for Home Support Services,* London: HMSO.
SSI/NHS Executive (1993) *Assessment Special Study*, London: Department of Health.
SSI/NHS Executive (1994) *Implementing Caring for People: Impressions of the First Year*, report of 14 special studies carried out by the Social Services Inspectorate and the NHS Management Executive, London: Department of Health.
Taylor, M., Hoyes, L., Lart, R. and Means, R. (1992) *User Empowerment in Community Care: Unravelling the Issues*, Bristol: School for Advanced Urban Studies, University of Bristol.
Warburton, W. (1993) 'Performance indicators: what was all the fuss about?', *Community Care Management and Planning*, **1** (4), pp. 99–105.
Wilkin, D., Hallam, L. and Doggett, M. (1992) *Measures of Need and Outcome for Primary Health Care*, Oxford: Oxford University Press.
Wilson, G. (1993) 'Users and providers: different perspectives on community care services', *Journal of Social Policy*, **22** (4), pp. 507–26.

Chapter 7

Outcome Measurement in the Management of Social Rented Housing

Peter A. Kemp

7.0 Introduction

Outcome measurement is in its infancy in the management of social housing. Insofar as anything approaching outcome measurement is undertaken, it is largely confined to the production and publication of a limited number of performance indicators. These performance indicators were introduced on a mandatory basis in the early 1990s. It is no coincidence that this new development occurred at a time when social housing was undergoing a major restructuring process, which is still under way.

The first section of this chapter therefore outlines the wider context within which performance indicators were introduced. It briefly outlines the history of social housing in Britain and sketches out some key features of this area of the welfare state. The second section examines the various stakeholders in housing management in respect of both local authorities and housing associations. The third section discusses the notion of outcome within the context of housing management. The fourth describes the system of performance indicators (PIs) that has been established and the uses to which it is put. The fifth section examines some of the main strengths and weakness of the PIs and the difficulties of analysing them in the real world of social housing management. The sixth section sets out some conclusions.

7.1 Outcome Measurement in Context

Social housing accounts for nearly a quarter of all dwellings in Britain, the great majority of such accommodation being owned and managed by local authorities.

Local authority housing has a long history, stretching back to the late nineteenth century, at which time about nine out of ten dwellings were rented from a private landlord and almost all of the remainder were owner occupied. Local authorities accounted for an estimated 24000 dwellings in 1914 (Merrett, 1979). The emergence of local authorities as major providers of rented accommodation really occurred after the First World War, when Exchequer subsidies for the construction of new housing to let were first introduced. Although initially conceived of as a temporary response to the postwar housing shortage, subsidized council housing soon became a major provider of housing to let. By 1939 local authorities accounted for 10 per cent of all dwellings (Merrett, 1979).

After the Second World War, the Labour Government gave local authorities the main responsibility for dealing with the postwar housing shortage. Under the temporary building licensing system, four-fifths of new construction was reserved for local authority output, with the private sector making up the remainder. Local authority house building continued to rise under the Conservative governments of the early to mid-1950s, peaking at 229000 completed dwellings in 1953 (Merrett, 1979).

Since the mid-1970s local authority housing has come under increasing attack, from both the Left and the Right. It has been criticized for being inefficient, paternalistic and for failing to offer choice to tenants. As David Donnison (1987) has pointed out, the response of the Left has been to 'call in the community', by arguing for decentralization and more intensive and localized housing management (Power, 1987), for tenant participation and the introduction of tenant cooperatives (Clapham, 1989). On the right, while there has been some attempt to embrace these options, the main response has been to 'call in the market', by seeking to demunicipalize the existing stock, cutting back on new construction by local councils, by promoting housing associations as the main provider of new social housing to rent, by selling off dwellings to sitting tenants under the right-to-buy programme, by introducing new financial regimes for both local authority housing and housing associations, by the introduction of compulsory competitive tendering, and by the introduction of mandatory performance indicators (see Cole and Furbey, 1994).

Housing associations are non-profit organizations that provide subsidized housing to rent for low-income households; they also act as developers and managers of low-cost home ownership schemes. Housing associations have had a long history but were of relatively minor importance as housing providers until 1974. The Housing Act of that year introduced a capital grant which enables housing associations to build new dwellings or acquire and rehabilitate existing ones. The availability of this grant has enabled the housing association sector to expand considerably (Best, 1991). This expansion has been facilitated by the Housing Corporation, a government agency which has responsibility for promoting, supervising and funding housing associations.

Housing associations have found favour with both Conservative and Labour Governments. Labour has tended to see housing associations as a preferred alternative to private landlords, while the Conservatives have viewed them as being preferable to local authorities as providers of housing to let. Prior to 1980, housing associations generally performed roles that were complementary to those provided by local authorities, but since then they have increasingly been promoted by government as a substitute for council housing.

Reform of Social Rented Housing

Major changes are currently under way in the provision of social rented housing and in the way in which it is managed. Taken together these developments amount to the most radical reform of rented housing since the early 1920s. Although the final outcome of these emerging developments and their impact on management performance is not obvious, what is clear is that they are intended to have a significant effect on the efficiency and effectiveness with which social rented housing is managed.

The White Paper *Housing: the Government's Proposals* put forward plans for a radical reform of social rented housing (DoE, 1987a). The legislative framework for this reform was subsequently provided by the 1988 Housing Act and the 1989 Local Government and Housing Act. The main thrust of the reform is the demunicipalizing of social rented housing and a corresponding shift towards a more pluralist and market-orientated system of provision. The government has sought to shift local authorities away from their role as providers, preferring them to act as enablers, facilitating provision by other agencies, including housing associations and the private sector (DoE, 1987a). This new strategy applies both to *new* social rented housing provision and to the *existing* stock of local authority housing (see Kemp, 1989).

As intended by the government, housing associations have taken over from councils the role of being the main providers of *new* social housing to rent. The new financial regime for housing associations was introduced to facilitate this expansion of their role. At the same time, local authorities have been discouraged by a new financial regime for capital spending and by other means from building new houses to rent. For example, only 25 per cent of receipts from the sale of council houses can now be used by local authorities for capital projects; the remaining 75 per cent has to be used to redeem their debt.

For the *existing* stock of municipal housing, two new measures – Tenants' Choice and Housing Action Trusts – were introduced by the Housing Act 1988 with the aim of transferring estates to new landlords and in particular to housing associations. Under Tenants Choice, landlords which have been approved by the Housing Corporation may bid for local authority housing subject to a ballot of the tenants concerned. Housing Action Trusts are special-purpose bodies set up by the Secretary of State to take over the ownership of local authority housing in designated areas, with the aim of undertaking an improvement programme and diversifying ownership.

While these two policy instruments have not to date been much used, local authorities have themselves developed the approach of voluntary stock transfers (VSTs). These have mainly involved the sale by councils of their entire housing stock to newly established housing associations, under the Housing and Planning Act 1986. By the end of December 1994, 35 local authorities had transferred their housing stock in this way.

As well as *transfers* of existing council housing to new owners, measures have also been introduced aimed at improving value for money in the management of the *retained* stock of municipal housing. The three main policy instruments for this purpose are: (i) the new financial regime for local authority housing revenue accounts; (ii) the introduction of compulsory competitive tendering (CCT) from April 1996 onwards (DoE, 1992); and (iii) the publication of annual statutory reports to tenants setting out specified information on housing management (see below).

The introduction of CCT in housing management is part of a wider process of introducing CCT in local government under the Citizen's Charter. CCT is intended to build upon the new financial regime (NFR) and the statutory performance indicators by 'maintaining and enhancing existing good management practice and providing a means by which the poorest performing authorities can raise their standards of management so that tenants receive a better service in future' (DoE, 1992, p. 3). Thus CCT is at least to some extent viewed as an instrument for improving performance and outcomes in the management of social rented housing.

The 1995 housing White Paper has endorsed the demunicipalization strategy and given support to the proposal that local councils should seek to sell their stock to independent housing companies. In addition, it announced that private organizations will be allowed to compete for the capital grants which were previously available only to housing associations. These private organizations will be subject to the same scrutiny from the Housing Corporation as housing associations already receive (DoE, 1995).

New Financial Regimes

The new financial regimes are important to outcomes in housing management not merely because they provide the financial context within which local authorities and housing associations operate. They have been explicitly designed to introduce or increase the incentives for social housing landlords to improve performance and to enhance the outcomes of housing management.

Local authorities

The Local Government and Housing Act 1989 introduced a new financial regime for local authority housing revenue accounts, which came into operation in April

1990. A key element of the NFR is the ring fencing of the housing revenue account (HRA) to keep it completely separate from the other local authority accounts. Ring fencing the HRA has two aspects.

First, the HRA has been more clearly defined as a 'landlord account' such that only costs which are incurred by the local authority *as a landlord* are to be charged to the account (Warburton, 1991). Thus the costs of street lighting and doctors' surgeries, which in some authorities had been charged to the HRA, were instead to be charged to the local authority's general fund and be paid for out of local taxation. Second, under the new financial regime local authorities are prohibited from making transfers from the general fund to the HRA to subsidize rents (previously known as rate fund contributions).

These two features of the NFR were at least in part seen as ways in which the costs of housing management could be more closely related to the service provided; neither subsidized by nor subsidizing the local authority's general fund. In theory, this should mean that council tenants and management staff now have a clearer understanding of the relationship between costs and services and, hence, a more strongly vested interest than previously in housing management performance and outcomes.

As well as ring fencing the HRA, the NFR involves a consolidation of previous subsidies to local authority housing into a single HRA subsidy (see Hills, 1991; Warburton, 1991). The amount of HRA subsidy to which a local authority is entitled is determined by the size of the deficit (or surplus in the case of a negative subsidy entitlement) on its notional HRA. However, the notional HRA is by no means the same as the actual expenditure made and income received by the authority in its HRA. In the notional HRA, reckonable expenditure includes amounts for expenditure on rent rebates, charges for capital expenditure and allowances for management and maintenance spending. Reckonable income includes interest from receipts and assumed levels of rental income. Allowances for management and maintenance expenditure are calculated annually by the Department of the Environment for each local authority. However, authorities are not required to set their expenditure at these guideline levels.

The Department of the Environment also sets guideline rents for each local authority every year. Guideline rents are calculated from a complex formula based on each local authority's contribution to the national capital value of the council stock (which is estimated from valuations of dwellings sold under the 'right to buy'). Each year the Secretary of State determines a rent increase over the previous year's rent for each local authority (see Warburton, 1991).

The calculation of each local authority's notional rent income assumes that 2 per cent of its stock is empty. In other words, the calculation of each authority's subsidy entitlement assumes that it is collecting rent from 98 per cent of its dwellings. This means that authorities with a void rate of more than 2 per cent will have to charge a higher rent than they otherwise would have needed to do in order to make up the difference.

The subsidy calculation also makes the same allowance for rent arrears. In other words, it assumes that authorities collect all of the rent from 98 per cent of their dwellings. To the extent that an authority does not collect this amount of rent, the actual rent which it must charge will have to be increased to make up the difference.

Both the empty property and rent arrears assumptions in the subsidy calculation are designed to provide authorities with an incentive to improve the efficiency of their housing management in these two areas. In effect, they are performance benchmarks which local authorities have a financial incentive to attain.

Housing associations

The objectives of the NFR for housing associations are to increase the amount of rented housing which associations can produce for any given level of public expenditure and to create incentives for associations to 'deliver their services in the most cost-effective manner, bringing to bear the disciplines of the private sector and strengthening the machinery of public support' (DoE, 1987b, para. 2).

The NFR for housing associations is largely concerned with capital funding of development, but it also involves significant changes to revenue funding. In outline, the main changes introduced in April 1989 are as follows (see Gibb and Munro, 1991; Hills, 1991).

An increasing share of the total housing association approved development programme is being moved towards a mixed funded basis. Instead of associations being 100 per cent publicly funded through a combination of housing association grant (HAG) and public sector loan, the capital costs not covered by HAG are to be met by borrowing from the private sector.

Whereas previously HAG was flexible in that it was adjusted to whatever amount of allowable development costs could not be serviced out of the income from the registered fair rent, from April 1989 it has been largely fixed in advance. Consequently, under the NFR over-runs in development costs have to be met, in full or in part, by the association. Hence the NFR provides new financial incentives to help ensure that housing associations are efficient developers.

The average level of HAG has been significantly reduced, from about 85–90 per cent of the total development costs to an average of about 60 per cent. This has meant that the same amount of subsidy could be stretched over a larger number of new dwellings. But lower HAG per dwelling has also meant that rents under the NFR have to be significantly higher in real terms than previously. Indeed, housing association rents have increased much faster than either retail price inflation or earnings since 1989. Hence, housing association tenants are paying much more for a similar level of service.

New lettings by housing associations were deregulated from 15 January 1989. Instead of their rents being set independently by the rent officer service, housing associations are now responsible for setting their own rents. This has two aspects: they must decide not only what rents to charge in order to cover their costs (the actual amount of rent per dwelling per week) but also devise a rent scheme for determining the relative rents for different types of property in different locations. The deregulation of rents was necessary to enable the three changes to capital funding set out above to be introduced.

Under the previous regime, a revenue deficit grant was payable by the Housing Corporation, in certain circumstances, where the rental income was not sufficient to cover the revenue expenditure. This grant is now being phased out. Again, the removal of this subsidy takes away an important cushion for associations and means that they have to be much more careful to ensure that their revenue exceeds their outgoings.

7.2 The Stakeholders

The stakeholders in social housing management are many and various. However, local authorities and housing associations are neither equally nor fully accountable to all of them. Moreover, the nature of the stake which these agencies have in the management of social housing differs between them. And in some cases these stakeholders have competing interests.

Tenants

In both the local authority and the housing association sectors an obvious group of stakeholders is the tenants who are housed by these landlords. In December 1993, there were 4724000 tenants renting their home from local authorities in Britain and a further 874000 renting from housing associations.

It is clear that social housing tenants have an interest in efficient and effective management of their homes. As highlighted above, the new financial regime was designed to give them a more direct and stronger financial interest in the economic and efficient management of their homes by their landlords.

The extent to which the NFR has succeeded in this objective is to some extent blunted by the Housing Benefit scheme, which provides rent rebates and allowances to low-income tenants. Under this scheme as presently designed, Housing Benefit recipients can receive up to 100 per cent of their rent in benefit. Moreover, for all recipients, the scheme covers all of any subsequent increase in their rents. Hence, the marginal cost of housing is nil for tenants on Housing Benefit (Kemp, 1992).

Moreover, the amount of leverage that social housing tenants can exert on their landlord is relatively limited. Although progress has been made, tenant participation in housing management is still relatively weakly developed. Tenant membership of housing association management boards is limited and appears to have little impact on the decisions that are made (Bines *et al.*, 1993).

Given a situation of excess demand for rental housing and a relatively limited range of suppliers, there is little competition between landlords for tenants: rented housing is a sellers' market. Hence it is difficult for tenants to take their custom elsewhere, other than by purchasing their dwelling under the right to buy, provided that they can afford to do so.

The aim of *Tenants' Choice* was ostensibly to give council tenants the right to choose an alternative landlord. But in practice the Act gives potential alternative landlords the right to submit a bid to take over council housing (Kemp, 1989). These bids are then subject to a ballot among the tenants, but the rules are stacked in favour of the transfer: in order to prevent it from happening, at least 50 per cent of eligible tenants must vote against the transfer, otherwise it goes ahead. In fact, very little housing has been transferred to alternative landlords under the Tenants' Choice procedure, largely because council tenants do not wish to change their landlords. Indeed, tenant satisfaction surveys carried out by numerous local authorities since the 1988 Housing Act came into effect have found very high levels of satisfaction; these local surveys confirm the picture presented by independent research (Maclennan *et al.*, 1989; Bines *et al.*, 1993; Hedges and Clemens, 1994).

Apart from existing tenants, it can be argued that potential tenants, such as households on housing waiting lists, constitute another group of stakeholders. Potential or future tenants do not necessarily have a stake that is identical with that of existing tenants. This is demonstrated in relation to voluntary stock transfers, most of which have gone ahead after the existing tenants were given promises of future annual rent increases of no more than a certain percentage above inflation for a set period after transfer, while new (post-transfer) tenants faced significant real rises to finance the stock transfer and subsequent investment programmes.

Social landlords must consider the long-term care and use of the stock, as well as equality of opportunity and potential consumers (e.g. people on the waiting list) and not just the concerns of the immediate consumer. Pleasing existing consumers may mean failing to satisfy potential consumers of the service.

Housing Officers

Another group of stakeholders is the housing staff who work in housing management. In 1994, 65700 full-time equivalent staff were employed in housing by local authorities (CSO, 1995), while 59600 were employed by housing associations (Housing Corporation, 1995).

Senior housing staff commonly employ indicators to monitor their organization's housing management activities and the performance of individual staff or area offices.

Councillors and Housing Association Board Members

Basic performance indicators on rent arrears, lettings and repairs have long been included in reports to the housing or relevant committee of local councils and to housing association boards. Indeed, it is one of the key functions of council housing committees and association boards to monitor performance on housing management.

Local authority housing managers are accountable to local councillors, while housing association staff are accountable to housing association committee members or boards. Councillors are of course periodically subject to local ward elections. In contrast, while housing association committees are elected into office by the annual general meeting of their association, this is often little more than a formality. In practice, they are placed onto committees on the recommendation of existing committee members or senior staff of the association. Housing association board members are ultimately responsible to the Housing Corporation.

Councillors are rarely elected on housing issues alone and are responsible to the whole electorate and not just to their tenants. In contrast, housing association board members are responsible for organizations that are first and foremost providers of housing.

The Housing Corporation

As the government agency with responsibility for the registration and supervision of housing associations and for allocating housing association grant, the Housing Corporation in England and its Scottish and Welsh equivalents – Scottish Homes and Housing for Wales – have an explicit stake in the outcome of housing management by housing associations. Indeed, it was because of its supervision role that the Corporation recently introduced defined performance indicators which associations are required to collect for submission in an annual return.

The Housing Corporation is in turn accountable to the Department of the Environment, while Scottish Homes is responsible to the Scottish Office and Housing for Wales to the Welsh Office. Unlike its English or Welsh counterparts, Scottish Homes is a major social housing landlord in its own right and consequently has a stake in the management of its own stock.

The Audit Commission

The Audit Commission was set up in April 1983 under the Local Government Finance Act 1982. It appoints auditors to local authorities in England and Wales (the Accounts Commission performs a similar function in Scotland). It also has a remit to carry out studies designed to enable it to make recommendations for improving the economy, efficiency and effectiveness in the provision of local authority services.

The Commission has undertaken a number of studies of housing management by local authorities (e.g. Audit Commission, 1984, 1986a). It has recently reached an agreement with the Housing Corporation under which it will provide advice about value-for-money measures and practices which housing associations should adopt (Edmonds, 1995).

Government Departments

Several government departments have an interest in housing management outcomes. Most obviously, the Department of the Environment (and its predecessors), which has responsibility for housing and local government, has had an interest in housing management since at least 1919 when explicit Exchequer subsidies for social housing were first introduced. For much of the early history of council housing, the relevant central government department was more concerned with the *construction* of dwellings than with their subsequent *management* (Power, 1987). Even so, the rent which local councils charged for their accommodation, whom they housed and how the dwellings were managed has increasingly been a matter of concern to the Department of the Environment, as well as to the Department of Social Security and the Treasury.

The Treasury has an interest in the rent that local authorities and housing associations charge for a number of reasons. First, both types of landlord receive public money and hence the Treasury has an interest in ensuring that it is spent efficiently. Second, rent levels have important consequences for Housing Benefit expenditure. Other things being equal, if rents go up, the cost of Housing Benefit also increases. This has implications for the cost of social security (and therefore for the Department of Social Security) and hence for the public sector borrowing requirement. Third, rent increases have an impact on the retail price index, which is a key economic indicator for macro-economic management. Moreover, since a number of pensions and other benefits are linked to the RPI, rent increases indirectly impact on public spending, another key macro-economic indicator (Meen, 1994).

Private Lenders

Following the introduction of the new financial regime for housing associations, private lenders have become important stakeholders in the management of social rented housing. The future stream of rental income on associations' properties provides the security for the loans which private lenders make to housing associations. Lenders therefore have a clear interest in the efficient management of the stock; not just in rent collection, but also in the lettability of the stock and its long-term repair and maintenance.

Given that approximately three out of five housing association tenants are receiving Housing Benefit, private lenders also have a clear interest in the level of payments which are made under the scheme. A number of key private lenders have cautioned against the introduction of new cuts in Housing Benefit as they would help to undermine the rental income stream and hence the security of the loans which they make to housing associations.

Private Contractors

An emerging set of stakeholders in housing management are the private contractors who have or will be bidding for housing management contracts under CCT in council housing. Both local authorities and housing associations have used private contractors in the past, mainly for undertaking repair work. The introduction of CCT, however, involves private contractors (and housing associations) bidding for the work of managing local authority housing. Their ability to win or retain contracts may be affected by their track record in undertaking housing management.

7.3 Outcomes in Housing Management

Outcome measurement is a relatively new phenomenon in the management of social housing. Prior to the 1970s, central government advice was periodically offered to local authorities by, for example, the housing management sub-committee of the Department of the Environment's Central Housing Advisory Committee. But for the most part, housing management was left very much to local discretion. Partly this reflected an era when central–local relations were less fraught than they are today. Since the late 1970s, however, there has been a 'nationalization' of housing policy (Murie, 1985) whereby central government has increasingly controlled and intervened in local authority housing. It has also reflected a belief in the competence, and the place within the welfare state, of local government. Moreover, it has also reflected a belief that good practice in the management of rented housing was to be found in council housing and not in the private sector (Kemp and Williams, 1991).

The move towards a concern with the three Es (effectiveness, efficiency, economy) and with outcomes in housing management reflects the decline in confidence in the efficiency of the public sector, growing intervention by central government in local government, and a renewed belief in the efficacy of markets. Whereas previously the public sector in housing was seen to be the solution to the private sector problem of slum housing, increasingly the private sector – both in terms of provision and in terms of management techniques – has been seen to be at least part of the solution to the problem of public housing (Kemp, 1991).

The nature of central advice and involvement has likewise changed. Initially, the concern was with the dissemination of advice about effective housing management policies and good practices. From the 1980s, the concern increasingly became focused on the three Es. The Audit Commission published an influential report on housing management in 1986 – tellingly entitled *Managing the Crisis in Council Housing* – which examined the organization and performance of housing management by local authorities.

In the mid-1980s, the Department of the Environment subsequently commissioned a major study by Glasgow University of the nature and effectiveness of housing management, which compared the performance of local authorities and housing associations (Maclennan *et al.*, 1989). It was no coincidence that the study was commissioned at a time when the government had criticized local authorities as paternalistic and inefficient and decided to focus new social housing provision on housing associations instead. However, the report found that housing management performance was not a function of organizational form. In some respects, local authorities were doing better and in others worse, than housing associations. Moreover, there were just as important variations within as between these two types of landlord.

The Glasgow University comparison of housing management performance also found that there was little systematic use of performance monitoring and targets in either housing associations or local authorities. It also noted that there were no structural incentives for them to be efficient or effective landlords. One of its recommendations was that social housing landlords should be required to publish performance indicators (Maclennan *et al.*, 1989).

The Department of the Environment subsequently commissioned the Centre for Housing Policy at the University of York to examine housing management performance under the new financial regimes (Bines *et al.*, 1993). The research found that there had been a significant movement towards a performance culture in social housing management. Many local authorities and housing associations had introduced systems for monitoring performance in certain areas of housing management. The use of personal and departmental section targets had increased greatly since the Glasgow study five years before. The great majority of both types of landlord were producing internal management information on voids. Three-quarters of councils and two-thirds of housing associations had established target periods for reletting empty dwellings. Most organizations had set procedures for checking for delays in repairs. Three-quarters of local authorities and two-thirds of housing associations had a formal system for assessing tenant satisfaction with the repair service.

The York study found that, in some respects, housing management staff were also more performance orientated compared with the findings of the Glasgow study. For example, the proportion of housing officers who felt that training could help to improve their performance had increased from a half in 1987 to four-fifths in 1991. Most staff were aware of the new performance indicator requirements and the majority of them thought that performance indicators were a useful management tool, even if they were suspicious of the government's motives for introducing them. Compared with the Glasgow study, housing officers were much more able to talk about their organization's objectives and felt they knew what they were (Bines *et al.*, 1993).

On the other hand, there was relatively little agreement between the officers in any one organization about what its objectives were. Since effectiveness has been defined as the extent to which an organization meets its objectives (Audit Commission, 1986b) the lack of clarity or agreement about objectives, while understandable, is something which social housing landlords could usefully address.

While many local authorities in particular had carried out customer satisfaction surveys, these seem to have been mainly one-off exercises rather than part of a regular review process. Moreover, the promotion of tenant participation remained relatively undeveloped, especially among district councils and the smaller housing associations (Bines *et al.*, 1993).

It was also noticeable that the areas in which social landlords were collecting performance data were relatively limited in scope. Apart from the information which organizations are required to collect to complete mandatory returns to the Housing Corporation or Department of the Environment, performance monitoring was largely confined to a few key indicators in repairs, rent collection and void control. It is easy to see why. Tenants' satisfaction with the overall service is strongly related to their satisfaction with the repairs service. Rent collection and void control both have revenue implications for landlords while empty properties can be a visible sign of apparent landlord performance. Moreover, as discussed above, the NFR creates incentives for local authorities to keep their voids and arrears to below 2 per cent. The evidence of the York study suggests that this had led some organizations at least to place a new emphasis on collecting the rent and reducing void levels (Bines *et al.*, 1993).

However, many social landlords were not collecting information on some aspects of housing management which are essential to a full awareness of performance. For example, many organizations were unable to say what proportion of their offers of accommodation were refused. Two-fifths of associations and one-third of authorities were unable to specify how many repair requests were received in the financial year 1990–1. Three-tenths of local authorities and one-third of housing associations were unable to say what percentage of repairs were completed within their target time periods. Three in ten authorities and one in ten associations were unable to say what proportion of voids were actually let on target and one-third of authorities and one-tenth of associations were unable to specify what percentage of vacancies were pre-allocated.

Information on transfers of existing tenants within their stock was particularly lacking, perhaps because little information about transfers was then being requested by the Department of the Environment or the Housing Corporation.

While the majority of housing associations monitored their lettings to minority ethnic groups (about which information is collected by the Housing Corporation), only one-third of local authorities did so (information about which is not collected by the DoE). There was thus an extent to which data collection was driven by the mandatory returns which social landlords are required to make rather than by the need to undertake comprehensive performance monitoring and assessment (Bines *et al.*, 1993).

7.4 The Performance Indicator Regime

Section 167 of the Local Government and Housing Act 1989 introduced a new requirement for local authorities to produce an annual report on housing management to be distributed to its tenants as from September 1991. A consultation paper published in October 1989 set out two objectives for the production and distribution of the performance indicator reports:

(1) to provide information to tenants about the performance of their landlord, with the aim of promoting tenant interest and involvement; and
(2) to improve standards of housing management, as a response to customer demand, through the use of performance targets.

In March 1990 the Department of the Environment issued *The Report to Tenants etc Determination 1990* which listed the information that local authorities were required to include in their Report to Tenants under the 1989 Act. Circular 19/90, which was issued in September 1990, set out further information which local authorities might consider including in the reports, including data on performance targets and relevant local information.

Although these reports to tenants were seen as forming part of the Citizen's Charter (Marsh *et al.*, 1993), a separate set of Citizen's Charter housing performance indicators was subsequently devised by the Audit Commission. Under the Local Government Act 1992, the Audit Commission has a duty to specify a list of performance indicators which every local authority in England and Wales will then be obliged to report each year from April 1993. Local authorities are required to publish their performance indicators locally, while the Audit Commission has a duty to publish national summaries of the information in order to facilitate comparisons between authorities (Audit Commission, 1992).

Housing associations moved into the performance indicator regime at a later date than local authorities. The Housing Corporation placed a requirement on housing associations, with effect from October 1991, to issue specified information to all tenants who request it and to inform all of their tenants of this right. They were, however, under no obligation to publish this information to the outside world.

Then in July 1994 the Housing Corporation published a consultation paper which proposed that a range of PIs and contextual data be published for the 250 larger housing associations and those with development programmes, using data that were collected as part of its annual survey of housing associations for 1994. It also proposed to publish a further four PIs for the same group of associations in late 1995. The majority of respondents to the consultation paper (69 per cent of whom were housing associations) welcomed the proposal to publish the PIs. The PIs for 1994 were subsequently published in early 1995 (Housing Corporation, 1995).

Garner (1995) has put forward a number of reasons why an emphasis on management performance and a scrutiny of management costs has come to the fore in the housing association sector. Two of these have already been mentioned: the fact that management costs are reflected in rent levels and hence in Housing Benefit expenditure; and the Citizen's Charter and related developments.

In addition, housing associations are now operating in a much more competitive environment. They are competing against each other for grants from the Housing Corporation to undertake development and the introduction of CCT means that some of them at least will be competing with local authorities, other associations and private sector firms for housing management contracts.

Moreover, private lenders are now scrutinizing their accounts and indicators of management performance such as rent collection and voids. If they are to obtain private loans to continue their development plans, associations have increasingly to demonstrate their ability to collect the rent from which the repayments on these loans is made.

Finally, there has been a growing debate about the 'unelected and unaccountable state'. This debate relates to the shift away from democratically accountable local authorities to housing associations whose committees are much less accountable to their local communities. It has led to pressure on housing associations for them to be more open to public scrutiny and accountable to the consumer and to others who have a stake in housing association performance.

7.5 Outcome Measurement?

Outcomes have been defined by the Audit Commission (1986b) as that which is achieved by producing services. To what extent do the housing management performance indicators produced, for example, by housing associations tackle the questions of *outcomes* as distinct from the more easily measurable *inputs* (resources used to produce a service) and *outputs* (the service that is produced)?

We explore this issue by examining the published performance indicators for housing associations in 1994 (Housing Corporation, 1995). The main indicators

Table 7.1 Housing association performance indicators in 1994

Rental stock:
total number of rental dwellings
dwellings vacant and available for letting
dwellings for elderly people
dwellings for wheelchair users
total number of hostel bedspaces
hostel bedspaces for elderly people
hostel bedspaces for people with wheelchairs
Rents:
average assured weekly rents charged
rent collected as percentage of the rent due
average time taken to relet available dwellings
Lettings:
nominees from local authorities
statutorily homeless households
households transferred from within the association
direct applicants
referred through mobility schemes or from other associations
Black and minority ethnic households
total number of lettings
Repair service:
target times for response repairs (emergency, urgent, routine)
percentage of repairs completed within target (for each category)

Source: Housing Corporation (1995).

are listed in Table 7.1. They are categorized under four headings: rental stock, rents, lettings and the repairs service.

The first point to note is that many of these PIs are not really *performance* indicators as such. Rather, some of them are pieces of contextual information (e.g. the percentage of lettings to direct applicants). It is very helpful, indeed essential, to have these data but they are not indicators of management performance.

The second point to note is that the published PIs each provide insights into certain, different aspects of performance, but they do not in themselves completely capture performance. For example, the percentage of repairs completed within target is certainly an important indicator of how well an association is doing at repairs, but it says nothing about either the quality of the repair work or its cost; and nor does it say anything about whether the maintenance staff were on time for their appointment, whether they were polite to the customer or cleared up any mess before they left the dwelling. Hence even if an association is completing 100 per cent of its repairs within the target times, this does not necessarily mean that it is providing a good overall repairs service.

Third, although some of the PIs are about inputs (e.g. number of staff) and others are about throughputs (e.g. the reletting times) and some deal with outputs (e.g. the number of lettings), none of them is about *outcomes*. Indeed, there has been very little discussion of what is an outcome of housing management and still less of what would count as a 'good' outcome.

These limitations are by no means peculiar to the published PIs for housing associations; they are commonly found in the PIs used in the public and non-profit sectors, but as a first step there needs to be a recognition that outcomes should be defined and identified. One way forward may be to define and assess outcomes in terms of the impact of housing management on the quality of life of social housing tenants, though this would have to be balanced against the cost of improving their quality of life and on whom those costs should fall (the tenant or the taxpayer). Of course, 'quality of life' would itself have to be defined and this is not unproblematic.

If housing management is viewed simply as rehousing, then outcomes would be defined as the impact on the general well-being or quality of life of the households rehoused. Thus it would be sufficient to ascertain whether a particular household's quality of life had improved as a result of being rehoused. There might be some respects in which a household's quality of life had improved and others in which it had deteriorated as a result of being rehoused by the local authority or housing association. Even so, it should in principle be possible to arrive at an evaluation that weighed up the net change in quality of life resulting from the rehousing. A similar evaluation could be applied to households which have been transferred from one dwelling to another within the landlord's own stock.

Social housing landlords that rely on 'points' systems to determine priority for rehousing or for transfers implicitly make such evaluations. In a points system, social housing landlords allocate points for particular circumstances – such as overcrowding, lack of standard amenities such as an internal WC or bath/shower, presence of children in the household, medical 'need' and so on – and then rank households according to their total number of points. The larger the number of points that a household has been awarded, the greater their priority and hence the sooner they are rehoused.

But rehousing is in essence a one-off process, while housing management is a service that is delivered over time, which involves more than simply rehousing. Thus rehousing is only one aspect of housing management. The quality of life of tenants after rehousing is affected by the other aspects of housing management, including the repairs service, the reletting of empty properties, rent collection and arrears recovery. The performance of social housing landlords in these areas is not in itself an outcome *of* housing management, but will affect the outcomes that *result from* housing management.

Thus the quality of life of tenants will be affected by the condition of the dwelling to which they have been rehoused. Dwellings last for many years and can deteriorate unless kept in a good state of repair. At its most extreme, substandard housing can affect the health of the occupants; indeed, it was partly because of this impact of poor housing on health that local authorities first began to be involved in housing activity. Thus, the impact of the repairs service on dwelling condition is an important element in the outcome of housing management. Outcome measures in housing management should therefore ideally include indicators of stock condition.

Rents also have to be considered as well as stock condition. Social housing is not provided free of charge: social housing tenants pay a rent and one that is subsidized (either implicitly or explicitly) by the general taxpayer in return for the services which they receive. The quality of life of tenants can be affected by the level of rent that is charged.

The level of rent – for a given level of housing management services – will determine the value for money (VFM) which the tenant receives: the higher the rent, the lower the VFM. Conversely, the rent will also affect the VFM which the taxpayer receives because – for a given level of service – the higher the rent, the lower the subsidy which will be required to fund housing management.[1] It follows that there can also potentially be a conflict of interest between tenants and taxpayers generally over the level of housing management service provided to tenants.

The level of rent in social housing can also have an impact on the non-housing aspects of the quality of life of social housing tenants, at least in respect of those who do not receive full Housing Benefit. Because social housing is allocated administratively on the basis of assessed need rather than through the market, tenants have relatively little control over the rent they pay and the level of housing management services which they receive. The higher their rent, the less they have to spend on non-housing items of consumption.

Because of the way that the Housing Benefit system operates, the level of income of social housing tenants (who are eligible and apply for it) should not fall below the relevant Income Support benefit rates, since at that point the scheme covers all of the rent. However, the withdrawal of Housing Benefit as income rises means that working tenants are little better off as a result of earning extra money: this is known as the 'poverty trap' or 'poverty plateau' (Deacon and Bradshaw, 1983). The higher the level of rents, the greater the number of tenants who will be entitled to Housing Benefit and hence will be affected by the poverty trap. It has been claimed that the poverty trap undermines work incentives (Wilcox, 1993). Thus one outcome of housing management, if that term is defined to include rent charging, may be to trap people in poverty; another may be to undermine work incentives. Thus there are interaction effects between housing management and other aspects of the quality of life.

Moreover, the less efficiently and effectively the rent is collected, the lower the value for money if it results in a higher rent having to be charged. Hence rent collection and arrears recovery are important aspects of housing management which will affect the outcomes that result from it.

Finally, the reletting of vacant properties is a crucial aspect of housing management. Slow reletting times result in lost rental income, increase the chances of empty dwellings being vandalized (which in turn will affect repair costs), and lengthen the time which households have to wait before being rehoused or transferred. Thus what is referred to as 'void control' can have an effect on the outcomes of housing management.

Problems in Assessing Outcomes

Quite apart from the lack of outcome measures in the PI regimes, a number of other factors make assessing performance difficult in housing management. Many of these are common to other service areas and will only be summarized here (see Kemp, 1995).

One immediate conceptual problem is that housing management is a complex and heterogeneous service. As a result, performance cannot, as Neil Carter (1989) has pointed out, simply be read off a dial or meter like electricity consumption. It follows, therefore, that it is not realistically possible to provide precise measures of performance in housing management, but only to provide an indication of it. That is to say, in examining performance in housing management, it is possible to deal only in performance *indicators* not in performance *measures*; or, as Klein and Carter (1988) have put it, we have to rely on 'can-openers' which may suggest areas where more in-depth scrutiny is required, rather than on 'meters' which precisely show achievement. Thus while definitive judgments are not feasible, qualified assessments are possible.

A related point is that performance is a contestable notion (Klein and Carter, 1988). It is laden with value judgments and open to differing interpretations, as well as being subject to ambiguity. How are judgments to be made about what constitutes good performance and what is poor performance? By what criteria is a given level of achievement to be judged? Is a rent arrears figure of 2 per cent of the total rent collectable a good or a poor level of performance?

The York report – following the Audit Commission (1986a) – attempted to get around this by using a relative, rather than an absolute, measure of performance. The top 25 per cent of performers on various indicators were defined as good performers, the bottom 25 per cent as poor performers and the middle 50 per cent as medium performers. One problem with this approach, of course, is that no matter how much improvement is made across the board in absolute terms, there will by definition always be both poor and good performers (Bines *et al.*, 1993).

A further difficulty concerns the quality of housing management, which is much more difficult to capture in a performance indicator than more readily quantifiable aspects of performance. Moreover, quality is an elusive concept and difficult to define.

In housing management there is continuing interaction between the provider and the consumer rather than simply a one-off transaction, and hence quality should be defined to include not just the service itself but the way in which it is delivered. In other words, the process by which the service is delivered is itself part of the service (Carter, 1989). One implication of this is that consumers may be satisfied with what is otherwise a relatively poor housing management performance because of the manner in which that service is provided – and vice versa.

Assessing effectiveness is made difficult by the fact that an organization's objectives may not be clearly defined, may not be mutually compatible and may not be known or even shared by all or most of the people working in the organization. The Glasgow study found that housing officers were often unclear about what the housing management objectives of their organization were (Maclennan *et al.*, 1989). Although the York study found that housing officers were much more able to talk about their organization's housing management objectives than was true of staff interviewed in the Glasgow study five years before, there was very little unanimity about what those objectives were (Bines *et al.*, 1993). However, this is not a problem that is peculiar to social housing landlords.

A further important difficulty, as Price Waterhouse (1992, p. 2) have pointed out, is that there is:

> ... no generally accepted definition of what constitutes a standard unit of housing management output and in practice there appears to be considerable variation in both the range and level of services provided.

As a result, landlords may vary in their housing management expenditure not only because of differences in the economy and efficiency of their operation, but also because the level and quality of service they provide vary. Thus 'outputs' are difficult to define, measure and hence cost, not to mention compare across different organizations.

One further very important concern is that any examination of service efficiency or service effectiveness must take into account what the Glasgow report called the 'degree of difficulty' of the housing management task (Maclennan *et al.*, 1989). The context within which different social landlords manage their housing stock can vary substantially. Housing estates may, for example, be located in very deprived inner-city areas characterized by high levels of crime, vandalism and unemployment; or they may be located in prosperous, leafy suburbs where unemployment and other indicators of social deprivation are low. The difficulty which social landlords face in managing their housing can be expected to vary such that it is harder to achieve a given level of performance in an area of relative social deprivation compared with one which is relatively prosperous.

The concept of the degree of difficulty of housing management is important because it draws attention to the fact that housing management performance and outcomes are not only a function of ownership or organizational size and structure, or of the policies and practices of housing managers, yet these are the features that are frequently stressed in critiques of public sector performance.

The Housing Corporation explicitly accepts that the degree of difficulty varies, by employing higher housing management expenditure benchmarks for associations that face extra management costs caused by estate difficulties or tenants who require extra management effort. According to the Housing Corporation, these assessments of the severity of need faced by an association represent a judgment 'as to whether the circumstances in which an association operates justifies a higher than average level of expenditure on housing management' (Housing Corporation, 1989, p. 5).

To facilitate comparisons of performance, the Housing Corporation has recently commissioned research with the aim of creating a classification of housing associations. The aim of the research was to group associations into categories or 'families' of similar associations, so that like-with-like comparisons may be made (Walker, 1994). This exercise appears not to have produced an intuitively meaningful classification of housing associations, perhaps because there is so much diversity between the 2000 or so associations that exist.

It has been suggested that comparisons of housing associations on their management performance involve what are essentially comparisons between different types of apple rather than between apples and pears. If this is so, then to continue the metaphor, these apples are growing on trees in orchards which have soils of different levels of fertility. Thus some kind of classification or weighting system is needed to take these different circumstances into account before conclusions are drawn about how well housing associations are performing.

Perhaps the most fundamental difficulty confronting the evaluation of housing management performance is that of identifying the causal mechanisms that have produced the outcomes that have been identified. Research on housing management has not been able to explain outcomes in other than a statistical sense. Using regression analysis it has been possible to identify factors which co-vary with particular housing management indicators, but this is not the same as explaining why these associations exist. To do this we need hypotheses about why a particular outcome is likely to result from a particular process and in what circumstances (Kemp, 1995).

7.6 Conclusions

The use of performance indicators and outcome assessment has developed later in housing than in some of the other areas of the welfare state such as health care and education. Moreover, it is still in its infancy in the sense that few of the PIs that social housing landlords are now required to produce are outcome measures. Instead, they are more to do with inputs, processes and outputs, while many of them are simply contextual data. Outcome measurement and assessment in housing, therefore, are still relatively undeveloped.

Although there was initially some scepticism about the motives of government in requiring social housing landlords to produce publicly available PIs, the value of PIs has now largely been accepted within social housing. Much of the debate is now focused on the cost of collecting the information needed to compile them and on their uses and abuses and on which indicators are the most useful. But there has been relatively little discussion, even in the context of what would be the most 'useful' PIs, about the need for *outcome* measures or indeed about what counts as an outcome of housing management. In part, this failure reflects the relatively limited debate about the intended outcomes of social housing in general and social housing management in particular. It also reflects the fact that outcomes are not easily captured in simple statistics and are perhaps best assessed through specially commissioned studies rather than through the routine collection of PIs.

Note

1. This evaluation is complicated by the fact that housing subsidies can be provided to the dwelling (which will affect the level of rent to be charged) and to the tenant via Housing Benefit. Since 1989, the reduction in bricks-and-mortar subsidies to local authorities and housing associations has not only increased rents but also Housing Benefit payments. The government has acknowledged that the net public expenditure saving from this process is rapidly diminishing.

References

Audit Commission (1984) *Bringing Council Tenants' Arrears under Control*, London: HMSO.

Audit Commission (1986a) *Managing the Crisis in Council Housing*, London: HMSO.

Audit Commission (1986b) *Performance Review in Local Government*, London: HMSO.

Audit Commission (1992) *Citizen's Charter Performance Indicators*, London: Audit Commision.

Best, R. (1991) 'Housing associations: 1890 to 1990', in Lowe, S. L. and Hughes, D. J. (Eds) *A New Century of Social Housing*, Leicester: Leicester University Press.

Bines, W., Kemp, P. A., Pleace, N. and Radley, C. (1993) *Managing Social Housing*, London: HMSO.

Carter, N. (1989) 'Performance indicators: "back-seat driving" or "hands off" control?', *Policy and Politics*, **17** (2), pp. 131–8.

Central Statistical Office (1995) *Annual Abstract of Statistics*, London: HMSO.

Clapham, D. (1989) *Goodbye Council Housing?*, London: Unwin Paperbacks.

Cole, I. and Furbey, R. (1994) *The Eclipse of Council Housing*, London: Routledge.

Deacon, A. and Bradshaw, J. (1983) *Reserved for the Poor: the Means Test in British Social Policy*, Oxford: Basil Blackwell and Martin Robinson.

Department of the Environment (1987a) *Housing: the Government's Proposals*, London: HMSO.

Department of the Environment (1987b) *Finance for Housing Associations: the Government's Proposals*, London: Department of the Environment.
Department of the Environment (1992) *Competing for Quality in Housing*, London: Department of the Environment.
Department of the Environment (1995) *Our Future Homes*, London: Department of the Environment.
Donnison, D. (1987) 'The community-based approach', paper presented at the *City Renewal Through Partnership* conference, Glasgow, 6–10 July.
Edmonds, D. (1995) 'Describing housing association performance', paper presented to the *Performing Miracles?* Symposium, London, 26 April.
Garner, C. (1995) 'Putting performance indicators in context', paper presented to the *Performing Miracles?* symposium, London, 26 April.
Gibb, K. and Munro, M. (1991) *Housing Finance in the UK: an Introduction*, London: Macmillan.
Hedges, B. and Clemens, S. (1994) *Housing Attitudes Survey*, London: HMSO.
Hills, J. (1991) *Unravelling Housing Finance*, Oxford: Clarendon.
Housing Corporation (1989) *Higher Management Allowances*, Circular HC 10/89, London: Housing Corporation.
Housing Corporation (1995) *Housing Associations in 1994. Housing Association Profiles: Performance Indicators and Supplementary Tables*, London: Housing Corporation.
Kemp, P. A. (1989) 'The demuncipalisation of rented housing', in Brenton, M. and Ungerson, C. (Eds) *Social Policy Review 1988–9*, London: Longman.
Kemp, P. A. (1991) 'From solution to problem? Council housing and the development of national housing policy', in Lowe, S. G. and Hughes, D. J. (Eds) *A New Century of Social Housing*, Leicester: Leicester University Press.
Kemp, P. A. (1992) *Housing Benefit: an Appraisal*, London HMSO.
Kemp, P. A. (1995) 'Researching housing management performance', *Urban Studies*, **32** (4–5), pp. 779–90.
Kemp, P. A. and Williams, P. (1991) 'Housing management: a contested history', in Lowe, S. G. and Hughes, D. J. (Eds) *A New Century of Social Housing*, Leicester: Leicester University Press.
Klein, R. and Carter, N. (1988) 'Performance measurement: a review of concepts and issues', in Beeton, D. (Ed.) *Performance Measurement: Getting the Concepts Right*, London: Public Finance Foundation.
Maclennan, D. *et al.* (1989) *The Nature and Effectiveness of Housing Management in England*, London: HMSO.
Marsh, A., Niner, P. and Symon, P. (1993) *An Evaluation of the First Year Experience of the Local Authority Reports to Tenants Regime*, London: HMSO.
Meen, G. (1994) 'The impact of higher rents', *Housing Research Findings*, No. 109, York: Joseph Rowntree Foundation.
Merrett, S. (1979) *State Housing in Britain*, London: Routledge & Kegan Paul.
Murie, A. (1985) 'The nationalization of housing policy', in Loughlin, M. *et al.* (Eds) *Half a Century of Municipal Decline 1935–1985*, Hemel Hempstead: Allen & Unwin.
Power, A. (1987) *Property Before People: the Management of Twentieth Century Council Housing*, London: Allen & Unwin.
Price Waterhouse (1992) *Empirical Study into the Costs of Local Authority Housing*

Management, report to the Department of the Environment, London: Price Waterhouse.

Walker, R. (1994) 'Putting performance measurement into context: classifying social housing organisations', *Policy and Politics*, **22** (3), pp. 191–202.

Warburton, M. (1991) *What Price Council Housing?*, London: National Consumer Council.

Wilcox, S. (1993) *Housing Benefit and the Disincentive to Work*, York: Joseph Rowntree Foundation.

Chapter 8

Measuring Outcome in Schools

Ana Rico

8.0 Introduction

The aim of this chapter is to analyse the main conceptual and practical problems of outcome measurement in education. The particular emphasis will be on assessing the comparative effectiveness of schools, an issue that has received considerable attention in Britain now that schools are required to publish their examination results. Since 1991, such results have been presented by the government in the form of 'league tables'. One of the central goals of such government initiatives has been to evaluate the performance of schools with a view to enhancing choice, control and accountability in the British educational system (UK Government, 1992). However, as we shall show, the proper assessment of school effectiveness can be extremely complex. Crude rankings based on single indicators of school outcomes can be extremely misleading, leading to faulty inferences about performance, and seriously dysfunctional consequences. Therefore, in contrast with most of the chapters in the book, the emphasis here will be on *interpreting* outcome measures, rather than on the measurement process itself.

To this end, educational researchers have invested considerable effort in developing techniques which translate crude measures of outcome – such as examination success rates – into sensible indicators of school effectiveness. Multi-level modelling techniques represent the fruits of such efforts, in so far as they constitute the best statistical device produced to date to evaluate school effectiveness. However, the sheer complexity of such sophisticated statistical techniques has often prevented the diffusion of multi-level contributions outside the academic domain. This chapter will therefore seek to explain in an accessible form how the multi-level methodology can lead to more sensitive outcome measurement in the educational sector.

The structure of the chapter is as follows. The following section discusses outcome in the educational sector, and the stakeholders who might care about outcome. The next section discusses how outcome might be measured, and the core of the chapter is then a discussion of how multi-level techniques can be used to analyse outcome. The chapter ends with a discussion of what action might be taken as a result of the multi-level analysis, and some more general conclusions.

8.1 What is Outcome in the Educational Sector?

As with most of the public sector, the social impact of a school is clearly multidimensional. In principle, therefore, a variety of outcome measures are required to capture properly the multiple dimensions of educational outcome. For instance, the two most influential British studies of school effectiveness (Rutter *et al.*, 1979; Mortimore *et al.*, 1988) included a broad range of measures of outcome relating to academic attainment (reading, writing, mathematics, oral skills) and social achievements (attendance, behaviour, delinquency, self-esteem, attitude towards school). Even such comprehensive batteries of outcome measures do not, however, exhaust the large numbers of school outcomes of potential interest. We could, for instance, also be interested in the capacity of schools to foster other student abilities such as creativeness, interpersonal relations, team work, participative skills, leadership initiatives, capacity for cooperation, self-organization, and so on.

Notwithstanding these considerations, however, the debate on school effectiveness in the UK has focused mainly on a single outcome measure: namely, examination success rates. This preoccupation became more marked after the passing of the 1980 Education Act, which required schools to publish their examination results. This initiative emphasized the considerable political commitment to exam success rates, which was subsequently reinforced by a requirement that league tables should be published, as set out in the Parent's Charter (Department of Education and Science, 1991). In practice, these developments have served to concentrate school effectiveness research efforts on the issue of examination results.

The second reason for retaining such a limited focus is practical. As the study by Gray and collaborators demonstrates, information on other relevant outcome measures is simply not systematically collected (Gray *et al.*, 1986). This is in spite of the manifest unease amongst schools and teachers concerning the value of exam results as the sole measure of outcome.

In spite of its limitations, however, the use of exam success as an outcome measurement scheme can be defended on three counts. First, as stated in Chapter 1, univariate measures have the advantage of being easy to produce and clearly understandable. In the second place, as school effectiveness research has consistently demonstrated, examination results do have a relevant social impact, in that they are important determinants of the employment prospects of school leavers (Willms, 1986; Raffe and Willms, 1989; Garner and Raudenbush, 1991).

The third reason for favouring exam results as a measure of educational outcome is the relatively well-developed British examination system. Unlike many other countries, the academic capabilities of secondary school students in the UK are tested through externally set and graded examinations based on a published syllabus. Moreover, the form of the exams does not restrict answers to a predetermined set of possibilities, instead requiring students to exercise complex problem-solving skills. Independent examination boards set and grade exams in a uniform way nationwide, to the extent that information on the commonest errors committed by students is published, with a view to improving future teaching (Fitz-Gibbon, 1991).

Such tight connection between assessment and teaching, which is not found in many other countries, reinforces the validity of exam results as a relevant measure of the quality of teaching. However, this is not to say that examination results should be taken as the sole, or even the main, outcome measure relevant for the evaluation of school performance (Cuttance, 1992), and the search for broader measures of outcome must continue.

In discussing outcome measurement in schools, it must be kept in mind that there is a broad range of potential stakeholders. Most immediately, students constitute the current users of educational services, while their parents also have an intimate interest in the performance of their schools. Moreover, parents of children under school age as well as future parents represent the interests of future users of schools. In a similar vein, parent associations are important as representatives of the common interests of current and future parents.

Second, teachers and their professional associations are crucial as direct providers of educational services, and school governors and head teachers as the managerial authorities of the school. Third, Local Educational Authorities (LEAs) represent democratic control over those schools that have not 'opted out' of local government control. Those that have are directly accountable to the central government, through the medium of the Funding Agency for Schools.

Fourth, the central government (and in particular, the Department for Education) is more generally concerned at a number of levels. Its schools inspectorate seeks to ensure that basic standards are maintained. It promotes reforms to improve the quality and equity of the educational system, and determines the contents of the syllabus, through its agency, the School Curriculum and Assessment Authority. More generally, educational reformers, professionals and researchers share with the government the role of informing school improvement schemes. Finally, as one of the largest and most fundamental investments made by all societies, education is always likely to attract the keenest interest from employers and society at large.

All these interested parties can be expected to share the common aim of improving educational outcomes. But they probably have different ideas about more specific issues, say, how those outcomes should be distributed, the means by which school improvements should be promoted or the priorities for improvement efforts. In this respect, the debate on the appropriateness of raw examination results as measures of school effectiveness constitutes a good example of the potential for conflicts between stakeholders. For instance, a broad majority of parents will probably consider the raw examination results of schools as relevant to their interests, even if it just reflects the higher intellectual ability or socioeconomic background of the pupil intake. However, local authorities, inspectors, managers and researchers, who adopt a more global view of the educational process, may be interested less in school success in absolute terms, and more in the value added to what students themselves bring to the educational process (Murphy, 1992).

8.2 Why Measure Educational Outcomes?

Outcome measurement in the educational sector can serve a wide variety of ends which cannot be discussed in detail here (see, e.g., Mayston and Jesson, 1991). Instead, this section focuses on those potential roles of outcome measurement schemes more directly related to the evaluation of the comparative effectiveness of schools. Why should this be desirable? To start with, the broader goals of securing political control and external accountability of the educational services are specially relevant after the enactment of the 1988 Reform Act, which – through the Local Management of Schools initiative – devolved important managerial and financial powers to schools. In addition, the Act introduced the right of parents to send their children to the school of their choice, with the idea of reproducing the role that consumers' preferences play in the marketplace. In this context, the league tables of school examination results have two functions. First, they are expected to provide parents with some of the data necessary to inform their choice. And second, they are intended to promote the more general control and accountability of the increasingly autonomous school authorities to society at large.

Given the important political and resource allocation roles that these outcome measurement schemes are expected to play, it is therefore of crucial importance that they are very carefully designed. Unfortunately, as we shall explain, the crude league tables of schools based on raw examination results do not satisfy this criterion. Most crucially, raw examination results are heavily dependent on the school's intake of pupils, as reflected in the characteristics of its catchment area (Gray *et al.*, 1986). Research on school effectiveness has consistently shown that students' characteristics constitute the main determinant of educational attainment. Therefore, any judgment about school performance will be misleading unless school exam results are adjusted to take account of the different characteristics of the pupil intake. The inability of crude league tables to accommodate this complication is the prime motivation for the multi-level modelling methodology described below.

To illustrate the problem of interpreting exam results, consider two hypothetical schools. The first is highly effective, but its intake contains an unusually high concentration of problem students. It therefore secures relatively modest exam results, notwithstanding its high quality. By way of contrast, a highly selective school might secure good exam results even if it is ineffective, simply because of its ability to 'cream off' high achievers from its catchment population. Clearly, comparison of these two schools on the basis of exam results alone may lead to completely false inferences about school performance.

For this reason, it has become accepted that fair comparisons of school effectiveness should be based on the *value added* by schools to student educational progress. In the context of exam success, the value added by a school implies the extent to which exam results are influenced by factors directly under the control of the school. The measurement of value added therefore requires a methodology which adjusts for differences in students' characteristics. However, in spite of the broad consensus among educational professionals and researchers on the virtues of value added as the correct approach to outcome measurement, subsequent policy statements by the government – and in particular the 1988 Education Reform Act – have not so far adopted the principles of value added.

An additional crucial role of outcome measurement in the educational sector is to inform initiatives for improving educational practice. If it is possible to isolate policy characteristics that are common to the most effective schools, then they can serve as models of 'best practice'. Their educational practices can be transferred to less successful schools, and thereby improvements in the educational system as a whole can be secured. Similarly, the impact of major educational reforms – such as the introduction of comprehensive schooling during the 1970s – can be evaluated by comparing school results before and after the introduction of reforms. In this way, outcome measurement can also lead to important advances in educational processes.

8.3 Modelling Outcome in the Educational Sector

The different ideas and interests involved in the educational field are reflected in the debate surrounding outcome measurement models. The principal arguments in this debate mainly relate to three crucial questions. (1) What are the relevant dimensions of educational outcome and how can we best measure them? (2) Which of the available methods should be used to analyse outcome? Of particular importance here, given the nature of outcome measurement schemes in the educational sector, is that the method chosen should allow fair conclusions to be drawn about the comparative effectiveness of schools. In this respect, a proper analysis of school results involves the isolation of the effect of the school from that of other determinants of outcome. Finally, (3) how should the knowledge obtained on school outcomes and processes be used to secure improved educational services?

In fact, these three questions correspond to the three key stages of outcome measurement outlined in Chapter 1, namely measurement, analysis and action. The successful completion of these three tasks is crucial to guaranteeing adequate political and managerial control over public services. We therefore now consider them in turn.

The Measurement Problem

The first important measurement issue refers to which dimensions of outcome should be considered. The views of educational professionals and researchers in this respect represent a useful corrective to the dominant emphasis on exam results in the political and public debate. In this sense, the main claim of educationists, as summarized by Peter Mortimore's remarks, is the following: 'the adoption of a broad range of outcome measures is essential if studies are to address, adequately, the all-round development of students, and if they are to be used to judge the effectiveness of schools' (Mortimore, 1992, p. 156).

Therefore, although we shall only discuss the problems involved in the measurement of exam results, it is nevertheless important to keep in mind that the task of producing and measuring other complementary educational outcomes constitutes a crucial challenge for the future. Indeed, the complexity of this formidable challenge is merely emphasized by exploring the considerable difficulties involved in the relatively simple task of producing adequate measures of school exam results.

The main problem in relation to exams is that of translating the examination passes obtained by each school into a single unidimensional index of exam success. There are several aspects relevant to this problem. The first one refers to the scaling of grades obtained in different types of public examinations. For example, in the UK at age 16 these used to include the GCE O level (the General Certificate of Education), the CSE (Certificate of Secondary Education) and the 16+ exams. Several scales and indicators have been used by researchers, LEAs or statisticians to reconcile scores on different schemes (Gray *et al.*, 1986). Among them, the scale designed by the Inner London Educational Authority (ILEA) is typical. The ILEA scores attributed to the grades obtained in three different public examination systems were given in Table 8.1.

In spite of being widely accepted, the ILEA scores highlight the problem of

Table 8.1 ILEA scores for public examination grades

Examination	*Grade*							
GCE O level	A	B	C	D	E	–	–	U
16+	A	B	C	2	3	4	5	U
CSE	–	–	1	2	3	4	5	U
ILEA score	7	6	5	4	3	2	1	0

applying what is ultimately an arbitrary system of weighting to grades obtained in different public examinations systems (Gray *et al.*, 1986). In the UK this practical problem has to some extent been alleviated by the more recent introduction of homogeneous systems of examinations, known as the General Certificate of Secondary Examination (GCSE) in England and Wales, or the Standard Grade in Scotland (Cuttance, 1992).

However, even where a single examination scheme is in place, there are likely to be variations in marking practices across administrative boundaries. The second difficult aspect of scaling therefore refers to the practice of equating marks across examination boards in order to aggregate them into a single index (Goldstein, 1984). Obviously, the various subjective criteria applied in each board to award marks are likely to vary across boards. This introduces an error of measurement in exam success scales. This error can be corrected for by adjusting for the boards at which pupils presented (Cuttance, 1992).

Another related aspect of scaling is far more problematic both in practical and conceptual terms. It refers to the equal weight given to the grades obtained in every subject. This practice fails to take into account the fact that schools may place different emphases on different subjects depending on their particular objectives. Therefore, a school with low overall exam success rates may well be above average in one or more subjects central to its academic objectives, such as mathematics or English. In this sense, the practice of giving equal weight to all subjects may not respect different school objectives. Aggregate effectiveness scores may therefore misrepresent the effectiveness of schools in particular subjects.

In fact, the preliminary findings of recent school effectiveness research in this respect point to the existence of differential school effectiveness in different academic subjects (Mortimore *et al.*, 1988; Reynolds, 1992a; Goldstein *et al.*, 1993). Such results emphasize the need to consider school exam results for individual subjects as a complement to aggregate exam results. This view is endorsed in the government requirements that the results of schools in each of the core subjects of the new National Curriculum should be published alongside aggregate exam success rates (DES, 1991).

The final problem in connection with the measurement of exam results is the variability of exam success rates of schools over time. Usually, comparisons of schools are restricted to the results achieved in a single year. However, the little empirical evidence existing on this topic suggests that there are significant variations in the results achieved by schools over different years (Goldstein, 1987; Nuttall *et al.*, 1989; Willms and Raudenbush, 1989). If this is the case, longitudinal studies considering school results through time may be required to get a fair picture of the effectiveness of each school.

The Analysis Problem

The key issue in the analysis of educational outcomes concerns how raw examination results might be transformed into sensible indicators of the value added by schools to the educational progress of their students. This requires an adequate statistical analysis of the various determinants of outcomes. In particular, appropriate interpretation of school success rates requires that the effects of those determinants of outcome that are under the control of schools should be isolated from the effects of other influential factors not under their control. The statistical techniques usually used to effect this are various forms of regression analysis.

However, the application of traditional regression methods to the analysis of school outcomes suffers from several important problems. The key to these problems is the hierarchical structure of the educational system, in the sense that individual outcomes are determined to some extent by the individual, to some extent by the teacher and to some extent by the school. This hierarchical structure should be taken into account by the statistical model used to analyse outcomes. However, conventional regression techniques are not well suited to dealing with hierarchical, multi-level data. They can therefore lead to erroneous interpretations of the outcomes found within a hierarchical structure. For this reason, educational methodologists have dedicated considerable effort to the development of what have become known as multi-level modelling techniques, which constitute an extension of regression methods specially designed to deal with hierarchical data.

The central point of multi-level methodologists is that fair indicators of the value added by schools should include consideration of the full range of determinants of outcomes. The factors that are thought to influence outcomes act mainly at two levels: (1) the level of the individual characteristics of students, and (2) the level of school characteristics and policies. (For convenience, this discussion omits consideration of the teacher – an intermediate level.) In statistical terms, student characteristics are known as micro-variables, which define the intake of schools; school-level factors are termed macro-variables. Accordingly, the effect on outcomes of variables acting at the individual level is studied through statistical analysis of what are termed micro-parameters, while the effect of factors acting at the level of the school is modelled by school macro-parameters.

Micro-parameters in multi-level modelling

Two micro-variables are generally considered important to describing the background of pupils at entry to school: the prior attainment of students, and the socioeconomic status of their parents. Measures of prior attainment are usually obtained from the tests administered to students at entry to the school, and they reflect the intellectual ability of students as well as their prior schooling experiences. Socioeconomic background measures include information on parents' professional occupations and levels of education, and represent the social influence of the family on student progress. These two variables are generally accepted to have an effect on outcomes over and above the influence of the school.

Thus, what we find here is one of the analytical problems outlined in Chapter 1, namely that of the joint influence of several factors on outcome. Families, students' intellectual ability, prior schooling experiences and current school processes act together to produce outcomes. In addition, student social and intellectual background differs across schools, giving rise to a different environment for each school. Such heterogeneity makes the task of achieving a given target level of effectiveness harder for some schools than for others.

The statistical adjustment of outcomes for the differing intakes of schools seeks to disentangle the influence of the school from the joint influence of individual level factors. At the micro level, the multi-level model can be expressed as follows:

$$\text{Exam results} = a + b_1\,(\text{prior attainment}) + b_2\,(\text{social circumstances}) + e \quad (1)$$

In this equation, a, b_1 and b_2 constitute the school micro-parameters, while e represents the random variability in individual outcomes within each school. This random variability is expected to be high because the statistical analyses are usually based only on a small sample of pupils from each school. As stated in the introduction to this book, high random variability creates problems for reliably estimating the effect of schools on outcomes. However, one of the important advantages of multi-level techniques is their ability to take appropriate account of high random variability.

The term a is the school micro-intercept, which represents the effectiveness of each particular school compared with pupils of nationally average intellectual and social background. The magnitude of a in each school constitutes a crucial piece of information for ranking schools in value-added league tables. The micro-intercept constitutes the main indicator for judging the *average* value added by the school, because it isolates the specific influence of the school on outcomes from that of its intake composition. Multi-level techniques provide reliable estimates by allowing the value of the intercept to vary randomly across schools, thus accommodating the heterogeneity of school environments.

The school micro-slopes are b_1 and b_2, which model whether schools are differentially effective for pupils of different intellectual ability and social background. Therefore, while school micro-intercepts measure the first dimension of school effectiveness – namely the average quality of educational provision in each school – school micro-slopes measure the *equity* dimension of school effectiveness (Cuttance, 1992). In other words, they indicate how equitable is the distribution of school outcomes among different types of students.

Multi-level modelling techniques also allow school micro-slopes to vary across schools, so that the specific contribution of each school towards equity in educational outcomes can be analysed. Accordingly, schools with flatter slopes (i.e., with smaller values of b) would be promoting similar results for all pupils, independently of their social and intellectual characteristics, thus contributing to equity in educational outcomes. In contrast, schools with steeper slopes would be favouring the progress of particular types of pupils at the expense of other pupils, thus promoting an inequitable distribution of outcomes within the school.

The determination of whether school micro-slopes vary across schools is a crucial question within school effectiveness research, not only because it is interesting for its own sake, but also because it has serious consequences for attempts at producing school rankings. For if the equity dimension of school effectiveness is found to differ across schools, it will not be possible to rank schools according to only the first dimension of school effectiveness (i.e., average quality). In short, schools would be ranked differently, depending on which types of pupils were of interest. A bidimensional classification of schools will therefore be required, as illustrated in Figure 8.1.

	EQUITY DIMENSION	
QUALITY DIMENSION	High quality and disequalizing	High quality and equalizing
	Low quality and disequalizing	Low quality and equalizing

Figure 8.1 The equity and quality dimensions of school performance
Source: Cuttance (1992, Figure 4.4).

Macro-parameters in multi-level modelling

Thus the first step in the statistical analysis of school outcomes involves the multi-level estimation of the two intake-adjusted dimensions of school effectiveness: quality and equity. As we have seen, this involves isolating the effectiveness of each school from the effect of individual-level factors, and requires the proper estimation of two types of micro-parameters: school micro-intercepts and school micro-slopes. However, to get a more complete picture of the determinants of school effectiveness, it is important to analyse the effects of school level factors on school effectiveness.

The second step in the analysis of outcome therefore seeks to discriminate between those school-level factors (macro-variables) which are under the control of schools from those that are not. Accordingly, two types of macro-variables can be distinguished. The first represents the aggregate social and intellectual composition of the school, which is known to have an effect on the results obtained by individual students of varying social and intellectual background. An example of these compositional or contextual effects arises from the finding that a particular student of any given background will have better results in a school where the average socioeconomic status or intellectual ability of the pupil body is higher than in a school of lower social or intellectual composition. Although an important determinant of outcome, the aggregate composition of the school is in general not under the control of school authorities (except to some extent in selective schools). Therefore, the analysis of value-added indicators of school effectiveness should take account of such uncontrollable school-level factors.

The second type of macro-variable refers to the school practices and policies which are likely to be under the control of schools, such as classroom management policies, teaching practices, and so on. The effect of these school factors on outcomes reflects the true effectiveness of the school to foster the educational progress of their students.

In the light of these considerations, a second multi-level equation is used to estimate the effects of the two types of macro-variables:

$$\text{School micro-intercepts} = c\,(\text{school composition}) + d\,(\text{school policies}) + u \qquad (2)$$

What we are analysing in this equation is the relative contribution to effectiveness of those school-level factors which are under the control of schools. In particular, the magnitude of the macro-parameter d represents the best possible measure of the average value added by schools to the exam results of their students. Similar equations can be produced to explain the corresponding effect of school policies on the equity dimension of school effectiveness. This can be done by simply substituting the school micro-slopes for the first term of the equation (school micro-intercepts), in the following way:

$$\text{School micro-slopes} = c\,(\text{school composition}) + d\,(\text{school policies}) + u \qquad (3)$$

Again, the equation analyses the extent to which school authorities are responsible for the prevailing level of equity in the distribution of educational outcomes within each school. This information is crucial to the evaluation of schools' effectiveness, given that one of the explicit objectives of the British public sector is to foster an equitable distribution of public service outcomes. To date, however, official comparisons of school effectiveness have disregarded this second dimension of school effectiveness.

Combining micro- and macro-effects in multi-level modelling

Finally, in a third analytical step, the different macro-equations for the micro-intercept (equation 2) and the micro-slopes (equation 3) can be combined with the single micro-equation described before (equation 1) to estimate the effects of individual and school-level factors simultaneously. This combination offers the most comprehensive way of analysing the value added by schools to the educational progress of their students, as it takes explicitly into account the fact that educational outcomes are jointly determined by factors acting at different hierarchical levels.

Conventional regression methods suffer from important problems when trying to estimate the influence of factors acting at the individual and school levels. Multi-level models have been developed specifically to overcome such problems. They are also able to estimate reliably the relative contribution to school performance of different school policies. This is the central objective of the macro-equations presented above. As we shall see in the next section, the information on the relative effectiveness of educational policies can offer useful policy guidance on school improvement initiatives.

In summary, the satisfactory analysis of school exam results is a rather complex enterprise. First, adequate multi-level modelling of all the determinants of outcome is expensive in terms of data and expertise. Second, if crucial information on any of the determinants is missing, school effectiveness cannot be reliably estimated, and the school rankings produced may be unfair. British multi-level research on school outcomes is still far from achieving all the demanding requirements of the multi-level approach. There is therefore plenty of room for improvement in the analysis of school outcomes. However, the rate of developments in this field during the last decade has been extraordinary, to the extent that we might reasonably expect that all the requirements for producing fair comparisons of school effectiveness will be in place in the near future.

Acting on Educational Outcome Measurement

Proper measurement and analysis of school outcomes can generate important information for improving school effectiveness. In this respect, the role of outcome measurement schemes in clarifying the effects of school, teacher and student background on educational outcomes is much more important than simply setting league tables. If used properly, they can enable improvement efforts to be targeted at families, teachers and school authorities on the basis of a sound understanding of the areas where improvement is possible.

In this context, each of the stakeholders in the educational sector has a relevant part to play in the action stage. For instance, the study by Mortimore *et al.* (1988) found that the most effective schools in their study involved parents, teachers, school governors and authorities (and to some extent, children) in the decisions and activities of the school. By the same token, the authors claim that the performance of the less effective schools could be promoted through the participation in improvement schemes of all these actors, basing their recommendations on the policies and practices found in the most effective schools. In this respect, the significant advances in the analysis of outcomes introduced by multi-level methodologists make a fundamental contribution to knowledge concerning the policies and practices which make schools effective. The main problem with the technique is its statistical sophistication, which precludes fluent communication between outcome analysts and policy makers. In the future, it is almost certain therefore that much effort will have to be expended on disseminating multi-level research findings in an accessible form.

A second related problem – common to most statistical techniques – is the following. Although multi-level studies have generated a great deal of knowledge about the associations between outcome and various environmental and administrative variables, much less is known about why the relationships exist. For example, it may not be enough to know that there exists a positive relationship between a participative school culture and educational outcome. It may also be necessary to understand why participation improves performance if the finding is to be helpful in improving outcome in poorly performing schools. Multi-level analysis is therefore only the start of the improvement process, and more effort will be necessary to translate its findings into concrete improvements. One way of doing this is to undertake careful qualitative investigation of the processes occurring in the most effective schools. In this respect, the fruitful qualitative exploration by Levine and collaborators (Levine, 1992) of effective American schools can serve as a model.

An alternative way of promoting school improvement may be through the enactment of parent choice. Belief in the potency of parental choice constitutes the core of the UK Government's policy with regard to the action stage, now that parents have the right to express a preference for the school their child should attend. The publication of league tables of comparative school effectiveness is intended to inform parental choice, so that they can select the school most appropriate for their child. In this 'quasi market' for education, it is expected that the schools favoured by clients' preferences will grow while the less effective schools will be pushed out of the market by the most effective ones. However, this action strategy presents considerable problems within the public sector field. First, as we have explained above, it is not easy to recognize the most effective schools, because a proper evaluation requires a detailed knowledge of students' characteristics and school policies. This information is not yet available for most British schools. Second, as Mortimore and collaborators (1988, p. 289) remark, the most effective schools 'cannot be stretched like elastic to make more room for more children'. It may be that by expanding, they would risk losing the very qualities that made them effective, for, according to the authors' research findings, 'the smaller schools were, on average, more likely to be effective than were the larger ones'.

A third problem associated with parental choice is that it conflicts to some extent with the importance of equity inherent in much educational policy. The principle of enhancing choice has until now tended to promote those schools with higher raw examination results, ignoring the equity dimension of school effectiveness. The potential conflict between equity and efficiency reflects a conflict between stakeholder objectives which has not yet been explicitly addressed by the UK Government.

The substantial existing body of multi-level findings on the impact of comprehensive reforms on educational outcomes (see, e.g., Willms, 1986 and McPherson and Willms, 1986) may constitute the first step towards solving such conflicts. The implementation of the parental choice reforms can now be investigated along similar lines. The results of both reforms can therefore be contrasted so as to inform future improvement efforts. In this way, the rigorous evaluation of educational outcomes can help push forward the debate on educational strategy from the field of political opinion and ideology to the field of informed, rational choice.

8.4 Conclusions

The main conclusion from this chapter is that outcome measurement schemes, if appropriately interpreted, can play a useful role in controlling and improving educational provision. However, the satisfactory interpretation of educational outcomes is not a simple task. It requires the application of statistically sophisticated methods of analysis, and is expensive in terms of data, expertise and computational requirements. However, multi-level methods represent a significant improvement in the power and precision of statistical methods of analysing outcome. Such methods allow researchers adequately to model hierarchical data, so that the relative importance of individual and organizational factors in explaining educational outcomes can be reliably estimated.

The importance of isolating the relative contribution of individual versus organizational factors is paramount, because, as multi-level research has consistently shown, the specific effects of the school on outcomes tend to be small relative to the impact of factors acting at the level of individual students. Therefore, if the results of educational providers are not adjusted by the different composition of their catchment populations in terms of individual characteristics, any judgment about their performance will be unfair, and may lead to ineffective policy responses.

However, the effect of the school on outcomes, although relatively small, is highly relevant because it applies to all the pupils in a school, and can therefore have a marked impact on the performance of the educational system as a whole.

In this respect, multi-level methods offer the additional advantage of being well suited to detecting effects of relatively small magnitude. Furthermore, multi-level research can determine which factors contribute to school effectiveness, by isolating the policies and practices which are associated with effective schools.

To conclude, multi-level methods have significantly increased the range of research questions which can be addressed by empirical enquiry. They can potentially clarify some hitherto intractable questions regarding the comparative effectiveness of schools. However, this potential has only begun to be exploited by educational researchers, and the future agenda for multi-level research in the field of outcome measurement is still large. Many of the most important questions in this field therefore still await conclusive empirical answers. This relatively slow progress can be attributed to three facts. First, multi-level computational developments are relatively recent, so that some lapse of time is needed before researchers can take them on board. Second, the sheer complexity of the multiple, interlocked determinants of educational outcomes makes the development of multi-level models difficult, notwithstanding the existence of the necessary methodologies. Third, multi-level methods are relatively expensive in terms of data requirements, and the continuing lack of information on many important activities and outcomes further constrains their application to school effectiveness issues.

The first problem will easily be solved as more effort is dedicated to spreading multi-level modelling techniques through the research community. Fortunately, there are already some excellent contributions in this respect, which present multi-level methods and research findings in an accessible form (see, e.g., Bock, 1989; Paterson, 1991; Paterson and Goldstein, 1991; Cuttance, 1992; Reynolds, 1992a). Similarly, the second problem will not constitute an insurmountable barrier for multi-level research, although the complexity of the educational domain will always present a challenge.

It is therefore only the third problem – the lack of data – that may represent a more serious obstacle for future research in the field of school outcomes. In this respect, the information innovations introduced in most parts of the British public sector in connection with the Citizen's Charter are to be welcomed, in that they will facilitate more comprehensive exploration of the determinants of public sector outcomes. As Culyer *et al.* (1990, p. 5) claim in connection with the parallel health reforms, 'the general effect of the reform is to place much greater emphasis on the measurement of process and to encourage audit of activity and cost'. In the schools sector, the new flows of information may open up similarly promising avenues of research on comparative performance, given that the necessary statistical methodology is already in place.

Acknowledgement

The help of Graham Vullianny, who presented a seminar on this topic and offered invaluable guidance, is gratefully acknowledged.

References

Bock, R. D. (Ed.) (1989) *Multi-level Analysis of Educational Data*, London: Academic Press.

Culyer, A. J., Maynard, A. and Posnett, J. (1990) 'Reforming health care: an introduction to the economic issues', in A. J. Culyer, A. Maynard, and J. Posnett (Eds) *Competition in Health Care: Reforming the NHS*, London: Macmillan.

Cuttance, P. (1992) 'Evaluating the effectiveness of schools', in Reynolds, D. (Ed.) *School Effectiveness: Research, Policy and Practice*, London: Cassell.

Department of Education and Science (1991) *The Parent's Charter*, London: DES.

Fitz-Gibbon, C. T. (1991) 'Multi-level modelling in an indicator system', in Raundenbush, S. W. and Willms, J. D. (Eds) *Schools, Classrooms and Pupils: International Studies of Schooling from a Multi-level Perspective*, New York: Academic Press.

Garner, C. and Raudenbush, S. W. (1991) 'Neighbourhood effects on educational attainment', *Sociology of Education*, **64** (4), pp. 251–62.

Goldstein, H. (1984) 'The methodology of school comparisons', *Oxford Review of Education*, **10** (1), pp. 69–75.

Goldstein, H. (1987) *Multi-level Models in Educational and Social Research*, London: Griffin.

Goldstein, H., Rasbash, J., Yang, M., Woodhouse, G., Pan, H., Nuttall, D. and Thomas, S. (1993) 'A multi-level analysis of school examination results', *Oxford Review of Education*, **19** (4), pp. 425–33.

Gray, J., Jesson, D. and Jones, B. (1986) 'The search for a fairer way of studying school examination results', *Research Papers in Education*, **2**, pp. 91–122.

Gray, J., Jesson, D. and Sime, N. (1990) 'Estimating differences in the examination performance of secondary schools in six LEAs', *Oxford Review of Education*, **16**, 137–58.

Levine, P. (1992) 'An interpretative review of US research and practice dealing with unusually effective schools', in Reynolds, D. (Ed.) *School Effectiveness: Research, Policy and Practice*, London: Cassell.

Mayston, D. and Jesson, D. (1991) 'Educational performance assessment: a new framework of assessment', *Policy and Politics*, **19**, pp. 99–108.

McPherson, A. and Willms, J. D. (1986) 'Equalization and improvement: some effects of comprehensive reorganization in Scotland', *Sociology*, **21** (4), pp. 509–39.

Mortimore, P. (1992) 'Issues in school effectiveness', in Reynolds, D. (Ed.) *School Effectiveness: Research, Policy and Practice*, London: Cassell.

Mortimore, P., Sammons, P., Stoll, L., Lewis, D. and Ecob, R. (1988) *School Matters: the Junior Years*, London: Open Books.

Murphy, J. (1992) 'Effective schools: legacy and future directions', in Reynolds, D. (Ed.) *School Effectiveness: Research, Policy and Practice*, London: Cassell.

Nuttall, D. L., Goldstein, H., Prosser, R. and Rasbash, J. (1989) 'Differential school effectiveness', *International Journal of Educational Research*, **13**, pp. 769–76.

Paterson, L. (1991) 'An introduction to multi-level modelling', in Raudenbush, S. W. and Willms, J. D. (Eds) *Schools, Classrooms and Pupils: International Studies of Schooling from a Multi-level Perspective*, New York: Academic Press.

Paterson, L. and Goldstein, H. (1991) 'New statistical methods for analysing social structures: an introduction to multi-level models', *British Educational Research Journal*, **17** (4), pp. 387–92.

Raffe, D. and Willms, J. D. (1989) 'Schooling the discouraged worker: local-labour markets effects on educational participation', *Sociology*, **23** (4), pp. 559–81.

Reynolds, D. (1992a) 'School effectiveness and school improvement: an updated review of the British literature', in Reynolds, D. (Ed.) *School Effectiveness: Research, Policy and Practice*, London: Cassell.

Reynolds, D. (Ed.) (1992b) *School Effectiveness: Research, Policy and Practice*, London: Cassell.

Rutter, M., Maugham, B., Mortimore, P., Ouston, J., Smith, A. (1979) *Fifteen Thousand Hours. Secondary Schools and their Effects on Children*, London: Open Books.

UK Government (1992) *Choice and Diversity: a New Framework for Schools*, London: HMSO.

Willms, J.D. (1986) 'Social class segregation and its relationships to pupils' examination results in Scotland', *American Sociological Review*, **51**, pp. 224–41.

Willms, J.D. and Raudenbush (1989) 'A longitudinal hierarchical model for estimating school effects and their stability', *Journal of Educational Measurement*, **26**, pp. 1–24.

Chapter 9

In Search of a Representative Measure of Poverty

Jonathan Bradshaw, Laura Bouwknegt and Hilary Holmes

9.0 Introduction

Poverty is not really a measure of outcome. Indeed many of the measures discussed in this chapter are based on income and *in*come is quite clearly an *in*put. Nevertheless an explicit objective of many policy interventions is to prevent or reduce poverty. It is probably the major objective of the social security system which takes a third of all public expenditure in the UK. It is an important consideration in fiscal policy and because poverty is at the heart of so many problems in modern Britain it is a relevant issue in the evaluation of almost all social and economic interventions.

The notion of poverty also implies a moral imperative. If we define someone as poor we mean that he/she is living so far below the standards of the rest of us that there is a collective duty to respond to that person's need. Poverty is a call to (collective) action and the test of the outcome of that collective action is the extent to which poverty has been diminished or abolished. Given the importance of poverty and this moral imperative it is vital that we know how to measure it.

Poverty can be measured directly by investigating the actual living standards and lifestyles of people and identifying those who are relatively and unacceptably deprived. These types of measure are attempts to devise real outcome measures. However, more usually poverty is measured indirectly by the use of income (or expenditure). In this case a measure of input is being used as a proxy indicator of a standard of living. This chapter explores the consequences of using a variety of measures of poverty for the size and structure of the poor population in the UK.

9.1 Background

For nearly a century social scientists have sought to define and measure poverty. Indeed in the UK this effort has been one of the major preoccupations of research and scholarship in social policy. The stream of research has passed through a number of intellectual phases. The most distinguished pioneer of all this effort and one of the founding fathers of empirical social policy research was Seebohm Rowntree (1901, 1941, 1951). His 1899 study of poverty in York set the style and standard of the investigation of poverty for over half a century. The use of baskets of goods (budget standards) by him and other prewar researchers dominated thinking about poverty and even informed the scales of benefit recommended by Beveridge in 1942, which were more or less implemented in the National Assistance scale rates in 1948 and are still influencing the scales of Income Support which now determine the living standards of one person in six in the UK.

In the postwar period poverty research re-emerged with a new conceptualization and empirical thrust. Abel Smith and Townsend (1965) pioneered the method of measuring poverty that related income to the scale rates of assistance benefit. This technique eventually became the standard government approach to the measurement of poverty and lasted in the Low Income Families (LIF) statistics until the series was abandoned by the government in 1985. (Note however that the series has since been sustained by the Institute of Fiscal Studies with the support of the Social Security Committee of the House of Commons [1992]).

Then Peter Townsend (1979) sought to articulate empirically his concept of relative deprivation and developed a 12-item social deprivation index.

In recent years there has been a relative dearth of new poverty research in the UK. This has no doubt been one consequence of the political environment illustrated by a government member (John Moore) declaring 'the end of the line for poverty' and that 'individuals and organizations concerned with poverty were merely pursuing the political goal of equality'. Nevertheless the development of empirical techniques for the investigation of poverty has gone on. In addition to the development of social indicator methods mentioned above there have been four main approaches. We discuss them in turn.

Measures Based on a Proportion of the Average

There has been increasing use of measures that draw a line on income distribution and count the number of families and individuals below that line. It has become one of the most prevalent techniques in comparative poverty research (O'Higgins and Jenkins, 1989; European Commission, 1991; Mitchell, 1991) and the Households Below Average Income (HBAI) statistics that replaced the LIF series as the official count of the poor in the UK is based on this method. There has been a fantastically arcane but empirically and politically very important 'stocktaking' debate about the methodology for deriving the HBAI figures. This has ranged over the income definition, the treatment of outliers, the choice of price indices, the equivalence scale, whether mean or median should be used as the base, the most appropriate threshold, the treatment of the self-employed and of housing costs and many other aspects concerned with the sensitivity of the results (DSS, 1991, 1992, 1993; Social Security Committee, 1991; Townsend, 1991). The process was one of the few productive exchanges between the academic community and the government in this area of policy in the last decade or so and the outcome has produced a better and more coherent set of statistics.

This kind of measure has also been used in international comparative research on poverty and has raised similar issues. In particular Mitchell (1991) and Bradshaw (1993) have explored the sensitivity of the results of the analysis of poverty and inequality to the threshold and equivalence scale being used. Gustafsson and Lindblom (1993) have shown that the minimum income threshold varies in different countries and that the choice of which threshold to use makes a good deal of difference to the rank ordering of countries. Saunders *et al.* (1992) have shown how sensitive international comparisons are to the range of resources that are included in the income definition.

Measures Based on Expenditure

Most studies based on the proportion of the average have been based on income not expenditure, although the European Community Combat Poverty Programme was an exception (European Commission, 1991). Nevertheless the analysis of expenditure to explore poverty has a tradition most recently found in the UK in Bradshaw *et al.* (1987), Bradshaw and Morgan (1987), Bradshaw and Holmes (1989). This programme of research has led eventually to the rediscovery of the budget standards methods pioneered by Rowntree at the turn of the century (Bradshaw, 1993; Oldfield and Yu, 1993). This approach had been relegated to the scrap heap in postwar poverty research in the UK, partly because of its association with minimum subsistence concepts (and no doubt also because of the tedium involved in drawing them up and keeping them up to date).

Research on the Experience and Consequences of Poverty

There is not as much research on this subject as there should be but among the smaller scale studies that have been undertaken there are those which have been illuminating in explaining labour supply behaviour (McLaughlin *et al.*, 1989), take-up behaviour, reviewed by Craig (1991), poverty and health behaviour (Graham 1989), patterns of money management (Pahl, 1989) and stress (Bradshaw and Holmes, 1989).

Consensual Measures of Poverty

Following Townsend's original deprivation index work the techniques for representing relative deprivation have been further developed, twice by Mack and Lansley (1985) and Gordon *et al.* (forthcoming) but also by Townsend (Townsend *et al.*, 1987; Townsend and Gordon, 1991).

Some of the most interesting work on poverty has attempted to compare and contrast the results produced using some of the many approaches that have been used to measure poverty. Much of this research has been based on the conceptual challenge of Ringen (1988) suggesting that the link between direct measures of poverty (consumption) and indirect measures of poverty (income) has been neglected in research. Examples of this comparative work include Deleeck *et al.* (1991) in their seven-nation study; Ringen (1988) using a variety of measures of deprivation from the Swedish living standards survey; Hagenaars and deVos (1988) using a variety of Dutch measures; Hutton (1991) who sought to integrate two sources of data on poverty at an aggregate level; Erikson and Uusitalo (1987) and Hallerod (1991) using the Swedish level of living survey; and Townsend and Gordon (1991) using a data set derived from a survey in London.

9.2 Objectives

These latter types of study which seek to evaluate the representativeness of different measures of poverty have as part of their agenda an attempt to establish one or more measures that are acceptable as a 'best' measure for national and comparative research. This article follows the work of Hagenaars and deVos (1988) who compared the prevalence of poverty in Holland using different measures. We have developed this approach using UK data and have adopted a larger variety of family types and a larger set of poverty measures.

In the days when assistance board officers and others had, in home visits, to discriminate between the deserving and undeserving poor there was an attempt to identify reliable indicators of poverty. Whether or not a household possessed a sewing machine was at one time considered a crucial determinant. In more modern times this kind of effort has continued in social indicator methods and in particular the assessment of the number or type of assets that a household has access to (with singular lack of success). This chapter similarly attempts to investigate whether it is possible to identify an indicator of poverty that best represents the great variety of alternative measures. So we are pursuing the same tradition but in this case we seek an empirical rather than a practical device. If we can demonstrate that one measure tends to cover for the great variety of measures that are used in the secondary analysis of large data sets then we have made a significant contribution to reducing the costs of research on poverty. More seriously and practically we have demonstrated the sensitivity of whatever measure the investigator relies on. The idea is that having identified the best, in the sense of the most representative measure, this could in future be used with confidence as the stalking horse for poverty measures.

9.3 Methods

The analysis is based on the Family Expenditure Survey (FES) which is an annual survey of the income and expenditure of about 7000 households in the UK. Its primary purpose is to inform movements in the retail price index but it is widely used in government and outside to investigate poverty, inequality and living standards and forms the basis of the official HBAI figures. Although the FES has detailed data on income, expenditure and household composition it has limitations for the study of poverty. People who do not live in private households are excluded from the survey. This category includes people living in hostels, boarding houses or other institutions as well as the homeless. Also there are only limited data in the study on lifestyle, activities and asset ownership, and no data at all on attitudes, feelings or beliefs. We use data from 1991.

In order to avoid the complications of measuring income and expenditure for households containing more than one unit the analysis was restricted to single-unit households. All single-unit families with children all under 16 were included and in addition families with children aged 16–18 were included if none of the children was in employment. Households with more than two adults and two adults of the same sex were excluded. These exclusions amounted to about 15 per cent of households in the FES. The family units left were distributed as shown in Table 9.1. The age-groups for the elderly are chosen to reflect the pension ages of men and women in the UK. All the other groups have adults under pension age. People who are working include the self-employed. Those not working are either unemployed but seeking work, or sick or injured and seeking or not seeking work, or the retired or unoccupied. The families with children are not differentiated beyond the third child in the family (or beyond the second child in a lone-parent family) in order to retain reasonably large groups.

The income definition used in this study is 'normal' disposable income, that is income from all sources after the deduction of income tax and national insurance contributions. Normal income is measured over a period of 13 weeks in the FES and differs from current income in treating those unemployed for less than 14 weeks as being normally employed. It is thus less influenced by temporary fluctuations than current income, and thought to provide a more representative measure of poverty (Isherwood and van Slooten, 1979).

Some of the measures used in the analysis involve the deduction of net housing expenditure. After deducting the housing expenditure from normal disposable income there were 27 cases with negative income and for analytical purposes these incomes were set at £1.

There are a large number of possible measures of poverty that could be derived from the Family Expenditure Survey. In this study six distinct classes

Table 9.1 Characteristics of family types

Type	*No.*	*%*
1. Elderly single man over 65 or woman over 60 (ES)	1039	17.9
2. Elderly couple, man over 65, woman over 60 (EC)	578	10.1
3. Single, working (SW)	737	12.7
4. Single, not working (SNW)	176	3.0
5. Couple, one earner (C1W)	437	7.5
6. Couple, two earners (C2W)	920	15.8
7. Couple, no earners (CNW)	159	2.7
8. Lone parent with one child, working (LW1C)	62	1.1
9. Lone parent with two or more children, working (LW2C)	58	1.0
10. Lone parent with one child, not working (LNW1C)	94	1.6
11. Lone parent two plus children, not working (LNW2C)	83	1.4
12. Couple with one child, one earner (C1W1C)	166	2.9
13. Couple with two children, one earner (C1W2C)	251	4.3
14. Couple with three plus children, one earner (C1W3C)	90	1.5
15. Couple with one child, two earners (C2W1C)	341	5.9
16. Couple with two children, two earners (C2W2C)	435	7.5
17. Couple with three plus children, two earners (C2W3C)	128	2.2
18. Couple with one child, no earners (CNW1C)	25	0.4
19. Couple with two children, no earners (CNW2C)	20	0.3
20. Couple with three plus children, no earners (CNW3C)	10	0.2
Total	5809	100

have been employed. Poverty lines based on:

(1) proportions of income or expenditure;
(2) food expenditure ratios;
(3) fixed costs to income ratios;
(4) expenditure to income ratios;
(5) an index of access to assets;
(6) official minimum.

These are now discussed in turn.

Poverty Lines Based on the Proportions of Mean (or Median) Equivalent Income (or Expenditure)

Because they are still conventionally used in official studies, and despite the criticism of them, the DSS (McClements) equivalence scales for before and after housing costs were used to adjust income (and expenditure) for the number of adults and number and ages of children in the household (see Table 9.2). An

Table 9.2 Equivalence scale values (couple =1)

Category	*Before housing*	*After housing*
First adult (head)	0.61	0.55
Spouse of head	0.39	0.45
Child 0–10	0.20	0.20
Child 11–15	0.26	0.27
Child 16–17	0.36	0.38

equivalence scale adjusts household income to take account of the relative needs of different households. Thus for example if a childless couple needs £100, then a single person only needs £61, but a couple with one child under 10 years needs £120 to achieve an equivalent income.

The proportion of the (sub)samples in poverty by these measures is summarized in Table 9.3 and shows that, depending on which measure is used, the proportion of all families living in poverty would vary between 8 per cent if the poverty threshold is 'less than 40 per cent of median income after housing costs' and 37 per cent if the threshold is 'less than 60 per cent of mean income after housing costs'.

Furthermore, the proportion of different family types defined as living in poverty would also vary sharply with the measure chosen. Thus 84 per cent of non-working lone parents with one child are living below 60 per cent of mean equivalent income before housing costs, while only 63 per cent are living below 40 percent of median equivalent expenditure. Therefore the measure chosen alters not only the estimated number in poverty but also the composition of the poor group.

Yet there is an argument to be made in support of any of these measures. The choice between the threshold of 40, 50 or 60 per cent of income or expenditure is an arbitrary one depending on how exclusive the concept of poverty that is desired. Nevertheless it is an important choice, particularly where a threshold is near the benefit scales that large numbers of families are dependent on, such as the retirement pension or income support for lone parents. A threshold drawn either side of those levels will make a great deal of difference to the number and composition of families defined as living in poverty.

The merits of the median and the mean were debated at length in the HBAI review. The median is generally thought to be a better measure of central tendency in the distribution of income. Nevertheless, because of the skewed nature of the distribution and the insensitivity of the median to outliers, the DSS concluded that mean was the better base for the threshold. They argued that if the median was used when looking at poverty over time, changes in incomes above the median would have no impact on the measure of poverty or on how

Table 9.3 Proportion of families in poverty

Category	*Before housing costs (%)*	*After housing costs (%)*
Income less than		
40%	17	19
50%	25	29
60%	33	37
of mean equivalent income		
Income less than		
40%	11	8
50%	16	18
60%	24	27
of median equivalent income		
Expenditure less than		
40%	21	
50%	28	
60%	36	
of mean equivalent expenditure		
Expenditure less than		
40%	14	
50%	21	
60%	28	
of median equivalent expenditure		

low-income households compare with the population as a whole.

The arguments in favour of taking income before and after housing costs have also been rehearsed in the HBAI review and by Johnson and Webb (1990). Many households have little choice over their housing costs and an increase in housing costs will typically represent a fall in living standards. Furthermore, housing costs vary in ways (by region, tenure and life cycle) that do not reflect variation in quality. On the other hand, housing costs are a consumption item over which households do, in the long term, have choice and for owner-occupiers the cost includes the accumulation of an asset which will eventually bring lower real costs for the same quality of housing.

The respective merits of income and expenditure have been less discussed. The argument in favour of expenditure is that it is thought to be a better measure of long-term control over resources – it reflects better than income both the capacity to borrow and consumption power. On the other hand, expenditure at an individual level (at least as it is collected in the FES), is subject to large fluctuations owing to the purchase of expensive commodities during the diary fortnight, or seasonal factors (e.g. in fuel expenditure) and expenditure does not include saving, which is arguably a component of future well-being.

By rank ordering the prevalence of poverty for each family type it is possible to determine which measures within this class are the most stable and thus best represent the class as a whole. In general both before- and after-housing cost measures are required because they produce rather different rankings of the proportion of different types of families in poverty. For mean equivalent income we have chosen 50 per cent on the grounds that it has become a conventional threshold. For the ratio of median equivalent income we have chosen the 60 per cent threshold on the grounds that it is the most stable in its rank ordering.

The expenditure-based measures produce quite different results from the income measure for some family groups, and the mean and median measures produce different rankings. On those grounds both the mean and the median at the 50 per cent level were selected to represent this class of measures.

Food Expenditure Ratios

This measure of poverty is still the basis of the USA's official poverty line. It is based on the fact that the proportion of income spent on food increases as income falls. Families who spend the same proportion of their income on food are thought to have the same living standard. Because expenditure on food is related to the size and composition of a family, equivalence scales are in a way a natural part of the measure. The choice of what food expenditure to income threshold is taken as the poverty line is in the end an arbitrary one. There is a technique, S-curve analysis, through which it may be possible to identify an income threshold where food expenditure as a proportion of all expenditure falls rapidly as the need for food is satisfied and income is freed to be spent on other commodities. This technique was not tried here on the grounds that previous research (Bradshaw *et al.*, 1987) had found it difficult to establish such thresholds for a variety of family types. Instead, on the basis of observation of the distribution of the ratios, we have taken ratios of 20, 25, 30 and 35 per cent spent on food.

The results for the whole sample are presented in Table 9.4. Depending on the measure used the proportion in poverty would vary from 9 per cent to 53 per cent. Food expenditure as a proportion of total expenditure tends to produce more pensioners in poverty and fewer lone parents and couples with children than food expenditure as a proportion of income. The ranking of different family types tends to vary more with the food expenditure as a proportion of expenditure ratios. On these grounds, food expenditure over 35 percent of income was chosen to represent the class.

Table 9.4 Food expenditure ratios

Category	*Before housing costs (%)*	*After housing costs (%)*
Food expenditure as % income:		
More than 35%	10	17
More than 30%	15	24
More than 25%	24	33
More than 20%	36	45
Food expenditure as % of expenditure:		
More than 35%	9	
More than 30%	18	
More than 25%	32	
More than 20%	53	

Fixed Costs/Income Ratio

This measure extends the food expenditure to income ratio measure into the analysis of a wider range of 'necessities'. There is a choice about what items should be included in the category of necessities. Hagenaars and deVos (1988) included housing, municipal levies, energy, insurance payments, telephone, public transport, educational costs and expenditure on pets – on the grounds that these were the items that respondents said they could not cut down on. In this study we have taken three measures. First, expenditure on housing (including rates), energy and food. Second, housing, energy, food and clothing. Third, expenditure on housing, fuel, food, clothing and public transport. Although clothing is a necessity, clothes expenditure is positively related to income (i.e. the higher the income the more is spent on clothes) and clothes expenditure is highly influenced by taste and choice. Public transport may be an essential cost of working, living and going to school – though the location of the dwelling and the need to use transport may already be taken into account in the costs of the dwelling. In order to exclude families who are obviously not poor but who have a fixed-costs-to-income ratio which is high by choice, all families with equivalent income of more than 1.5 times the mean were excluded. The results for the sample as a whole are summarized in Table 9.5. To represent this class we chose expenditure on housing, energy and food only and the more than 60 per cent ratio.

Table 9.5 Fixed-costs-to-income ratios

Category	*Percentage spending more than* 60%	55%	50%
Housing energy and food	24	33	41
Housing, energy, food and clothes	33	44	53
Housing, food, energy, clothes and public transport	38	48	57

Total Expenditure Income Ratio

This method defines a household as poor if its total expenditure is greater than its income. The ratio is calculated by dividing the total expenditure of a household by their net disposable income before housing costs. Where the result exceeds 1, then a family is spending more than their income and this ratio is taken as the poverty threshold. There is evidence that families at the lower end of the distribution tend to spend in excess of their income through borrowing and dissavings. But the relationship between income and expenditure is complicated by other factors. First, in the FES, expenditure data are collected using a diary of a fortnight's expenditure which does not cover the same period for which income is assessed. Second, expenditure includes 'lumpy purchases' such as a car, foreign holiday or a washing machine which at an individual level will distort the relationship. Third, a well-off family also may tend to spend more than their income because they have easier access to borrowing and dissavings. In order to control for the latter problems, again families were excluded where expenditure exceeded income but their income was more than 1.5 times the mean equivalent income. Overall 29 per cent were defined as poor using this measure.

An Index of Relative Deprivation

Relative deprivation occurs when a family lacks resources which are common in the society of which they are part. The limitations of the FES preclude the establishment of the kind of deprivation index derived by Townsend (1979) and Mack and Lansley (1985). In this study the deprivation index is derived from the ownership of five durable consumption goods, namely: telephone, refrigerator, washing machine, television and car. Each family is given one point for each of these commodities that they possess. The lower the household's score the more deprived the family is. The median score using this index was 5 and a score of 3 or less was taken as the poverty threshold. The overall proportion with assets of less than the threshold for the relative deprivation index was 18 per cent. The problem with this index is that the components are the commodities that are most commonly possessed and ownership is high for all families. There is also no information in the FES on whether the family lacks an item through choice or because they cannot afford it, or about the quality or state of repair of an asset.

Official Minimum

Although the UK does not have an official minimum income below which people are regarded as poor, as we have seen the scale rates of income support can be used to represent such a minimum. They are the minimum level of social security benefits paid to people without resources who are not in the labour force, and they are also related to scales used to assess entitlement to housing benefit and family credit for those with low earnings. An income support entitlement was calculated for every family on the basis of the number and ages and marital status of the members of the family and then compared with net income after the deduction of net housing costs. We did not attempt to replicate fully the highly detailed comparison of requirements and resources actually involved in estimating entitlement to income support. So the resulting figures are not good enough to be used to compare with earlier years' figures or to calculate non-take-up. But they are adequate for the purpose of this analysis.

The convention when using the official minimum is to present the proportion of families with incomes (a) below the minimum, (b) dependent on the minimum and (c) below the minimum plus a proportion of it. The basis for including those with incomes above the minimum is that families who are actually on income support have incomes rather above the scale rates as the result of income from disregarded capital or earnings. The overall proportions are given in Table 9.6 (the figures are cumulative).

The characteristics of the families with incomes below income support are rather different from those on income support and up to 40 per cent above it. Those below income support are more likely to be pensioners, singles and

Table 9.6 Percentage in poverty using the official minimum

Category	%
Income below income support level	12
Income below income support or on IS	20
On IS and/or below 110% of it	24
On IS and/or below 120% of it	25
On IS and/or below 130% of it	27
On IS and/or below 140% of it	29

couples not working and less likely to be non-working lone parents and couples with children (because they are most likely to be on income support). The other measures of the official minimum were more stable and so the below 110% of income support level was chosen to represent the class.

9.4 Comparing the Results

In order to assess the extent to which different poverty measures produce similar results to one another we need to compare the results produced by them. So far we have derived 48 different measures of poverty and in order to compare the results we selected the poverty measure that best represented each subgroup or class of poverty measures. Twelve representative measures of poverty were derived in this manner. They were:

- P1 50 per cent of mean equivalent income before housing costs;
- P2 50 per cent of mean equivalent income after housing costs;
- P3 60 per cent of median equivalent income before housing costs;
- P4 60 per cent of median equivalent income after housing costs;
- P5 50 per cent of mean equivalent expenditure;
- P6 50 per cent of median equivalent expenditure;
- P7 food expenditure more than 35 per cent of income before housing costs;
- P8 food expenditure more than 35 per cent of income after housing costs;
- P9 fixed costs as a proportion of income of more than 60 per cent;
- P10 total-expenditure-to-income ratio of more than 1.00;
- P11 relative deprivation index;
- P12 official minimum less than 110 per cent.

There are considerable differences in the proportion of poor households according to the different measure employed. Table 9.7 shows that for the whole sample the proportion varies from 10 per cent of families for P7 (the measure based on food expenditure more than 35 per cent of income before housing), to 29 per cent for P10 (the expenditure-to-income ratio measure). The table also shows that proportions of different groups in poverty also change with the definition. Thus 58 per cent of elderly singles are poor according to P2 while only 1 per cent are poor according to P7. Furthermore the rank ordering of the proportions who are in poverty alters for different family types. There are some quite large discrepancies in the rank ordering of the household groups by different poverty measures. For example on P5 and P6 (less than 50 per cent of mean and median equivalent expenditure) couples not working with one child are less likely to be defined as poor than they would be by P1, P2, P3 or P4. On food expenditure (P7 and P8) pensioners are further down the ranking than on other measures. In general the relative deprivation index (P11), the fixed-costs-

Table 9.7 Proportions of families defined as poor according to different measures

Group	*P1*	*P2*	*P3*	*P4*	*P5*	*P6*	*P7*	*P8*	*P9*	*P10*	*P11*	*P12*
1. ES	46	58	46	54	74	62	1	3	55	5	38	52
2. EC	35	45	45	40	29	18	9	23	39	32	11	24
3. SW	14	17	14	16	34	23	3	5	19	8	28	13
4. SNW	64	67	63	65	76	64	6	13	37	16	52	48
5. C1W	10	14	10	13	11	5	6	14	19	28	9	11
6. C2W	3	4	3	3	3	1	4	5	6	16	3	3
7. CNW	34	37	33	35	23	18	14	26	25	38	10	27
8. LW1C	40	34	40	32	40	29	7	15	18	34	27	40
9. LW2C	40	44	38	41	22	17	26	36	28	48	17	43
10. LNW1C	77	77	77	77	71	62	25	25	23	36	55	84
11. LNW2C	78	81	78	75	60	41	49	48	36	60	40	92
12. C1W1C	28	30	28	28	11	8	24	37	16	56	14	21
13. C1W2C	23	25	23	23	7	3	28	44	11	68	7	18
14. C1W3C	28	28	28	27	7	6	42	57	17	79	11	20
15. C2W1C	4	5	4	5	1	0	8	15	7	47	4	4
16. C2W2C	6	8	6	6	1	0	19	30	10	63	2	3
17. C2W3C	15	18	14	17	2	1	39	47	8	71	1	8
18. CNW1C	84	84	84	80	20	12	56	72	28	92	28	60
19. CNW2C	80	80	80	75	25	20	70	75	15	90	30	65
20. CNW3C	60	60	60	60	30	10	60	30	90	90	20	50
All	25	29	25	27	28	21	10	17	24	29	18	24

Key:

ES	elderly single
EC	elderly couple
SW	single, working
SNW	single, not working
C1W	couple, 1 earner
C2W	couple, 2 earners
CNW	couple, no earners
LW1C	lone parent, one child, working
LW2C	lone parent, 2 or more children, working
LNW1	lone parent, 1 child, not working
LNW2	lone parent, 2 or more children, not working
C1W1C	couple, 1 child, one earner
C1W2C	couple, 2 children, one earner
C1W3C	couple, 3 or more children, one earner
C2W1C	couple, 1 child, two earners
C2W2C	couple, 2 children, two earners
C2W3C	couple, 3 or more children, two earners
CNW1C	couple, 1 child, no earners
CNW2C	couple, 2 children, no earners
CN3WC	couple, 3 or more children, no earners

P1	50% of mean equivalent income before housing costs
P2	50% of mean equivalent income after housing costs
P3	60% of median equivalent income before housing costs
P4	60% of median equivalent income after housing costs
P5	50% of mean equivalent expenditure
P6	50% of median equivalent expenditure
P7	food expenditure more than 35% of income before housing
P8	food expenditure more than 35% of income after housing
P9	fixed costs as a proportion of income of more than 60%
P10	total-expenditure-to-income ratio of more than 1.0
P11	relative deprivation index
P12	official minimum less than 110%

to-income ratio (P9) and the total expenditure-to-income ratio (P10) all seem to produce rather dissimilar rankings from the other poverty measures.

In order to identify a measure that best represents the others, the next matrix, in Table 9.8, explores the coincidence of poverty. That is, it shows how much of the poverty according to the measure on the horizontal line would also be revealed by the measure of poverty on the vertical line. For example P7 (food expenditure more than 35 per cent of income before housing costs) would pick up 74 per cent of the poverty measured by P4 (60 per cent of median equivalent income after housing costs). In contrast P7 would only pick up 8 per cent of the poverty defined by P9 (fixed costs as a proportion of income of more than 60 per cent). The measures that appear to pick up least of the poverty revealed by other measures are P10 (total-expenditure-to-income ratio of more than 1.00), P11 (relative deprivation index) and P7 (food expenditure more than 35 per cent of income before housing costs). In addition the coincidence between P5 and P6 (both based on 50 per cent of equivalent expenditure) and P7 and P8 (the food expenditure to incomes ratio) appears to be low. This is no doubt because those with low overall expenditure are not likely to have high food expenditure as a proportion of income. The measure that appears to have the best coincidence overall is P12 (the official minimum 110 per cent of the income support rates). This is the measure that the government has abandoned in favour of the HBAI figures. Of the four measures based on the HBAI methods P1 and P2 (50 per cent of mean income before and after housing costs) provide marginally more coincidence than P3 and P4, which are based on the median.

It would be reasonable to expect that measures which define a larger proportion of the population as poor would have a larger coincidence than measures which include a lower proportion as poor. But that is not the case with the measures considered. P10 (total-expenditure-to-income ratio) has the largest proportion defined as poor and relatively low coincidence with the income measures. P12 (official minimum less than 110 per cent) has nearly the same proportion who are poor as P3 (60 per cent of median equivalent income before housing costs) and better coincidence. P7 (food expenditure more than 35 per cent of income before housing costs) which has a very low overall proportion in poverty, also has relatively high coincidence with other measures.

Another way of examining the coincidence of the measures is to take one measure as a base measure and examine what proportion of the poor by other measures are poor by this measure. This is shown in the vertical columns in Table 9.8. Thus, for example, P12 (the official minimum less than 110 per cent of income support rate) picks up only about two-thirds of P1 and P2 (the HBAI measures). In contrast P1 (50 per cent of mean equivalent income before housing costs) picks up 87 per cent of the P12 poor. In fact P1 to P4 are most successful overall in picking up those defined as poor by other measures.

Table 9.8 Coincidence of poverty (percentages)

Households defined as poor using	*also defined as poor using*											
	P1	*P2*	*P3*	*P4*	*P5*	*P6*	*P7*	*P8*	*P9*	*P10*	*P11*	*P12*
P1	100	80	99	81	51	50	23	26	28	21	36	63
P2	92	100	79	93	50	46	21	28	35	23	34	63
P3	99	92	100	80	51	51	23	25	28	21	36	63
P4	93	97	93	100	49	46	21	28	34	22	33	66
P5	79	77	79	77	100	75	7	8	42	5	39	47
P6	82	78	82	79	91	100	5	6	38	3	39	46
P7	76	74	77	74	65	71	100	60	8	30	9	18
P8	73	71	73	73	60	66	92	100	14	43	9	21
P9	69	70	69	71	75	76	70	67	100	56	24	28
P10	61	59	61	60	47	52	77	79	52	100	8	17
P11	77	79	77	75	77	81	92	71	72	59	100	32
P12	87	85	87	87	78	81	76	72	70	60	77	100

9.5 Conclusion

Poverty is not easy to define or measure. Many different measures have been used in both research and policy to identify the poor population in society and to compare the poor between societies. This chapter has compared poverty estimates using a number of alternative poverty measures which can be derived from the UK Family Expenditure Survey. There are of course a range of other measures that it would have been nice to have included in the comparisons if they had been available. Nevertheless the chosen range included both direct and indirect measures of poverty, social indicators, income and expenditure and relative and absolute measures. The most obvious measure missing from the armoury is a subjective measure of poverty and it would have been better to have been able to assess a more sophisticated index of relative deprivation.

The selected poverty measures used produced proportions in poverty ranging from 10 to 29 per cent of the population. They also produced different proportions of the poor made up of different family types. Some measures produced less consistent results than others. The food-expenditure-to-income-after-housing-costs ratio, the fixed-costs-to-income ratio, the total-expenditure-to-income ratio and the index of relative deprivation seemed to produce rank ordering and numbers most unlike the other measures.

The other measures produced rather similar rank orderings. Couples with children and lone parents out of the labour market tended to have the largest proportion who are poor, followed by the single unemployed and then single pensioners. The groups least likely to be poor were childless couples who were both working and couples with children who were both working.

The measure that best represented the other measures overall as assessed by its level of coincidence with the other measure was the official minimum (P12) – a method of measuring poverty that used to form the basis of the UK Government's approach. The income threshold measures that have replaced it were best at picking up the poverty defined by other measures. Although the measures (before housing costs) and the official minimum produced very nearly identical proportions who are poor and the rank orders of the poverty groups were also nearly identical, there were still some considerable differences in the proportion of each family group considered poor. For example P3 defines 46 per cent of the single elderly as poor while P12 defines 52 per cent of them as poor and 84 per cent of couples not working with one child are poor by P3 while 60 per cent are poor on P12.

The conclusion is that it is not without risks to employ only one measure of poverty to identify the poor. The choice of measure will have consequences for the proportion and structure of the estimated poor population and therefore the policies that should be pursued to reduce or eliminate poverty. In the end the choice of poverty measure will be determined, if not by the availability of the data, then by the purpose of the research. We have not discovered the holy grail of poverty research – a single preferably simple measure of poverty. The search will go on but we suspect that Deleeck *et al.* (1991) will always be right: poverty is essentially an ambiguous notion – relative, gradual and multidimensional. In poverty research, the measure determines the result. This has implications for research at the national level and the official statistics on poverty but it also has implications for comparative research on poverty.

References

Abel Smith, B. and Townsend, P. (1965) *The Poor and the Poorest*, London: Bell.

Bradshaw, J. and Holmes, H. (1989) *Living on the Edge*, London: Child Poverty Action Group.

Bradshaw, J., Mitchell, D. and Morgan, J. (1987) 'Evaluating adequacy: the potential of budget standards', *Journal of Social Policy*, **16** (4).

Bradshaw, J. and Morgan, J. (1987) *Budgeting on Benefit*, London: Family Policy Studies Centre.

Bradshaw, J. (Ed.) (1993) *Budget Standards for the United Kingdom*, Aldershot: Avebury/Gower.

Bradshaw, J. R. (1993) 'Developments in Social Security Policy', in Dowes, C. (Ed.) *New Perspectives on the Welfare State in Europe*, London: Routledge.

Craig, J. (1991) 'Costs and benefits: a review of research on the take-up of income related benefits', *Journal of Social Policy*, **20** (4), pp. 537–65.

Deleeck, H., Van den Bosch, K. and De Lathouwer, L. (1991) *Indicators of Poverty and*

Adequacy of Social Security, Antwerp: Centre for Social Policy, University of Antwerp.

Department of Social Security (1991) *Households Below Average Income: Stocktaking*, London: DSS.

Department of Social Security (1992) *Households Below Average Income: a Statistical Analysis 1979–1988/89*, London: HMSO.

Department of Social Security (1993) *Households on Below Average Income: 1979–1989/90*, London: HMSO.

Erikson, R. and Uusitalo, H. (1987) 'The Scandinavian approach to welfare research', in Erikson, R., Hansen, E., Ringen, S. and Uusitalo, H. (Eds) *The Scandinavian Model: Welfare States and Welfare Research*, New York: Sharp.

European Commission (1991) *Final Report on the Second European Poverty Programme 1985–1989*, Com (91) 29, Brussels: EC.

Graham, H. (1989) 'Women and smoking in the UK: the implications for health promotion', *Health Promotion*, **3**, pp. 371–82.

Gustafsson, B. and Lindblom, M. (1993) 'Poverty lines and poverty in seven European Countries, Australia, Canada, and the USA', *Journal of European Social Policy*, **3** (1), pp. 21–38.

Hagenaars, A. and deVos, K. (1988) 'The definition and measurement of poverty', *Journal of Human Resources*, **23**, pp. 211–22.

Hallerod, B. (1991) *Den Svenska fattigdomen*, Lund: Arkiv.

Hutton, S. (1991) 'Measuring poverty using existing national data sets', *Journal of Social Policy*, **20** (2), pp. 237–55.

Isherwood, B. and van Slooten, R (1979) *The Definition and Measurement of Poverty*, London: Department of Health and Social Security.

Johnson, P. and Webb, S. (1990) 'The treatment of housing in official low income statistics', in *Poverty in Official Statistics*, London: Institute for Fiscal Studies.

Mack, J. and Lansley, S. (1985) *Poor Britain*, London, Allen & Unwin.

McLaughlin, E., Millar, J. and Cooke, K. (1989) *Work and Welfare Benefits*, Aldershot: Avebury/Gower.

Mitchell, D. (1991) *Income Transfers in Ten Welfare States*, Aldershot: Avebury/Gower.

Mitchell, D. and Bradshaw, J. (1992) *Lone Parents and their Incomes: a Comparative Study in Ten Countries*, Report to the ESRC, York: York University.

O'Higgins, M. and Jenkins, S. P. (1989) *Poverty in Europe – Estimates for 1975–1985*, paper presented at the Conference Poverty Statistics in the EC, Nordwijck, The Netherlands.

Oldfield, N. and Yu, A. C. S. (1993) *The Cost of a Child: Living Standards for the 1990s*, London: Child Poverty Action Group.

Orshansky, M. (1969) 'How poverty is measured', *Monthly Labor Review*, **92**, pp. 37–41.

Pahl, J. (1989) *Money and Marriage*, London: Macmillan

Ringen, S. (1988) 'Direct and indirect measures of poverty', *Journal of Social Policy*, **17** (3), pp. 351–65.

Rowntree, B. S. (1901) *Poverty: a Study of Town Life*, London: Longman Green.

Rowntree, B. S. (1941) *Poverty and Progress*, London: Longman Green.

Rowntree, B. S. and Lavers, G. R. (1951) *Poverty and the Welfare State*, London: Longmans.

Saunders, P. *et al.* (1992) *Noncash Income, Living Standards, Inequality and Poverty:*

Evidence from the Luxembourg Income Study, Social Policy Research Centre Discussion Paper 35, University of New South Wales.

Social Security Committee (1991) *Low Income Statistics: Households Below Average Income Tables 1988*, HC 401, London: HMSO.

Social Security Committee (1992) *Low Income Statistics: Low Income Families 1979–1989*, HC 359, London: HMSO.

Townsend, P. (1979) *Poverty in the United Kingdom*, Harmondsworth: Penguin.

Townsend, P. (1991) *Meaningful Statistics on Poverty*, No. 2, Bristol: Statistical Monitoring Unit, University of Bristol.

Townsend, P., Corrigan, P. and Kowarzic, U. (1987) *Poverty and Labour in London*, London: Low Pay Unit.

Townsend, P. and Gordon, D. (1991) 'What is enough? New evidence on poverty allowing the definition of a minimum benefit', in Adler, M., Bell, C., Clasen, J. and Sinfield, A. (Eds) *The Sociology of Social Security*, Edinburgh: Edinburgh University Press.

Chapter 10

Accounting for Outcomes: an Alternative Approach?

Rebecca Boden and Anne Corden

10.0 Introduction

The UK public sector in the past 20 years has seen rapid developments in management control and changing notions of public accountability. The fact that what used to be called public administration is now more often referred to as public sector management, or even New Public Sector Management (Hood, 1991) semantically demonstrates a real shift in focus from more traditional conceptions of administration as being based on 'probity and propriety' to the assessment of 'policy and performance' (Stewart and Ranson, 1988, p. 19).

One response to a perceived need for new techniques for better evaluation of policy outcomes and control over public sector resources has been a steady ingress of accounting personnel and skills into the public sector (Hopwood, 1984). It can even be argued that there has been a certain amount of capture of public sector management by the accounting approach (Power, 1994). The skills and techniques adopted are largely those of traditional private sector accounting.

This growing role and importance of accounting may be problematic. Accountings are essentially social products: what might suit the aims and objectives of the private sector may not be suitable for the public. More subtly, accounting technologies, like other technologies, cannot be thought of as socially neutral: the very fact of measurement and the form which that measurement takes can be a driver and shaper of policy and behaviour. Put simply, accounting technologies do not merely *measure* outcomes, but also *have the capacity to define* and *shape* them.

Extreme care must therefore be exercised in selecting accounting procedures fitted to the nature of the public, as opposed to the private, sector. The effects of accounting techniques on policy formulation and implementation must be explicit if proper account is to be taken of these on social outcomes. New ways of incorporating social aspects into conventional accounting processes must be sought.

This chapter argues that not only the utility of accounting technologies in terms of the measurement of outcomes, but also their imperative definitive force can be usefully harnessed to both explicate and achieve social objectives in the public arena. We argue that a practice known as social audit, adopted as an outcome measurement technique, could both enable sensible measurement of public sector achievements and put in place a process whereby goals and priorities could be discussed and determined. Social audit could therefore turn the disadvantage of accountancy – that it not only measures but also influences outcomes – into an advantage by facilitating and necessitating discussion on public sector objectives.

The chapter first explains why traditional private sector accounting techniques may be inappropriate for the public sector and goes on to discuss how social audit, and particularly social audit based on 'needs', may bridge this gap. The second part of the chapter uses data from a study of self-employed applicants for family credit, an income-related social security benefit for working parents, to demonstrate how social audit on the basis of needs satisfaction might be put into effect. The chapter ends with a discussion of possible ways forward.

10.1 Accounting and Public Sector Organizations

The Big State and the Accountants

The sheer scale of the modern state, in terms of commands over resources, access to national wealth and range of essential functions, presents a major challenge for ensuring efficient, effective and economical management. In the UK, the concern of successive Conservative Governments during the past 15 years has been that the state may be galloping out of control, consuming too large a portion of the national income and inappropriately dominating the private sphere. This has led to concern about how to limit or indeed reverse the growth of the state, and how to spend capped resources most effectively. For example, social security expenditure rose from 4.7 per cent of Gross Domestic Product (GDP) in 1949–50 to 12.3 per cent in 1992–3 (DSS, 1993). Part of the government response, in a revision of social security strategy in 1985, was to introduce tighter concepts of the targeting of benefits (DSS, 1985). These new strategies require new management control techniques and new sources of information.

Moreover, developing government notions of the role of the state and the way in which it should function have also led to changing notions of public accountability and demands for new techniques and skills. Privatization and the Next Steps Initiative have introduced greater elements of commerciality into many areas. Privatization has often required regulation, which creates demands for information and accountability. Similarly, the move to agency status creates notions of the customer–contractor relationship between citizen and state, and an agent–principal relationship between the agency and the state. This generates demands for information, means of management control and new forms of public accountability (Geddes, 1988; Coote, 1993; Skelcher, 1993). If the delivery of social security benefits, for example, is entrusted to an agency, the state will need means of assessing the performance of the agency and the citizen will need new ways of calling the agency to account for the public resources for which it is responsible.

Such demands for information, control and accountability have taken place in a context of governmental encouragement for the adoption of market principles in all aspects of the public sector. It is therefore not surprising that the techniques adopted have their origins firmly within the private sector and in private sector accounting (Hopwood, 1984; Power, 1994).

Is Accountancy the Answer?

There are two main problems in the adoption of private sector accounting techniques by the public sector. First, states are not private sector organizations, even if, like the Next Steps agencies, they are constituted in such a way as to emulate certain features of the private sector. The public sector exists for its own distinct purposes. As Stewart and Ranson (1988) put it: 'The public domain can be described as the organization of collective purpose, the area in which collective values are pursued. That is its rationale and its purpose' (p. 15).

Second, accounting is not a homogeneous, objective precision tool which can be applied with impunity to all organizations in all situations. It is both a product and a shaper of the social, economic and political environment (Hopwood, 1984). Accountings are, explicitly or implicitly, designed and produced with specific tasks in mind.[1] Thus whilst the principles and skills of quantification might have applicability in the public sector, it would be unwise to transfer these from the private domain unthinkingly and without appropriate adaptation.

Towards Appropriate Accounting

The watchwords in the new UK public sector accounting orthodoxy are economy, efficiency and effectiveness. *Economy* might be equated with doing things as cheaply as possible. This is often now validated via mechanisms such as market-testing.

Smith noted in Chapter 1 that *efficiency* is the relationship between inputs and outputs. In the private sector one measure of efficiency might be the ratio of production resources used (inputs) to finished products (outputs). Inputs and outputs can be expressed as monetary values. Public sector efficiency indicators (such as cases dealt with per member of staff) have also been developed (Lewis, 1986). At least two problem areas can arise with efficiency measures, even in the private sector. First, there may be externalities to the process (e.g., industrial pollution) which, because of the bounded nature of accounting, represent costs or beneficial outcomes which are never factored into the efficiency calculation. Second, some inputs and outputs may defy quantification.

Implicit in decisions about what outputs should be measured are statements about the purpose and objectives of organizations. Thus whilst industry exists to make things, it may also serve other purposes such as providing employment essential to a local infrastructure or contributing products essential to national strategies. Lack of care in the selection of output measures may affect organizational behaviour.

Measures of *effectiveness* are linked to measures of efficiency. Effectiveness can be defined as a measure of the extent to which an organization has met its objectives, based on a calculation of output weighted by quality. We might therefore think of effectiveness as a measure of *outcome*, a more subtle and complex measure of organizational performance than efficiency alone.

In the private sector measures of efficacy might be based on stated commercial objectives of, albeit imperfect, market-based competition and wealth maximization, as Smith (Chapter 1) suggests. In the public sector such criteria are inappropriate. Public sector objectives must therefore be defined if the quality of the output is to be assessed. The inherent difficulty of developing an appropriate measure of public sector outcomes using traditional profit-orientated accounting techniques has led to the domination of the work of bodies such as the National Audit Office by efficiency measures as opposed to outcome measures (Smith, Chapter 1). In this chapter we argue that social audit techniques may offer the necessary answers.

Accounting for 'the Social'

Attempts to expand private sector accounting to encompass considerations of an organization's activities in the wider social, political and economic domain are generally referred to as social accounting, or social responsibility accounting. With origins in the USA in the 1960s, social accounting tended to emerge as a responsive strategy by corporate management anxious to demonstrate commitment to issues such as pollution control rather than following the demands of social critics (Hopwood and Burchell, 1980). Social accounting is not therefore a homogeneous phenomenon: its formulations reflect the circumstances which give rise to it, and it is at least as much about defining the social nature of organizations as about their functioning (Hopwood and Burchell, 1980).

Social audit is a discrete area of social accounting and represents an attempt to utilize the audit approach of investigating, evaluating and reporting on the performance of an organization against a known set of criteria and standards (Power, 1994). It can therefore be described as an attempt to assess and evaluate the outcome of organizational activity. However, the impact of the *social* element is that such an audit is not bounded in the traditional sense to considerations of the financial performance of the organization.

There exists no coherent precise definition of social audit. Percy-Smith (1992) emphasizes that social audits frequently concern needs and how these are met by the public sector. Others have variously described social audits as challenges to the status quo rather than elaborations on the rationality of conventional managerial decisions (Hopwood and Burchell, 1980); as one-off rather than ongoing processes (Geddes, 1988); and as extending accounting to the consideration of non-financial or non-economic factors (Harte, 1986). Gray *et al.* (1993) prefer to use the term to describe the independent preparation and publication of information to aid democracy and accountability.

Early social audits emerged slowly in Britain and tended to build on traditional accounting techniques (Geddes, 1992). But an upsurge of social audits in the 1980s developed as a direct challenge to traditional accounting models. This newer approach stressed values associated with economic and social planning, and prioritized social need as a prime indicator in resource allocation; emphases which veered in the opposite direction to the political dominance of the market and private enterprise (Harte, 1986; Geddes, 1988, 1992; Turok, 1990).

In particular, the approach was adopted by local authorities and trade unions challenging local private sector plant closures (e.g., Edinburgh District/Lothian Regional Councils, 1985) and the nationalized industries (Hudson *et al.*, 1984). Social audit has also been used to defend the public sector against cut-backs in service provision (Geddes, 1992), to demonstrate the overall impact of government policies on a particular locality (Newcastle City Council, 1985), and to provide better models of state provision in a direct challenge to Conservative Governments' tendencies to apply uncritically private sector financial accounting principles to public sector activities, as typified by the Audit Commission's value for money approach (Kline and Mallaber, 1986). There have been interesting developments in social audit techniques in the voluntary and cooperative sectors, where organizations have sought ways of assessing business activity and its social impact in keeping with their own goals and objectives (Jefferis and Robinson, 1987; Zadek and Evans, 1993). Elements of the social audit approach, encapsulating the relationship between needs and resources, have been included in practical techniques for community profiling (Hawtin *et al.*, 1994).

Needs-based Social Audit

If organizational objectives are to determine the choice of output/outcome measures they have to be defined. In a crude sense the organizational objectives of a private sector company are to generate wealth for the shareholders. This objective might be attenuated by other factors, such as a requirement to be socially responsible, but the principal objective is unchanged.

It is possible to argue that whilst markets are constructed to meet demand, the public sector exists to meet need. As Stewart and Ranson (1988) put it:

> It is also possible to see the [public] domain as a public arena, not merely where the defects of the market can be corrected but where distinctive values can be realized.
>
> Thus, in the public arena many will assert the value of equity in meeting needs that cannot even be expressed in the market.... In the search for value for money, emphasis is placed on economy, efficiency and effectiveness. For at least the first two of those values the private sector model may suffice. Yet, if the value of equity is sought, distinctive management processes are required. Need has to become a management concept. (p. 15)

Thus, Stewart and Ranson go on to argue, in the market allocation is by demand; in the public sector, in pursuit of collective goals, allocation should be on the basis of need.

Percy-Smith (1992) also argues that the primary objective of the public sector is to meet need, and that this should determine the efficacy indicators adopted. She maintains that social audit is a valuable technique in emphasizing the concept of need in public sector management. It allows assessment of the promotion of values and principles, the extent to which objectives have been achieved, the costs of such achievements and their impact on other areas and can assist in future policy formulation.

Mushkat (1986) suggests that needs have three possible uses as indicators. First, they serve as an *ex post facto* measure of the effectiveness of a system in meeting its objectives; second, they feature in the determination of resource requirements, and third, they offer a means of setting future priorities. We support the view that using need as an indicator in social audits has potential value, and is consistent with the philosophy of developing appropriate accounting techniques based on the nature of the organization.

The use of needs indicators could also assist the positive development of accounting techniques as explicit policy shapers and drivers. The very process of defining the needs indicators would involve explicit discussion of policy objectives, direct policy makers towards listening to the various stakeholders concerned and encourage the public resolution of conflicting demands.

There is a long tradition of interest in the concept and measurement of human need, and the literature spans the fields of philosophy, economics, political science, sociology and social policy (Corden *et al.*, 1992). The debate is conducted at various levels. Argument as to whether social need is an 'objective' notion (Townsend, 1979), or a socially relative construction (Fitzgerald, 1977) raise all manner of theoretical and practical issues. Economists have tried to treat need as a special form of demand (Culyer, 1976), and thus operationalize the concept as a criterion for distribution (Nevitt, 1977). Doyal and Gough vigorously defend the concept of human needs as central to debates on policies about human welfare (1984) and develop a theory of need which can be operationalized to measure and compare levels of human welfare throughout the world (1991).

Arguments continue about what counts as need; meanwhile, the concept is increasingly used as the basis on which to allocate resources. Different ways of defining need are variously useful, according to context and the constraints of practice (Spicker, 1987). If need is to be used as the indicator in social audits then a heuristic device must be developed to enable the identification of need as part of the audit process. Moreover, this heuristic device should be of such a nature that it facilitates the use of social audit as not only a measurement technique, but also a means of advantageously shaping and defining policy.

Percy-Smith (1992) emphasizes the importance of utilizing a definition of need that contains a number of different dimensions. Drawing on Bradshaw's taxonomy of normative, felt/expressed and comparative need (Bradshaw, 1972), she acknowledges that the different perceptions of the various stakeholders may produce conflicting or at best non-congruent expressions of need. A process of reconciliation may therefore be necessary.

Martin (1982) takes further this discussion of the divergence of needs statements and makes use of Ife's (1980) model of social need: a three-way classification including stakeholder-defined need, caretaker-defined need, and inferred need. Caretakers are those who have a service or caretaking function, such as doctors; inferred need is that observed by administrators or researchers. Simplifying this framework, Martin discusses the definition of needs in terms of the relationship between actual or potential consumers and service providers. In common with Ife, she argues that this approach enables exploration of the relationship between source and sequence of need judgment, increasing our understanding of divergences of views between recipients and providers, and informing decision making about possible interventions.

Martin suggests that both service users and providers go through a sequence of judgments in defining need. For the consumer the first stage is the 'subjective experience of need' which is shaped by personal characteristics, social and cultural factors, and norms concerning living standards and quality of life. Consumers then go on either explicitly or implicitly to demand a service. That demand will be shaped by the availability or accessibility of help and some form of (perhaps implicit) cost–benefit analysis. Martin stresses that the factors determining demand are varied and socially determined, and a similar set of factors may influence whether the potential consumer moves to the final stage – utilization of service.

For the service provider, current norms and attitudes will also influence the perception of need or 'a problem'. Martin points to normative and comparative judgments (relating to Bradshaw's taxonomy of need) as being of importance here, and suggests that providers may be especially influenced by concern about 'adverse reactions' from potential consumers.

The second stage for providers is the definition of some appropriate response. If decisions have to be made about resource allocation, political power and considerations about public opinion or views of pressure groups may become important. Also critical is the availability of remedy – Martin suggests that agencies are less willing to identify need if no solution has been identified. Providers also have to make decisions about priorities: given limited resources how should they rank demands to satisfy needs?

Finally, service providers must decide on the means of service delivery, given the constraints of resources and priorities.

Martin's approach appears to us to offer one of the most workable methods for the identification of need for the purposes of constructing needs-based social audit indicators. Perhaps more importantly, it also offers the potential of *explicitly* using accounting technologies in policy formulation/implementation by making overt the discussion of organizational aims and objectives. This is an approach diametrically opposed to the definition of evaluative outcome measures with no *overt* reference to the aims and objectives of the organization, and offers the prospect of a system which is fundamentally democratic and user-orientated. Direct incorporation of the accounting methodology into the heart of the policy formulation process offers opportunities of deriving a measurement system which is more appropriate to the public sector.

The second part of this chapter uses data on self-employed applicants for family credit[2] to demonstrate that the identification of stakeholder needs and their reconciliation in order to produce usable outcome measures is a complex and subtly nuanced problem. The family credit data illustrate both the complexity of this task, and its feasibility. Social security provision involves an explicitly stated objective of meeting need. Even if social security policy has more discrete items on its agenda, such as social control (Dean, 1991), the explication of such unstated objectives can be made possible by an audit which seeks explanations for any failure to achieve the stated objective of meeting need. The following section is not a social audit *per se* but an illustration of a possible process of needs identification and types of indicators which might arise as a result. The discussion throughout draws on Martin's (1982) framework for exploring different judgments of social need.

10.2 A Social Audit of Family Credit?

Needs of Self-employed Applicants for Family Credit

There are considerable methodological problems in representing the needs of self-employed people for benefit support. First, the self-employed form a non-homogeneous group. The range of activities undertaken varies considerably as does its scale, rewards, degree of independence from business customers and stage of business development. Second, the self-employed people interviewed during the research were effectively self-selected. In applying for or receiving family credit they had already been defined, by themselves or by the Department of Social Security (DSS), as self-employed people who might benefit from family credit. Our discussion is therefore constrained by the acceptance of the selection of a needs community by reference to DSS criteria of who is needy. Acceptance of the family credit criteria, or at least the applicants' perception of these, as defining the needs community produces closure which defines some in and some out.

Third, even supposing that a common set of needs can be identified, self-employed people may not articulate them. For example, as a result of relative isolation or lack of collective organization the operation of power may ensure that not only are their needs organized off the agenda, but also that they are not perceived as needs in the first instance (Lukes, 1974). In this context the articulation of need may surface as gratitude for assistance. The fourth methodological difficulty relates to the problem of how their needs are to be identified and presented. Lack of overall group cohesiveness and organization of low-income self-employed parents reduces opportunities for group articulation. We as researchers attempted this task, but would be the first to recognize the limitations of this approach.

Finally, while we follow Martin's framework, the term 'user' is far from ideal in the context of family credit. In lone parent households the term 'user' is unambiguous. But in a heterosexual two-parent family roles and responsibilities may be divided or shared, most commonly with the woman as the statutory applicant and the man as the main earner, with either parent controlling expenditure of the benefit. The identity of the 'user' is therefore less distinct in such families, and there will be variety among families. Here we refer to the couple as the 'user', recognize that this is insufficient, but look to further opportunities to unpick this properly.

Among our potential service users we identified four types of need experience which might lead to 'demand' in the form of an application for family credit:

- need for income augmentation/stability;
- need for work;
- need for appropriate delivery of assistance;

- need for justice.

We discuss these in turn.

Need for income augmentation/stability

People who care for children might be expected to be fairly risk averse about income sources. Lack of appropriate economic resources was perhaps the most obvious single need which the applicants themselves identified. What was interesting was the variety in nature, pattern or form of this need.

For some the potential to become financially prosperous was circumscribed by the nature of their work. Whilst most small businesses did seem potentially viable as modest sources of income, capable of supporting the trader and his/her family without significant state assistance, they were experiencing financial difficulties for a variety of reasons: a down-turn in trade due to economic recession, or business start-up problems or expansion difficulties. In some cases the proprietors lacked the requisite skills to make significant progress, while others wished to remain operating on a very small scale.

The flow of income into the business could also fluctuate markedly. This was predictable if caused by factors such as the seasonal nature of trades, but some volatility was due to unpredictable demands for services, breakdowns in equipment or regulatory controls such as fishing quotas.

Therefore, to say that this group needed additional financial resources would be too simplistic. Business circumstances meant they might need short- or medium-term cash injections to assist business start-up, get through the initial difficult phase or see it through hard times. Sometimes additional cash was required to supplement business income, sometimes to supplement family income. There might also be a need to smooth income flows which fluctuated throughout the year. And some people had yet to generate sufficient cash resources to see them through seasonal downturns in business.

Need for work

There were strong and diverse expressions of wanting to work: to keep established businesses going, to overcome the difficult early period of business start-up or to make the transition from unemployment to self-employment. In some occupational groups, notably among farmers and fishermen, there were strong traditional ties with the 'business' as a way of life.

Starting new businesses, or keeping businesses going through hard times, requires high self-motivation, or can reflect desperation to avoid alternatives. Either way, the motivation to work and the importance of that activity is high. For this self-selected group then, we infer that the need for work was of some considerable importance.

Need for appropriate delivery of assistance

There are many issues and influences here that affect the sequence of judgments made that can eventually result in 'demand' for family credit.

First, there are issues of accessibility. To become aware of their own specific eligibility some self-employed people needed special promotional measures to overcome assumptions that self-employed people are excluded from social security schemes, or that 'business people' are not entitled to financial help. Beyond this, accessibility issues included further information material, application forms and written standard replies. People needed well-designed intelligible material. People with literacy problems, and those for whom English was not the first language, had special needs here. Some people preferred the telephone for enquiry, suggesting a need for a responsive and helpful telephone service from the Benefits Agency.

People needed appropriate procedural channels. The central postal scheme with telephone access was popular with some, but others wanted an opportunity to discuss their financial situation in a local office. Our research also demonstrated a need for agreement and cooperation between all parties involved at the 'user' stage, including a business partner or accountant. More fundamentally, couples needed a procedure that did not obstruct applications by challenging normal divisions of responsibility for business and household matters.

Since a key process in determination of eligibility for family credit is the assessment of income, applicants needed mechanisms for providing information about earnings which were within their means in terms of time, skills and expense. Few people in our study had high levels of accountancy or even book-keeping skills and their knowledge of specific family credit rules was often limited. Some who needed help in supplying income information had engaged professional assistance. In these circumstances they needed the DSS to work cost-effectively with their accountants. The commitment of time was also a major consideration: applicants were unwilling to enter into a time-consuming process for uncertain rewards and therefore needed enough information to enable them to evaluate the risks and benefits of applying. People needed to supplement their income immediately and those who had just made the move to self-employment needed a scheme that could assess their probable future earnings realistically.

Applicants needed to be aware of the time limits built into the application procedure, and to find these reasonable. They also needed certainty that their applications would be dealt with quickly and efficiently because crossing the threshold from unemployment and secure out-of-work benefits to uncertain and insecure low earnings could be a risky undertaking for people with family responsibilities. The question of time lags in dealing with applications is typically one of the measures of efficiency adopted by the National Audit Office (NAO, 1991).

Need for Justice

Finally, it might be argued that applicants have needs, in terms of the treatment accorded to them, which have roots in natural justice. Such considerations would include whether or not they are treated fairly, their case is assessed accurately and their rights acknowledged. Our research showed that not wanting 'charity' could put people off applying for income-related benefits. Fundamental considerations as to how far the application procedure meets needs for natural justice are whether the process is open, the rules explicit, bureaucratic decisions explained and justified, and whether there is a right to engage in a process of appeal and challenge, with the necessary access to resources that such engagement requires. If the procedures do not meet these requirements then they may be disempowering for the applicant. Furthermore, the process itself must be non-stigmatizing if the needs of justice are to be met.

Needs and the Department of Social Security

In this case study the Department of Social Security is a stakeholder on two counts. First, it has its own needs of the system. Some of these might usefully be thought of as system constraints – for instance the 'need' to be cost-effective. Second, the DSS has to represent the needs of other stakeholders by virtue of its position within government – for instance, it cannot ignore the needs of taxpayers/other claimants when making decisions on family credit. The stakeholder interests represented by the DSS may thus produce rather different interpretations of applicant needs than those of the applicants themselves. The process of reconciliation of conflicting needs statements thereby becomes crucial in policy definition and implementation.

Perception of need

Martin (1982) describes the perception of need by service providers as recognition that a problem exists to which they might make a response. Returning to Bradshaw's taxonomy of need, Martin distinguishes between normative and comparative assessments here. Normative assessments, based on social norms, imply whether or not the condition or characteristics of the potential user of a service deviate from those norms sufficiently to warrant service provider action. Comparative assessment involves some comparison of the potential candidates with those of other sections of society. There is plenty of scope for divergence of opinion here, and also a danger of making assessments on the basis of unquestioned assumption rather than explicit judgment. Moreover, resource constraints and whether an adequate response can be defined may drive the perception or formal recognition of need.

The perception of need which led specifically to family credit can be traced back to the 1985 White Paper on Social Security (DSS, 1985). This stated government's aim of targeting benefits at those perceived as needing them most, and in particular, families with children. There was also a statement of the desirability of encouraging high rates of participation in the labour market. People without employment were encouraged to move into work, including self-employment, and the availability of in-work benefits meant that families with children would generally be better off financially as a result. The government's perception of need here was thus both normative and comparative, and very much driven by policy based on explicit objectives. Further, the element of targeting implicit in this process suggests that perception was driven partly by resource constraints. Explication of service provider perception of need here demonstrates that social audit techniques might be used to unpick policy debates for analytical purposes, and possibly to aid democratic control.

Definition of response

Martin's second stage consists of the service providers, having identified a need, proposing an appropriate response. In order to meet the perceived need of targeting assistance to families with children and providing an incentive to enter the workplace, this response took the form of a benefit which aimed to encourage and facilitate labour market participation by supplementing the earned income of families with children, available to both employees and self-employed people. The rates of family credit are set so that families with children are, in the majority of cases, better off in work than out. The availability of family credit to self-employed people fits in well with stated aims of encouraging the enterprise culture.

Delivery systems

The third stage of service providers' activity is establishing appropriate delivery mechanisms: putting the desired response into practice (Martin, 1982). Decisions about delivery systems are determined by the inherent nature of the desired policy response, the characteristics of the users and their requirements of the system, organizational culture, resource and other constraints, and the power of other actors such as public opinion or external accountability mechanisms. Influences are both endogenous and exogenous, and the service provider has to meet a whole panoply of stakeholder needs, including its own.

The influence of exogenous imperatives other than those of service users should not be underestimated. For instance, social security easily attracts adverse publicity and the DSS is expected to be prudent with public money, making issues such as fraud and accuracy important. Similarly, the DSS is externally accountable through the National Audit Office and needs to meet the performance criteria laid down for them. Such influences are not necessarily in the best interests of individual service users. Social audit might be of real value in making such diverse stakeholder needs explicit, permitting analysis of the underlying power relationships.

One important measure of efficacy of delivery systems in National Audit Office type models is the take-up rate, used as a measure of success in delivering income-related benefits. However, such a measure is a limited proxy measure for efficacy and needs to be used with caution. A high take-up rate may suggest efficiency, ease of administration and low user costs. But apart from the methodological problems of calculating the take-up of family credit this indicator provides no information about people's degree of satisfaction, the real costs incurred in applying or the extent to which their situation improves. For the DSS it is imperative for reasons other than this traditional audit check that family credit take-up is high: if people do not claim family credit when entitled they are likely to be financially better off out of work and, the argument runs, the labour incentive collapses (Corden and Craig, 1991).

Administrative cost is a major constraint on benefit delivery systems. Cost is an indicator used by external agents such as the NAO, but the DSS would probably be concerned about cost without external scrutiny. The concern of service users here is likely to be that costs incurred in benefit delivery are not deferred onto themselves. In a system which uses crude measures of cost it might be tempting for providers to off-load costs onto the applicant, for instance, by shifting the balance of effort. Deferral of costs, by making the application process more time consuming, expensive and harder for applicants, might have an adverse impact on take-up rates. It might also make it easier for the articulate and well advised to make progress through the procedures and thus be unfair. However, an obsession with administrative costs should not privilege these over less easily quantifiable factors, such as quality of service, and should not ignore costs elsewhere in the system.

What has been said of costs is similarly true of speed. The applicant and DSS have greater congruity of purpose here as they both want to get matters resolved as quickly as possible. Having time constraints on both sides helps progress unless service providers' allocation of time between themselves and the applicants is uneven, placing undue pressure on the applicant. This is specially important when the process involves much interactive information seeking, as is often the case with self-employed people.

Take-up, administrative cost and speed are key indicators in the NAO type model of assessment. All are likely to be affected by the ease of administration. The administration of family credit for self-employed people is likely to be a fairly complex task and the system must be sufficiently sophisticated to cope with this. Whilst it is difficult to construct an indicator for ease of administration our research showed clearly some of the criteria that are important. First, the delivery system must be sufficiently open to enable people to identify their eligibility correctly and be motivated to apply. There are problems here with all non-universal benefits (Craig, 1991). Second, having stimulated appropriate applications the delivery system must successfully route applicants through the correct parts of the process. Third, because family credit is a means-tested benefit the system must efficiently elicit and accurately utilize earnings information: this can be problematic due to the diverse nature of the businesses, and the financial skills of the applicants. And finally, the DSS will be keen to ensure that fraud within the system is kept to a minimum.

Comparing the Needs of Users and Providers

From the above discussion of user and provider needs it is apparent that, as expected, there are areas of congruence and areas of conflict.

When they applied for family credit, the working parents wanted to be able to go on working; indeed most said they needed to work. For the time being they were self-employed and they wanted to continue as such. In accordance with policy aims of preventing poverty among children, the DSS also wanted the parents to work. Their choice of self-employment in comparison with working for an employer, while not a prime concern for the DSS, fitted in with the government's general aim of promoting 'enterprise'.

Applicants needed some stability of income at a level sufficient to meet their personal and business needs whilst the DSS wanted to maintain minimum living standards and work incentives. Within this general requirement, parents' needs varied. Some were looking for ways of smoothing fluctuations in income cycles; others needed short- or medium-term cash injections to help in early stages, or to tide them through lean periods. The policy response, a regular cash benefit paid at the same level despite fluctuating income, fitted the financial needs of some families better than others, although all were glad to have the benefit.

Service users needed to identify their eligibility quickly and wanted to understand the family credit scheme. Some wanted to be able to assess the level of the benefit which they might receive. The DSS needed this to happen to meet the policy aims of family credit, but there are major resource constraints here. It is hard to target small constantly changing populations with detailed information about a complex benefit scheme. There is conflict here between needs of users and resources of providers.

Families needed application procedures that did not present major challenges to their normal roles and responsibilities, both in household budgeting and in business matters. Where there is a woman, she is usually the formal applicant and for some families there was conflict between needs and provision here. The DSS has an interest in trying to resolve this conflict in order to increase take-up. Their response is likely to be via information presentation and design of promotional material. Again, there are cost constraints here.

Both users and the DSS needed a scheme that could respond quickly. Applicants had pressing financial needs, and the DSS wanted to maintain work incentives. Applicants needed the lowest possible share of the costs of application, but it was also essential for the DSS to keep their own costs down.

The DSS needed to impose an additional component of cost here – the need to prevent fraud. There might be no direct need experienced by applicants in prevention of fraud – indeed, the imposed cost could be detrimental when it deterred claims. On the other hand, there might be indirect results to applicants' advantage, if the 'image' of family credit can be maintained as a non-stigmatizing benefit associated with responsible family budgeting and good business practice. There is an interesting time factor here, in balancing the needs of current and future applicants.

Service users needed fair treatment to satisfy their requirements for equity with other citizens, workers, parents, taxpayers or contributors to national insurance. Whilst the principle of fairness underpins the philosophy of the DSS the practical need is also demanding. If schemes appear unfair, there will be confusion, non-compliance, challenge, dispute and dissatisfaction, all acting to increase costs, reduce response time and lower take-up. High take-up is primarily the DSS need – individual applicants may be unaffected by general overall levels of take-up. Here again, however, we may see indirect effects, or effects on future claimants. A benefit with high take-up among entitled people may be viewed as less stigmatizing than one where there is a known shortfall in take-up.

10.3 Summary

Public sector management is increasingly dominated by traditional accounting techniques which are used to evaluate performance. A principal difficulty is that the skills and techniques of the private sector are not directly transferable to the public sector. In particular, private sector techniques, with their emphasis on profitability as a measure of effectiveness, are of little value in evaluating policy outcomes.

An appropriate public sector measurement of outputs necessitates the evaluation of the extent to which the organization has met its primary goals. We have argued that the public sector exists to meet need, and therefore it is appropriate that the extent to which need is met should be the basis of efficacy measures.

A means must be found of identifying needs if they are to be used in any evaluatory process. We have argued that the very process of identifying and agreeing needs is complex but there is much to be learned from such an exercise. Moreover, such an approach beneficially utilizes the potential of accounting-based measurement systems to shape and define policy, reasserting a large element of democratic control and accountability. That is, using the social audit approach the very process of agreeing upon effectiveness indicators necessitates an explicit discussion of the purpose, aims and functions of the organization by all stakeholders.

Who should conduct such a process? Audits conducted by the organization responsible for service delivery are rejected by Geddes (1988) as doing little more than permitting the organization to effect greater control over its environment. Another suggestion is for those directly affected by the policy to fill this role. However, the targets of policy may lack the skills to be effective in such a situation (Percy-Smith, 1992). It does seem likely that individual targets of social security policy may lack the collective organizational structures and resources to perform such a task, particularly when they are as disparate as the self-employed applicants for family credit. We have seen that self-employed people in the family credit population often have modest skills of the kind necessary for such a task, little spare time and, by definition, no extra financial resources.

Perhaps the role might be filled by some independent auditors appointed by the delivery agency. Geddes gives more approval to an approach in which the organization is responsible for the audit, but conducts this in conjunction with outside actors including the policy targets. This model, he feels, is more in keeping with the democratic spirit of social audit. The approach reported here probably fits best within this type of model – independent research funded by the organization responsible for policy delivery (DSS), undertaken in conjunction with policy targets (self-employed parents on low earnings), and interested 'actors' (social security adjudication officers, local accountants, professional accountancy institutes). We have much sympathy, however, with the radical social audit approach which suggests that the audit should be community property, located between policy deliverers and recipients.

There is now the real possibility that techniques such as this may be adopted by policy makers. In November 1993 the UK Government announced that it was moving away from its traditional government accounting or financial reporting techniques, which account for cash and emphasize propriety in the handling of public money (Pendlebury, 1992). Resource accounting will be used instead (UK Government, 1994). Under such regimes policy departments will be given public money as a resource and asked to account for it at the end of the year in terms of the efficacy with which it has been used. The distinction is between those who can account properly for money to show there is no impropriety, and those who account for their actions in terms of the efficacy of their investment. If government departments are to demonstrate the efficacy with which they have spent public money they will need to find evaluative techniques which are congruent with their policy aims. The challenge will be to develop techniques such as social audit to such an extent that needs can be adequately identified, and efficacy adequately evaluated and even quantified.

Notes

1. The immediate origins of contemporary historical cost accounting lie in the desire of shareholders in nineteenth-century joint stock companies to ensure that the

professional directors fulfilled their stewardship responsibilities properly. Early emphasis was on the balance sheet as a record of the shareholders' assets and liabilities. As capital markets grew in importance in the years between the two world wars, so emphasis shifted to the profit and loss account as an indicator of financial performance expressed as profitability.

2. In a programme of research commissioned by the Department of Social Security we specifically examined the measurement of self-employed income within the family credit scheme. The work was undertaken by way of legal research, interviews with relevant policy makers, administrators and professional bodies, and a series of interviews with self-employed applicants for family credit. A full report of this work appears in Boden and Corden (1994). The views expressed in this chapter are those of the two authors and may not necessarily represent the views of the Department of Social Security.

References

Boden, R. and Corden, A. (1994) *Measuring Low Incomes: Self-employment and Family Credit*, London: HMSO.

Bradshaw, J. (1972) 'A taxonomy of need', in McLachlan, G. (Ed.) *Problems and Progress in Medical Care*, seventh series, London: Oxford University Press.

Coote, A. (1993) 'Needs must. . . .', *Social Work Today*, **25** (3), pp. 21–2.

Corden, A. and Craig, P. (1991) *Perceptions of Family Credit*, London: HMSO.

Corden, A., Robertson, E. and Tolley, K. (Eds) (1992) *Meeting Needs in an Affluent Society*, Aldershot: Avebury.

Craig, P. (1991) 'Costs and benefits: a review of research on take up of income-related benefits', *Journal of Social Policy*, **20** (4), pp. 537–65.

Culyer, A. J. (1976) *Need and the National Health Service*, Oxford: Martin Robertson.

Dean, H. (1991) *Social Security and Social Control*, London: Routledge.

Doyal, L. and Gough, I. (1984) 'A theory of human needs', *Critical Social Policy*, **10** (summer), pp. 6–33.

Doyal, L. and Gough, I. (1991) *A Theory of Human Need*, Basingstoke: Macmillan.

DSS (1985) *Reform of Social Security: Programme for Action*, Department of Social Security, White Paper, Cmnd 9691, London: HMSO.

DSS (1993) *The Growth of Social Security*, Department of Social Security, London: HMSO.

Edinburgh District Council and Lothian Regional Council (1985) *Rowntree Mackintosh plc, Edinburgh – the Consequences of Closure: a Social Audit*, Edinburgh: EDC/LRC.

Fitzgerald, R. (Ed.) (1977) *Human Needs and Politics*, Sydney: Pergamon Press.

Geddes, M. (1988) 'Social audits and social accounting in the UK: a review', *Regional Studies*, **22** (1), pp. 61–3.

Geddes, M. (1992) 'The social audit movement', in Owen, D. (Ed.) *Green Reporting: Accountancy and the Challenge of the Nineties*, London: Chapman & Hall.

Gray, R., Bebbington, J. and Walters, D. (1993) 'The external "Social Audits"', in Gray, R. (Ed.) *Accounting for the Environment*, London: Paul Chapman.

Harte, G. (1986) 'Social accounting in the local economy', *Local Economy*, **1**, pp. 45–56.

Hawtin, M., Hughes, G. and Percy-Smith, J. (1994) *Community Profiling: Auditing Social Needs*, Buckingham: Open University Press.

Hood, C. (1991) 'A public management for all seasons?: the new public management', *Public Administration*, **69**, pp. 3–19.

Hopwood, A. G. (1984) 'Accounting and the pursuit of efficiency', in Hopwood, A. G. and Tomkins, C. (Eds) *Issues in Public Sector Accounting*, Oxford: Philip Allen.

Hopwood, A. G. and Burchell, S. (1980) 'The idea of social accounting remains an illusive one', *Social Accounting, Public Finance and Accountancy* (September), pp. 12–18.

Hudson, R., Peck, F. and Sadler, D. (1984) *Undermining Easington: Who'll Pay the Price of Pit Closures?*, Durham: University of Durham for Easington District Council.

Ife, J. (1980) 'The determination of social need – a model of need statements in social administration', *Australian Journal of Social Issues*, **15** (2), pp. 92–107.

Jefferis, K. and Robinson, M. (1987) 'Social investment production', in Cochrane, A. (Ed.) *Developing Local Economic Strategies*, Milton Keynes: Open University Press.

Kline, R. and Mallaber, J. (1986) *Whose Value? Whose Money? How to Assess the Real Value of Council Services*, Birmingham: Local Government Information Unit/ Birmingham Trade Union Resource Unit.

Lewis, S. (Ed.) (1986) *Output and Performance Measurement in Central Government: Progress in Departments*, Treasury Working Paper No. 38, Operational Research Division, London: HM Treasury.

Lukes, S. (1974) *Power, a Radical View*, London: Macmillan.

Martin, E. M. (1982) 'A framework for exploring different judgments of social need', *Australian Journal of Social Issues*, **17** (3), pp. 190–201.

Mushkat, M. (1986) 'Needs identification and assessment in public planning: a discussion of some salient issues', *Teaching Public Administration*, VI (2), pp. 53–81.

NAO (1991) *Support for Low Income Families*, National Audit Office, London: HMSO.

Nevitt, A. A. (1977) 'Demand and need' in Heisler, H. (Ed.) *Foundations of Social Administration*, London: Macmillan.

Newcastle City Council (1985) *Newcastle upon Tyne: Social Audit 1979–84*, Newcastle upon Tyne: Policy Services Unit.

Pendlebury, M. (1992) 'Accounting for executive agencies in the UK Government', *Financial Accountability and Management*, **8** (1), pp. 35–48.

Percy-Smith, J. (1992) 'Auditing social needs', *Policy and Politics*, **20** (1), pp. 29–34.

Power, M. (1994) 'The audit society', in Hopwood, A. G. and Miller, P. (Eds) *Accounting as Social and Institutional Practice*, Cambridge: Cambridge University Press.

Skelcher, C. (1993) 'Involvement and empowerment in local public services', *Public Money and Management* (July–September), pp. 13–18.

Spicker, P. (1987) 'Concepts of need in housing allocation', *Policy and Politics*, **15** (1), pp. 17–27.

Stewart, J. and Ranson, S. (1988) 'Management in the public domain', *Public Money and Management*, (spring/summer), pp. 13–18.

Townsend, P. (1979) *Poverty in the United Kingdom*, Harmondsworth: Penguin.

Turok, I. (1990) 'Evaluation and accountability in spatial economic policy: a review of alternative approaches', *Scottish Geographical Magazine*, **106** (1), pp. 4–11.

UK Government (1994) *Better Accounting for the Taxpayer's Money: Resource Accounting and Budgeting in Government*, Cm 2626, London: HMSO.

Zadek, S. and Evans, R. (1993) *Auditing the Market: a Practical Approach to Social Auditing*, Gateshead: Traidcraft/New Economic Foundation.

Chapter 11

Societal Outcome Measurement: the European Dimension

Roy Carr-Hill and John Lintott with J. Bowen and M. Hopkins

11.0 Introduction

The focus of this chapter is the increasing tendency for a wide range of quality of life data to be reported at the European level. Problems of reliability and validity, discussed elsewhere in the book, are of course even more acute when making international comparisons but there are also 'cultural' disagreements over what ought to be measured in order to present a comprehensive picture, and over the most appropriate general approach.

In order to understand these debates about what ought to be measured and what is seen as the most appropriate approach, we first need to review the recent history of socioeconomic measurement on an international level.

The Social Indicators Movement of the 1960s

The resurgence of interest in a system of socioeconomic measurement across a broad range of subjects in the 1960s was due to:

- the redocumentation of poverty in several Western European countries and the parallel questioning of trickle-down theories;
- a growing concern about the environmental and other social costs of economic growth in general, and specifically the social dislocation generated by the space programme in the USA;
- the emergence of a youth culture questioning the purpose of economic growth.

Hence the concern to develop methods to monitor levels of living (UN, 1954) and the quality of life (OECD, 1970) and, *a fortiori*, provide a measure of social 'progress'. In particular, there was a stress on measuring the *outcomes* for individuals of *all* social programmes rather than the financial *inputs* or the (usually administrative) *activities* associated with any *specific* programme. The problem then becomes one of specifying exactly what are the outcomes that should be measured. Clearly, the choice of what components of well-being are to be measured by indicators – especially on an international level – is essentially a political one.

However, the difficulty of relating the activities of social programmes to individual well-being meant that there was an increasing divergence between the development of indicative social indicators for planning purposes and measurement of individual well-being. Indeed, there was a hiatus during the 1980s. There is a past to learn from!

Approaches: a Thousand Flowers Bloom

A classic division of analysis might be in terms of methods, theory and policy. Among the methodologists, there are those who have followed the survey route: there have been large numbers of surveys to document the 'objective' living conditions of individuals and households ('objective' in the sense that the measurement is made by someone else); equally, there have been a large number of attitude and/or opinion surveys and, sometimes, more systematic attempts to assess 'happiness' or 'satisfaction' in terms of scales. Others have been concerned with techniques for valuing the different components of the quality of life. The theoreticians, unsurprisingly, have been less concerned with data collection procedures and more concerned with monitoring collective attributes of a society – sometimes seen as national characteristics – such as the level of autonomy, or political participation; or with elaborating a model of social systems in order to identify its key attributes. The 'policy' group is concerned with providing simple policy tools – and so has focused on possible ways of modifying Gross National Product (GNP) to provide a better measure of welfare, or on combining 'objective' indicators into a composite in parallel with national income per capita, or on deriving measures specific to each programme.

But the crucial distinction is between those who emphasize the importance of a uniform method of valuing welfare and others. The majority of the work of the former has been based on the financial nexus and has led to proposals either for methods of extending GNP to reflect better economic welfare or for ways of valuing other, currently non-monetarized components, using the measuring rod of money.

Others have argued that we must escape from a system of data which is dependent on the national accounts, either through developing a system for monitoring living standards; or through constructing a different kind of composite based on a selection of key indicators; or through social surveys of some concept of the quality of life, whether 'objectively' measured or self-reported.

At the same time, it is remarkable that nearly every European government has, almost simultaneously, started the regular publication of a compendium of social statistics which presents a profile of social conditions.

In the following two sections we review developments in respect of each of these approaches. In section 11.3 we consider the ways in which European national governments have set about monitoring social progress; in section 11.4 we discuss the substantive importance of apparently technical problems and, in section 11.5 we set out what might and should be done in the future.

11.1 An Index of Economic Welfare

GNP is the measure most often used by the international community to assess economic progress. However, the development of national accounting upon which the GNP measure is based was marked by a number of debates, most notably between neoclassical economists interested in arriving at a measure of economic welfare and Keynesians concerned to create the tools required for demand management (Seers, 1976). The consensus which developed around Keynesian policies after the Second World War meant that the Keynesian view was the one embodied in the national accounting system adopted by most governments. National Income was therefore not intended as an index of welfare.

Attempts at Adjusting National Income

Nordhaus and Tobin (1973) suggested several modifications to National Income in order to reflect economic welfare more closely. First, expenditures were to be re-classified, with health care and education treated as investment in human capital, and certain expenditures such as on the police and on defence treated as 'intermediate', that is, not in themselves generating welfare. Second, imputations were introduced for the services of capital goods such as owner-occupied dwellings and durable consumer goods, for leisure time, and for some forms of non-market production. Third, some costs of urbanization were deducted.

While maintaining that GNP is deficient as a measure of welfare, Nordhaus and Tobin argued that it is sufficiently well correlated with their Measure of Economic Welfare (MEW) that it is in fact unnecessary to implement the latter. However the correlation is a likely consequence of the imputation methods used, and tends to disappear when short time periods are considered (Daly and Cobb, 1990, pp. 76–80).

A version of Nordhaus and Tobin's MEW was implemented for Japan for the years 1955, 1960, 1965 and 1970 (Economic Council of Japan, 1973). Imputations for leisure and housework were omitted, but some allowance was made for environmental damage. Again, a high degree of correlation was found between the resultant measure known as Net National Welfare (NNW) and GNP. However, NNW was found to grow much more slowly than GNP – which is probably the reason its use was discontinued.

Zolotas (1981) constructed an Index of the Economic Aspects of Welfare (IEAW) which shares many features with MEW/NNW, but is innovative in taking into account pollution costs and resource depletion. In spite of differences in the way they are constructed, growth rates of MEW and IEAW show a similar pattern in the USA.

The most recent attempt at a modified National Income is Daly and Cobb's Index of Sustainable Economic Welfare (ISEW) (Daly and Cobb, 1990; Cobb and Cobb, 1994). This is an attempt to draw on the best of previous work, while improving on its limited treatment of environmental issues and sustainability. The ISEW starts from personal consumption, which is weighted by an index of distributional inequality. Based on a search to quantify the annual welfare flow, and excluding the stock of capital welfare, a number of items are added:

- household labour, services derived from consumer durables and highways, public spending on health and education, and net capital growth;

while other items are subtracted:

- spending on consumer durables, defensive health and education, advertising, various urbanization costs, and pollution and resource depletion costs.

The ISEW is the most ambitious attempt so far to construct and estimate an index of welfare based on modified national accounting aggregates. Estimated for the USA for the years 1950–86, the ISEW grows more slowly than GNP, but still generally grows. A significant exception is the early 1980s, when there is a fall of some 6 per cent due to increased distributional inequality. An attempt to apply the ISEW to the UK showed a more dramatic divergence from GNP. The ISEW for the UK showed a steady decline over a 20-year period, and is now back to the level of about 1950 (Jackson and Marks, 1994).

Evaluation of National Accounts as the Basis of a Welfare Measure

Familiarity with aggregates such as GNP, and with its use as an imperfect welfare indicator, obscures the full extent of their shortcomings. Hueting (1991), for example, discusses some 15 objections to National Income as a measure of welfare. Many of these objections (about the classification of expenditures and imputations) are addressed, at least to some extent, by the indices discussed above.

But some of the objections (although described by Hueting as being of a 'technical' nature) are in a sense more fundamental, because they undermine the basis for using market prices at all. For example, GNP omits the consumer surplus, although this is part of welfare; it involves adding together different people's utilities, which is unjustified particularly where there is inequality of income; it ignores diminishing marginal utility – of individuals and of the economy as a whole; real GNP requires the use of price indices which can be calculated correctly only for a constant basket of goods; and the movement of activities between the unpaid and the paid sector is ignored.

Other problems arise in relation to the policy relevance of the national accounts. Seers (1976) emphasizes their close association with Keynesian demand management policies, and questions their appropriateness for use with other policies. The accounts are 'monistic' with their treatment of the whole nation as an appropriate object of analysis and presume a country which is 'economically independent'. In a period characterized by halting GNP growth, combined with increased inequality and poverty, restructuring of production, globalization and environmental problems which cut across national boundaries, this national emphasis is unjustified. It is more important to consider how the accounts should be extended, to monitor developments in the international economy on the one hand, and to disaggregate information by income classes and by production sectors on the other. This argument applies both to the current national accounts, and to the various attempts to create welfare indices out of them.

As Daly (1989) emphasizes, the purpose of the reform of the National Accounts should be to create a better measure of *income*, making it clear that much else needs to be done to arrive at a measure of *welfare*. In practice, however, even the best attempts so far at indices of welfare have been forced into arbitrary assumptions. For example Zolotas (1981) assumes that exactly half of all advertising is of a 'persuasive' kind (and thus should be excluded). Daly and Cobb assume that half of higher education spending is consumption and half investment. There are many other examples.

On the other hand, as we have seen, there is often a high degree of correlation between the conventional income aggregates and the modified versions. This results partly from their common core (most marketed production). In addition, large items such as the value of housework or of leisure are estimated essentially by multiplying the time involved by a measure such as the average wage rate. The latter is likely to change much more quickly than the former, and is of course highly correlated with National Income. Yet the pervasive use of money and prices as a method of valuing welfare may be becoming less and less relevant. In short, if one wants to measure well-being, don't start from here.

11.2 Identifying the Components of Well-being

The general argument in this section is that, in contrast with the GNP approach, there are several distinct components to the quality of life which have to be monitored. There have been three main strands: those based on a more or less theoretical account of need; those based on responses to social surveys, sometimes based on a theory of satisfaction; and those based on a normative view about what are the important components of quality of life in industrialized societies.

Theoretically Based Systems

The most well-known proposal for a theoretical approach is the 'basic needs' framework, based on the work of Abraham Maslow (1954). He proposed that human needs could be put in a hierarchical structure from physiological needs (hunger and thirst), safety needs (for security and avoidance of anxiety), belongingness needs (desire for affectionate relations), esteem needs (the respectful evaluation of oneself); and that human beings would seek to satisfy them in ascending order.

The idea was taken up by the International Labour Organization (1976). The basic needs approach to development includes two elements:

- certain minimum requirements of a family for private consumption, as well as certain household equipment and furniture;
- essential services provided by, and for the community at large, such as safe drinking water, sanitation, public transport and health educational and cultural facilities.

The idea of identifying separable needs, each of which has to be attained, is to be applauded. However, subsequent attempts to derive an index have encountered difficulties. The most recent example is the Human Development Index (HDI) promoted by the UN Development Programme which combines relative achievement of countries in terms of three different data series – life expectancy, adult literacy and GNP per capita – into an 'index'. Apart from the puzzle of why those who propose non-monetary indicators of well-being are none the less obsessed with constructing a single index, data quality is awful (Murray, 1991).

Doyal and Gough (1991) have attempted to elaborate a theory of need which might be a more appropriate basis for industrialized societies. They claim that Maslow's list is full of internal tensions, and that needs cannot be seen as real psychological 'drives' at all. Doyal and Gough reject arguments that 'basic human needs are nothing but a dangerous and dogmatic metaphysical fantasy' and that only expressed wants (or demands) are 'real'. Equally, they highlight problems of relativism, which is bound to be heavily value-laden with presuppositions. They argue instead that, whilst there is large cultural variation, there is a rock-bottom set of needs defined by the following proposition:

> So you can need what you want, and want or not want what you need. What you cannot consistently do is not need what is required in order

to avoid serious harm – whatever you may want.

(p. 42)

Avoidance of physical harm cannot be the only 'need': otherwise Huxley's *Brave New World*, which allows for some individual want satisfactions within a regimented system, would be Utopian – and obviously it is not. Doyal and Gough therefore argue for the importance of autonomous choices 'to have the ability to make informed choices about what should be done and how to go about doing it', even though this may result in some unhappiness. Like physical health, autonomy at its most basic level is rather negative – a loss or lack of control. What is crucial in their view is real opportunities to act and change one's life and conditions, both in day-to-day things and in the political arena.

Whilst acknowledging cultural relativity, they argue that there are some important universal characteristics of need-satisfiers. In particular, they argue that democratic structures, in addition to basic income and output, are a prerequisite for optimizing need satisfaction. Clearly, in political terms, the extent of real democratic participation depends upon the flexibility of the state and its structures, and on the viability of other forms of participation. Equally, the organization of society has to assure human rights and ecological sustainability. Measuring all of this is rather complicated.

Social Surveys of the Quality of Life

The number of surveys being carried out in Europe has, of course, mushroomed. Our concern here is with those which are explicitly concerned with measuring aspects of the quality of life. Two approaches can be identified: the subjective, and the objective.

The subjective approach is concerned with deriving satisfaction measures. A systematic approach to measuring happiness or satisfaction has been developed in the Michigan school, the major exponents being Andrews and Withey (1976). They argue, on the basis of small-scale survey work, that several domains contribute to the final outcome of happiness, and that responses to questionnaires about satisfaction in respect of each of these domains can be used to generate a happiness scale. On a theoretical basis, the fundamental issue is whether or not one believes that happiness can be boiled down to: adequate ECUs + health + hugs and kisses.

The practical problem is that, if direct questions about satisfaction are asked, nearly everybody responds satisfied, and a large proportion 'very satisfied'. This is partly because responses appear to measure social norms (of the 'can't complain' variety) rather than self-ratings of well-being. There is now a large literature on what affects expressed satisfaction and its relation to objective outcome in different fields (Thompson and Sunol, 1995).

The objective approach, based in Scandinavia, has been to argue that objective data on living conditions should be available to all citizens as a prerequisite in a representative democracy (Johannson, 1976). Again this appears laudable, but reliance on citizen reporting raises all the usual technical problems of social surveys, such as response rates. Moreover, one must question whether several of the important outcome indicators can be collected using a survey of either type, because the measurement of some crucial characteristics of modern society is not amenable to the survey method.

For example, during the 1980s in the UK, an indicator which excited great political attention was the number of deaths from hypothermia during the winter months. Yet it is not at all clear how such data can be reliably collected. Similarly, one might argue that the number of households without a home is a useful 'synthetic' indicator of well-being, in that it reflects the conjunction of a number of different problems. Again, this rate cannot be ascertained from a survey of individuals in private households or stable institutions. Indeed, it is not obvious how to collect accurate data on homelessness at all.

The OECD Approach: a List of Concerns

Rather distinct from either of these approaches has been the eclecticism of the UN Research Institute for Social Development in developing 56 indicators of the level of living in the 1950s (UN, 1954; McGranahan *et al.*, 1972). Their major problem was the quality of data available in developing countries.

For industrialized societies, it had been argued that there were several alternative visions of Utopia which are very specific to culture and time (Miles, 1985). Several different 'lists' have been proposed. However, there are 'areas of concern' which are more or less common across all these lists, and country representatives at the OECD were able to agree on a List of Social Concerns relatively easily.

Unsurprisingly these were grouped in a way that closely corresponded to the cabinet portfolios of the typical (OECD) government (health, education, employment, and so on). But at the same time the programme emphasized the measurement of well-being, so that it tried to proceed by breaking well-being down into various components and subcomponents, until a precise concept resulted which was capable of measurement.

In fact, although there was high-level commitment during the completion of the first stage – leading to the publication of *Measuring Social Well Being* (OECD, 1976) – the programme fizzled out during the 1980s. This was partly because governments became more concerned with the consequences of the oil price shock, and partly because it became obvious that very substantial statistical resources would be required to provide systematic data for many of the indicators proposed. The gap between the proposals and what could be derived from existing statistical series was well illustrated by the limited number of items which were included in the final publication of the programme (OECD, 1986).

11.3 Social Reporting Activities in Europe and North America

Information reported by international organizations such as the United Nations – including the International Labour Organization (ILO), the Food and Agricultural Organization (FAO), the UN Educational Scientific and Cultural Organization (UNESCO), the World Health Organization (WHO), the UN Research Institute for Social Development (UNRISD) – and by the World Bank, the Organization for Economic Cooperation and Development (OECD), the Nordic Council and the Statistical Office of the European Union (Eurostat) – is usually based on national data. Countries have adopted social reporting systems for similar reasons, such as social and political planning, for public information and for social control. However, the national programmes for social reporting vary according to the type and stability of the government in power, the industrial development and wealth of the country in question, and of course the history of the country with regard to each of these factors.

Nevertheless, all of the systems used and developed are based on a broad notion of 'social indicator reporting'. Moreover, the subject-matter of the various reports is fairly standard, concerning population; collectively provided or regulated social concerns (such as health, education, justice, housing, work and conditions, environment, production and consumption); and a certain amount of more qualitative information. But the approach to social reporting varies greatly from one country to the next, as does the amount of accompanying interpretive commentary. In the following paragraphs we identify five approaches adopted in developed nations. However, the categories described here are by no means exclusive, and a specific report may incorporate a number of different approaches.

Component-based Living Conditions Approaches

Principally using data from the national statistical compendia, such approaches are the mode widely adopted in Western Europe (Austria *Sozialstatistische Daten*, Denmark *Levevilkår i Danmark*, France *Données Sociales*, Germany *Datenreport*, Great Britain *Social Trends*, Italy *Statistiche Sociali*, Spain *Panoramica Social/Indicatores sociales*, Switzerland *Sozialindikatoren für die Schweiz*, as well as Australia *Social Indicators*, Canada *Perspectives Canada*, Japan *Statistical Indicators on Social Life* and USA *Social Indicators*), with there being a clear emphasis on *objective* statistical information with minimal interpretation or commentary. These reports are usually published regularly, and their subject-matter is mostly in line with the principal concerns of government departments (such as health, education, crime and justice, work). Austria, Germany and Great Britain use micro-census data specifically elicited for such purposes, and Germany also includes an element of subjective evaluation on the part of its respondents (see below).

Level of Living Research: the Resource Approach

This approach is basically confined to the Scandinavian countries (Denmark *Levevilkår i Danmark*, Finland *Suomalaisten Elinolot*, Norway *Levekårsundersøkelsen*, Sweden *Levnadsförhållanden*), and is fairly well developed in each of these (less so in Finland). Information is collected and reported by each of the national Statistical Offices. Also, the reports draw upon research institute information, especially in Denmark (annual surveys). The Nordisk Statistisk Sekretariat has also been publishing data for these countries since the mid-1970s. The preoccupations of all the reports are with 'level of living' in terms of comprehensive national statistics (on family, health, housing, environment, work, working conditions, education, etc.) with the emphasis being on *access to resources* and *inequality of distribution*. The justification for this approach is that, given adequate resources, people will dispose of them wisely for their optimal need satisfaction as autonomous individuals. Also included are certain more subjective data such as evaluations of working conditions and time budget information. The data are collected from official census and other sources, as well as interviews being conducted with a sample of the population. Attempts are made to achieve an element of continuity in the broader elicitation of data over time, but there is also a degree of specific focusing on different areas from one report to the next. All four Scandinavian countries have published regular reports since the mid- to late-1970s.

Quality-of-Life Research: the Needs Approach

Being concentrated specifically in Austria, Switzerland, Germany and The Netherlands, with elements also incorporated in Canada and the USA, this approach combines a mixture of objective and subjective data which seek to indicate well-being from a variety of perspectives. In contrast with the 'resource approach' outlined above, this method seeks to define a variety of desirable goals and then looks at *need fulfilment* in relation to these goals. The reports attempt to get away from the purely statistical approaches by including analytical commentaries, but obvious problems are encountered concerning first the essentially value-laden definitions of *needs*, and second the objectification of subjective attitudes, and the methodological problems associated with the subjective measurement of *satisfaction*. The data are obtained from national statistical compendia and combined with information from purpose-built micro-census sources. Austria (*Sozialstatistische Daten*), Germany (*Datenreport*) and The Netherlands (*De leefssituatie van de nederlandse bevolking*) have all published reports reasonably regularly since the mid-1970s.

Social Indicator Systems

Although all of the social reports mentioned here are, to a greater or lesser extent, based on social indicator-type systems, only those in Switzerland and Germany can be properly described as Social Indicator Systems. These are based upon the UN and OECD methods developed in the 1970s. The indicators are grouped into about 10 subject areas (there being a total of 196 indicators in Germany, 130 in Switzerland) covering a variety of social concerns. Although none is claimed to be more important than any other, the scales and values given to each are obviously value-laden. Similarly, there are methodological problems associated with subjective measures of *satisfaction* in that they tend to vary with, for example, the time of year. Germany published its 'German Welfare Surveys' in 1978, 1980, 1984, 1988 and 1990; Switzerland published a series of sector-specific reports in the early 1980s (*Sozialindikatoren für die Schweiz*), but has not repeated this, despite an extensive survey being conducted in 1987.

Other Systems

A number of other social reporting methods are used in different countries in Western Europe and beyond. Examples include the *Social Accounting Matrices* used in The Netherlands with a view to obtaining full social accounts with regard to sociodemographic, socioeconomic and labour statistics.

Coverage of specific social areas is included in a number of reports, such as regional issues (Great Britain *Welsh Social Trends*, France *Données Sociales Île de France*); population groups (The Netherlands on youth, elderly, immigrants, etc.), social security provision and social problems (Norway *Sosialt Utsyn*).

All of the Western European nations publish annual statistical compendia from which, along with national census data, the social reports draw heavily. These compendia tend to emphasize economic and quantitative data at the expense of more qualitative information. In addition, several nations have introduced register-based censuses in the last two decades too, owing to the impracticability of standard census methods. Other sources, besides administrative registers, include Household Budget surveys on consumption and income, and Labour Force surveys (all countries), time budgets, micro-censuses, and specific population group surveys (e.g. young or old people, or immigrant groups).

Despite the fact that the different member states of the European Union appear to have adopted very different approaches in choosing data for their social reporting, the resulting shape of each of the documents is very similar. To illustrate this, the chapter headings of the reports from nine nations have been compared with the list used by the OECD in their 1986 compendium in Table 11.1.

Table 11.1 Coverage of OECD concerns in nine countries

OECD Indicators	Austria: *Sozial-statistische Daten*	Denmark: *Leve-vilkår i Danmark*	Finland: *Suomalaisten Elinolot*	France: *Données Sociales 1993*	Italy: *Statistische Sociali*	Spain: *Panoramica Social*	United Kingdom: *Social Trends 1993*	Netherlands: *Social and Cultural Report 1992*	Norway: *Levekårs undersøkelse en 1987*
Length of life	3. Health	5. Health	2. Population 4. Health	5. Health	1. Population	5. Health 9. Social marginalization	7. Health	3. Health	13. Health
Healthfulness of life	3. Health	5. Health	4. Health	5. Health	3. Health	5. Health	7. Health	3. Health	13. Health
Use of educational facilities	4. Schooling and education	6. Education	5. Education	2. Education and training	4. Education	6. Education	3. Education	7. Education	12. Education
Learning	4. Schooling and education	6. Education	5. Education	2. Education and training	4. Education	6. Education	3. Education	7. Education	12. Education
Availability of employment	5. Employment/ working conditions	7. Work	6. Workforce	3. Job market	5. Employment	2. Employment	4. Employment	4. Employment	8. Employment
Quality of working life	5. Employment and working conditions	7. Work	6. Workforce	4. Working conditions	5. Employment	2. Employment	–	(4. Employment)	9. Physical working 10. Organizational
Use of time	12. Use of time/leisure	10. Leisure	11. Use of time/leisure	–	8. Leisure	3. Level of living	10. Leisure	8. Leisure	15. Leisure activities

Table 11.1 continued

Income	7. Social security	7. Work 8. Financial 9. Housing	7. Income	7. Budgets and estates	9. Income	4. Distribution of income	5. Income 6. Expenditure 8. Housing	5. Social security 6. Housing 10. Income	7. Wages and material goods
Wealth	7. Social security	8. Financial affairs	7. Income	7. Budgets and estates	9. Income	4. Distribution of income	5. Income 6. Expenditure	10. Income 11. Cultural changes	7. Wages and material
Housing conditions	9. Housing	9. Housing	8. Housing	8. Living environment	7. Housing	7. Housing	8. Housing	6. Housing	14. Housing conditions
Accessibility to services	9. Housing	10. Leisure	5. Education 8. Housing	2. Education 9. Social groups	–	4. Distribution of income 7. Housing	3. Education 10. Leisure	3. Health 8. Leisure	13. Health
Environmental nuisances	10. Infrastruc-ture and environment	14. Environment	9. Environment	–	–	–	9. Environment	–	–
Social attachment	–	5. Health	–	–	3. Health	9. Social marginalization	7. Health	–	–
Exposure to risk	11. Criminality	13. Personal safety	6. Workforce 10. Physical risk	5. Health	6. Justice	8. Public security 9. Social marginalization	7. Health 12. Crime 13. Transport	9. Justice	17. Violence and security
Perceived threat	–	13. Personal safety	–	–	–	–	–	9. Justice	–

11.4 Technical Problems in Developing Indicators

> The series a statistical office chooses to prepare and publish exercise a subtle and pervasive influence on political, social and economic development. That is why the apparently dull and minor subject of statistical policy is of crucial importance. (Seers, 1976, p. 3)

Deriving Indicators

Although the title of the section is 'technical' problems, the concern here is to identify the policy implications of some apparently technical choices made when devising indicators, when constructing composite indices and when monitoring the disadvantaged. There are several technical problems: we consider just three: objective and subjective data; reliance on existing data; formulating indicators.

Objective and subjective data

There is a general failure to incorporate both 'objective' and 'subjective' components into indicators. This is partly because of an over-rigid division between 'qualitative' and 'quantitative' methods of collecting data, and partly a failure to recognize that much of human behaviour is governed mainly by how a situation is perceived not by objective circumstances. For example, the recent European concern with 'exclusion' – although resulting from objective circumstances – is, at least in part, a subjective matter, in the sense that the criteria which identify the excluded are socially determined.

The usual difficulty with subjective data is that respondents are being asked their opinions about questions framed by a policy maker or researcher. Whilst there are other possible approaches (see below), they are time-consuming.

Reliance on existing data

As discussed elsewhere in this book, the content of most quality-of-life measures is dictated by data and measures that are readily available, rather than by the demands of prior theory. Etzioni and Lehman (1967), at the beginning of the 'social indicators movement', pointed to the problems this can cause, for example:

- 'fractional measurement', where there is a lack of correspondence between a concept and its operational definition (as with 'unemployment' and its measurement using social security statistics);
- 'indirect measurement' (e.g. measuring educational attainment by years of school), especially prevalent where data are used which were collected for some other purpose.

Worse still, many measures were in fact established on the basis of an outdated administrative or theoretical framework. As discussed above, there is a tendency for data series which are related to the national accounts to have been developed more systematically than others. And there is inevitable pressure to use existing data systems to derive social indicators, rather than to invest in expensive new systems.

Formulating indicators

In many cases the main concern is not with averages, but with the proportion of people who achieve an acceptable minimum standard – that is, with identifying poverty and marginalization. This concern is not simply with ensuring a basic income for everyone. It cuts across many other concerns, including for example basic literacy, avoiding early death, and the availability of transport for access to basic facilities. The emphasis is on individuals, looking at extremes rather than averages.

Absolute minima and culturally relative levels are inherently flawed. Instead, it is important to establish an 'optimal need satisfaction', beyond which level, more is not necessarily better (food, housing, etc.) and more can even mean worse. This means that in many cases neither a set of 'positive' indicators ('the proportion who are literate') nor a set of purely 'negative' indicators ('the proportion without adequate housing') will be sufficient. Instead, it implies relatively sensitive measurement of the proportions who are substantially below and substantially above some critical optimum.

Difficulties with Composite Indices

It is important to understand the processes and the systems that generate synthetic indices (Seers, 1985).

Choice of components

There is no consensus over what should be the components or the weighting procedures that should be employed in 'composite' quality-of-life indices:

- whilst everyone wants a certain minimum of several conditions, few can agree on what is the optimum level or what combination is required;
- whilst nodding in the direction of consumer sovereignty as the mechanism for choosing components and how to combine them, few have actually attempted to take that position seriously.

Indeed there is an argument that, in most indices, each of the components is the product of a gradual developmental process, in the course of which an implicit consensus emerged. Whether or not such components will always be relevant to different population groups is an important issue.

Trade-offs are obscured

As discussed above, although there is a very close correlation between life expectancy and *per capita* income, the relationship between economic growth and quality of life is not so simple. For example, Etzioni and Lehman (1967) argued against 'formalistic-aggregative measurement of collective attributes', such as the US crime index. This simply adds up a broad range of crimes, giving the same weight to a murder and a $50 theft.

The important point is that well-being is multidimensional, and its aspects are incommensurate because, although they are interrelated, they are not substitutes for each other. For example, income sufficient to ensure good nutrition increases life expectancy. But you cannot compensate early deaths with high income. Indeed, although continued use can lead to a complex index – such as GNP – being presented as being simple, the underlying presumptions are often quite complex and obscured.

Lack of disaggregration

Few quality-of-life indices address distributional aspects of the different components of the well-being of particular population groups. This is principally because of the difficulty of collecting sufficient nationally comparable data to yield meaningful estimates at the community level or for small groups. In practice, such indices can usually only be calculated for highly aggregated and often inappropriate geographic units of analysis.

Monitoring the Marginalized

The purpose of many of these systems is to monitor the living standards of those who are marginalized. This poses many practical difficulties both for administrative systems and social surveys. But, given increasing diversity within the population and an overall concern with empowerment, an important difficulty arises. This is that the categories used in administrative systems and in most social surveys are often contested by those being monitored. Problems of measurement then arise since the strongest groups tend to be the most vocal and visible, and they may also manipulate the facts – whilst asserting that participation of the subject community under study is vital.

Language and official categorization

A symptom of this contestation is the development of vocabularies which confront and challenge stereotypes. Thus, the politics of disablement movements (such as *Handicappés Méchants* in France) involves a criticism of terms which mark out disabled people as different and unequal. Equally, there is a concern with a confusion between the functional limitations affecting a person's body (impairments) with the socially imposed barriers stemming from the design of the physical environment and the attitudes of other people (disability). For example, in surveying disability, the OPCS asked 'What complaint causes you difficulty in holding, gripping or turning things?'. Yet one could equally ask 'What defects in the design of everyday equipment like jars, bottles and lids cause you difficulty in holding, gripping or turning them?' (Oliver, 1990, pp. 7–8).

Re-naming has played an equally central part in debates around lesbian and gay rights and anti-racism. Words with previously negative connotations, such as 'lesbian' and 'queer', are used to assert a positive collective identity. The word 'Black' has been similarly reclaimed.

Phenomena such as these can lead to exclusion from official statistics and national surveys which seek to provide a comprehensive picture of the health and social circumstances of the population. This may be either because of the criteria governing entry into the official statistics or social surveys, or because of the technical procedures used in sampling or data analysis. For example, there tend to be lower response rates in the UK among Blacks than among Whites. In part this is due to a concern that their reported experience will be drained of meaning through analysis by White researchers and that the information collected could be used by state agencies against the interests of minority ethnic groups. Clearly problems such as these will be exacerbated when seeking to compare international measures of well-being.

More sensitive social surveys

The problem of 'monitoring the disadvantaged' is only an acute form of the general problem of monitoring the quality of life where there is increasing attention being paid to user orientations. One possible proxy approach, in general, is that adopted in the survey conducted for ITV in 1985 (Mack and Lansley, 1985), and repeated in 1995 (Gordon and Patazis, 1995). Respondents were asked to select from among a long list those items they thought were essential for civilized living in today's Britain. They were then asked whether they had or had access to those items.

An extension of that approach – which has been tried within the health care context – is to ask people to name the most important subcomponents of any area of concern; and then to ask them how they rate their own performance in respect of each of these components (Ruta *et al.*, 1994). Whilst superficially appealing, the methodology makes many demands upon respondents. However, whichever avenue is adopted, the importance of focusing on user orientations and views about what constitutes the quality of life should not be ignored.

11.5 The Way Forward: Recommendations for Further Work

The purpose of this section is to suggest possible ways forward. As noted above, most governments of industrial countries now produce compendia of social statistics. These are very similar in their content and structure. They are, however, based mainly on administrative data, and include few indicators of outcome, in terms of social well-being. Clearly, comparability would be improved and more emphasis could be put on outcome measures.

A further set of issues arises in relation to the possibility of combining individual outcome measures into some kind of HDI-type index (see Section 11.2). Clearly, the HDI itself is inappropriate for industrialized countries, because only three series are included and richer countries score close to 100 per cent on all three. But in addition it uses a weighting scheme which is completely arbitrary.

Attempts to generate other composite indices have also tended to fail, partly because there is no agreed theoretical framework and partly because most of the components that could be included in such a composite index are themselves closely associated with GNP.

Indeed, the only possible way of incorporating a large range of concerns into an index with non-arbitrary weights is to modify the national accounting approach to incorporate a variety of environmental and social costs and benefits, along the lines of the UN's proposed Satellite System for Integrated Environmental Economic Accounting described by Bartelmus *et al.* (1991). However, as noted above, this approach is unlikely to yield a satisfactory index receiving widespread support in the foreseeable future.

In summary, the index approach is not realistic and is obviously not sufficient for the problem of monitoring the quality of life in the member states of the European Union. Work should be directed at improving the quality of individual social indicators.

Theoretical efforts – such as those based on basic needs – and the practical experience of social reporting across Europe converge on a number of general concerns, such as health, learning, work, leisure, the physical environment and the social environment. However:

- there are problems of comparability of data across Europe which need to be understood (even if they cannot be solved);
- there is considerable scope for combining and making the most of existing social reports;

- there needs to be an emphasis on indicators which measure well-being as directly as possible.

This book has suggested that there is a long way to go before the last point has been properly addressed. Yet, it is far more important and useful, for example, to have comparable data on people's health than on their health expenditures.

For many of the concerns discussed above, the basic source would have to be an international household survey. Such a survey might, for example, eventually cover autonomy and interpersonal relationships. However, the development of survey-based measures of the quality of life including both objective measures of living conditions and subjective estimates of satisfaction will not be easy or cheap.

Moreover, it would not be appropriate – nor indeed cost effective – to collect data for some of the concerns above from a household survey. Much information can be gleaned from existing data (as with energy) or new data-collection procedures (e.g., through collecting consumer data on the quality of services). However, the most important gaps in our existing knowledge relate to measures of inequality and exclusion. It is therefore these areas that are addressed in the EU framework IV programme of Targeted Socio-Economic Research.

The discussion earlier in this chapter has shown the difficulty of monitoring the disadvantaged. However, the concern with excluded minorities, as well as the concern with extending democracy, would suggest that it will be important to invest effort in ways in which social surveys categorizations can be implemented both within one country and cross-nationally.

Finally, it should not be forgotten that the original purpose of introducing data based on social indicators was to generate an informed public opinion (Nissel, 1970). That purpose is often lost in the development of social data compendia by various government bureaucracies, and even in the development of social surveys of the quality of life. These tend to remain top-down, despite the inclusion of bottom-up kind of questions such as 'are you happy/satisfied with . . .'. It is therefore important to re-focus any framework of social indicators more towards a user perspective. Thus, it is less a problem of new data and more a problem of collecting data properly. In our view, the key outstanding issue remains that of finding ways of extending democracy to data-collection procedures (Carr-Hill, 1978).

Acknowledgement

The authors are grateful to Eurostat who gave us the opportunity to pull together all this material, and to Vanda King for typing several drafts. We also want to thank especially James Bowen for providing the basic material for Section 11.3, and to Mike Hopkins and Deo Ramprahesh for very useful comments.

References

Andrews, F. and Withey, M. G. (1976) *Social Indicators of Well-Being*, New York: Plenum Press.

Bartelmus, P., Stahmer, C. and van Tongeren, J. (1991) 'Integrated environmental and economic accounting: framework for an SNA satellite system (SEEA)', *Review of Income and Wealth* (June).

Bauer, R. A. (Ed.) (1966) *Social Indicators*, Cambridge, MA: MIT Press.

Carr-Hill, R. A. (1984) 'Radicalising survey methodology', *Quality and Quantity: the European Journal of Methodology*, **18** (3), 275–92.

Cobb, C. W. and Cobb, J. B. (1994) *The Green National Product*, Lanham: University Press of America.

Daly, H. (1989) 'Toward a measure of sustainable social net national product', in Ahmad, Y. J., El Serafy, S. and Lutz, E. (Eds) *Environmental Accounting for Sustainable Development*, Washington, DC: World Bank.

Daly, H. and Cobb, J. B. (1990) *For the Common Good*, London: Green Print.

Doyal, L. and Gough, I. (1991) *A Theory of Human Need*, Basingstoke and London: Macmillan.

Economic Council of Japan (1973) *Measuring Net National Welfare of Japan*, Tokyo: ECJ.

Etzioni, A. and Lehman, E. W. (1967) 'Some dangers in "valid" social measurement', *Annals of the American Academy of Political and Social Science* (September), pp. 1–15.

Gordon, D., Patazis, C. *et al.* (1995) *Breadline Britain in the 1990s: a Report to the Joseph Rowntree Foundation*, Bristol: University of Bristol, Department of Social Policy and Planning.

Hueting, R. (1991) 'Correcting National Income for environmental losses: a practical solution for a theoretical dilemma', in Costanza, R. (Ed.) *Ecological Economics*, New York: Columbia University Press.

International Labour Organization (1976) *Employment Growth and Basic Needs: a One World Problem*, Geneva: ILO.

Jackson, T. and Marks, N. (1994) *Measuring Sustainable Economic Welfare – a Pilot Index 1950–1990*, Stockholm: Stockholm Environment Institute.

Johannson, S. (1976) *Towards a Theory of Social Reporting*, Stockholm: Swedish Institute for Social Research.

Mack, J. and Landley, S. (1985) *Poor Britain*, London: Allen & Unwin.

Maslow, A. (1954) *Motivation and Personality*, New York: Random House.

McGillivray, M. (1991) 'The HDI: yet another redundant composite development indicator', *World Development*, **19** (10), pp. 1461–8.

McGranahan, D. V., Richard-Proust, C., Sovani, N. V. and Subramanian, M. (1972) *Contents and Measurement of Socio-economic Development*, New York: Praeger, for UNRISD.

Miles, I. (1985) *Social Indicators for Human Development*, London: Pinter, for United Nations University.

Murray, C. J. L. (1991) *Development Data Constraints and the HDI*, Geneva: UNRISD.

Nissel, M. (1970) 'Editorial', *Social Trends No. 1*, London: HMSO.

Nordhaus, W. D. and Tobin, J. (1973) 'Is growth obsolete?', in Moss, M. (Ed.) *The*

Measurement of Economic and Social Performance, New York: NBER.

Oliver, M. (1990) *The Politics of Disablement*, London: Macmillan Education.

Organization of Economic Cooperation and Development (1970) *List of Social Concerns*, Paris: OECD.

Organization for Economic Cooperation and Development (1976) *Measuring Social Well Being*, Paris: OECD.

Organization for Economic Cooperation and Development (1986) *Living Conditions in OECD Countries: a Compendium of Social Indicators*, Social Policy Studies No. 3, Paris: OECD.

Ruta, D. A., Garratt, A. M., Leng, M., Russell, I. T. and MacDonald, L. M. (1994) 'A new approach to the measurement of the quality of life: the patient generated index', *Medical Care*, **32**, pp. 1109–26.

Seers, D. (1976) 'The political economy of national accounting', in Cairncross, A. and Puri, M. (Eds) *Employment, Income Distribution and Development Strategy: Problems of the Developing Countries*, London: Macmillan.

Seers, D. (1985) *The Political Economy of Nationalism*, Oxford: Oxford University Press.

Thompson, A. G. H. and Sunol, R. (1995) 'Expectations as determinants of patient satisfaction: concepts, theory and evidence', *International Journal for Quality in Health Care*, **7**, pp. 127–41.

United Nations (1954) *Report on International Definition and Measurement Standards and Levels of Living*, New York: UN.

United Nations Research Institute for Social Development (1977) *Measurement of Real Progress at the Local Level: an Overview*, Report UNRAISD/77/C.25, Geneva: UNRISD.

Zolotas, X. (1981) *Economic Growth and Declining Social Welfare*, New York: New York University Press.

Chapter 12

Conclusions and Prospects

Peter Smith

12.0 Introduction

All actions have consequences. But – certainly in systems as complex as the public services – it is often impossible to predict the consequences of our actions. Nevertheless we are often forced to act, even when the outcome is unknowable. The search for measures of outcome reflects a desire to offer some guidance, however imperfect, to those who are forced to act in the modern public sector.

The preceding chapters have documented the search for outcome measures across a vast canvas, the size of which is itself daunting. Authors have approached the issue from a variety of perspectives. However, there are some common themes which emerge from the programme of work summarized in this book. The purpose of this chapter is to offer some personal impressions.

12.1 What is Outcome?

Chapter 1 noted that, in practice, it is impossible to distinguish with any clarity between measures of output and measures of outcome. The approaches to outcome measurement described here occupy various positions along the output:outcome spectrum. There is generally a trade-off between the ease of obtaining a measure and how far it moves towards the outcome end of the spectrum. Thus, for example, examination pass rates are rather poor measures of outcome, but are readily available. Quality-adjusted life years should be excellent measures of the outcome of health care, but are extraordinarily difficult to make operational.

Several authors note the need to consider all aspects of outcome, and that – in practice – there is a tendency to concentrate on the readily quantifiable. For example, the criminal justice system is awash with various measures of the incidence of crime, but can tell us little about the quality of the justice it dispenses. In other words, it is generally easy to measure the quantity rather than the quality of services. Yet in programmes such as community care, effectiveness may be appalling if qualitative aspects are ignored.

12.2 Why Measure Outcome?

The new public sector management is predicated on the assumption that there is consensus as to what constitutes performance in the public sector, and that progress can be made towards its measurement. Our findings confirm that – on the contrary – there is often little consensus as to what constitutes outcome, and that its satisfactory measurement is astonishingly difficult. This is hardly surprising. Public sector enterprises consume inputs and produce outputs. By analogy with the First Law of Thermodynamics – which states that, in a closed system, energy cannot be lost – the sum of outputs must equal the sum of inputs. But some outputs – such as the time spent between patient visits by community nurses – may be of little value to anyone. What matters is whether society *values* the outputs of the public sector. The preceding chapters have exposed the diversity of opinions concerning valuation.

Yet there are two fundamental reasons why every effort should be made to measure outcome. The first is to identify effective modes of delivering public services; the second to identify the competence with which those services are delivered. The former is concerned with *allocative* efficiency, the latter with *managerial* efficiency. Both issues are of central importance. If public services are delivered inefficiently, in either sense, resources are being wasted. Moreover, the reputation of the public sector is tarnished. This in turn may give rise to public hostility to services funded out of general taxation. It is then quite possible that perfectly effective public services will be endangered, with adverse consequences for national well-being.

Because there is no consensus as to outcome, it follows that there can be no unique way of evaluating public services. Instead, the most that can be expected of an outcome measurement scheme is that it offers relevant stakeholders sufficient information to come to their own judgment about the services. It is then through the political process that the various views must be reconciled (Stewart and Walsh, 1994). But who are those with a legitimate part to play in the political process, and how can they effect change? I consider these issues below.

12.3 Who are the Stakeholders?

A recurring theme in the preceding chapters is the large number of diverse stakeholders in the public services, holding a vast range of expectations. This means that setting explicit objectives for many services is fraught with difficulty, and is the main reason for the lack of consensus as to what constitutes the components of outcome. Indeed it has been noted that there may even be reasons why politicians should wish to retain a degree of ambiguity about the purpose of the services under their control – as Disraeli commented, 'finality is not the language of politics'. It is therefore to be expected that any outcome measurement scheme which is to be used in the political process should retain a high degree of flexibility.

12.4 Outcome in the Public Sector – the State of the Art

The findings of my colleagues can be explored under three headings, requiring progressively more research effort to disentangle:

(a) the *concept* of outcome: what are the various dimensions of society likely to be affected by the programme under investigation?;
(b) the *measurement* of outcome: how might it be possible to quantify achievement along the dimensions identified?;
(c) the *analysis* of outcome: to what extent is it possible to interpret the outcome measures identified above?

For many programmes, progress in outcome research has barely reached stage (a): identifying the relevant concept of outcome. As a preliminary, this requires an analysis of the objectives of the service. Where stakeholders are easily identifiable, this may be straightforward. In health care, for example, patients are likely to value increases in the length and quality of life. However, even where the immediate beneficiaries are quite easy to identify, it can be surprisingly difficult to isolate objectives. For example, in community care it is not at all clear what long-run objectives are held by users and their carers.

However, if dimensions of outcome can be identified, the next stage is to seek to measure progress along those dimensions. Here, much depends on the extent to which output measures can be interpreted as reasonable proxies for outcome. Thus, for example, in the university sector, a vast apparatus has been set in place to measure and interpret research and teaching output. In social security, on the other hand, qualitative approaches to the analysis of the outcome of benefit payments may be more appropriate, and so the process of measurement is much less well developed.

Finally, even if outcome can be measured, there remains the problem of analysis – of identifying to what extent the outcome is the result of public sector activities. In secondary education, advanced multi-level statistical techniques can now be used to isolate with some precision the impact of teachers and schools from all the other social influences on educational attainment. In other areas – such as criminal justice – it is almost impossible to start thinking about how the joint efforts of the police, the courts, the probation service and the prison service combine with external factors to affect the nature of criminal activity.

In spite of the evident progress made in some areas, the general tenor of our findings is that analysis of outcome is in its infancy, and in many cases may never be tractable. This result is hardly surprising. Even in the private sector, although there may be a need from a marketing perspective to understand what customers value about the product, there is no need systematically to identify and quantify the outcome for customers. Consider, for example, the evaluation of the performance of a restaurant. Customers are likely to have a variety of reasons for dining there. These might include meeting friends; avoiding cooking at home; enjoying a gastronomic experience; satisfying nutritional requirements; making business deals; being seen at a fashionable venue; and so on. However, it is not necessarily the case that the successful restaurant should have to identify what these components of outcome are. Indeed, customers may very well not be able to articulate why they patronize the restaurant (customer surveys are notoriously difficult to design and interpret). Ultimately what matters is that customers – whatever their reasons – continue to be willing to pay for the restaurant's product. Any performance measures that are developed – such as indicators of quality – should therefore be indicative of a continuing willingness to pay. The consequent financial transaction offers an incontrovertible measure of the valuation placed on the restaurant's product.

'Outcome' is the analogous valuation placed by society on the activities of the public sector. Yet what our investigations have shown is that – just as in the private sector – there is no consensus as to what constitutes outcome. And crucially there is no financial transaction to act as the final arbiter. The closest analogy to the endorsement offered by a willingness to pay is – at best – the vote wielded by the electorate, and more general political action. However such activity is at best a very imperfect benchmark of public satisfaction. Realistically, therefore, the analyst examining outcome has no option but to delve directly into the preferences and perceptions of all those with a legitimate interest in the public sector.

12.5 Action on Outcome Measures

Perhaps the least developed aspect of researchers' thinking about outcome is the use to which any measures might be put. That is, using the framework of the control model presented in Chapter 1, most commentators have thought very hard about the *measurement* stage of control, and some have moved on to examine the *analysis* stage. Few, however, have had an opportunity to think about the *action* stage of control. Yet in some ways this is the key aspect of the control system. If we can measure and interpret but have no mechanism for changing the system then the entire outcome measurement exercise is futile.

Action on the basis of outcome measures can take a number of forms. If the measures are being used for research purposes, perhaps to inform policy makers about the relative merits of alternative modes of delivering services, then the action to be taken may be fairly straightforward, entailing persuading those delivering services to adopt the favoured methods.

If, on the other hand, the outcome measures are being used to help stakeholders form a judgment about managerial competence, then the actions to be taken are less clear cut. The role of outcome measures may be amongst the following:

- helping users to choose the relevant provider: for example, helping parents to select a school, or students to select a university;
- helping purchasers to select a provider on behalf of users: for example, guiding the referral practices of general practitioners, or the placing of community care contracts by local authorities;
- helping central authorities to control devolved units within an organization: for example, helping the Benefits Agency to control its local offices;
- helping politicians control the managers of services for which they are responsible: for example, helping housing authority members to secure control of their housing maintenance department;
- helping electors to vote.

This incomplete list illustrates the rich network of agency relationships that exists in the public sector. Outcome measures should play an important role in servicing those relationships. Yet frequently little thought has been given as to how outcome data can be presented and analysed so as to maximize the benefits to users. A striking example of this was the insistence of the British Government that only raw examination results should be made available to parents as a guide to choosing schools. Such data are of limited usefulness to parents, who want to know what educational value the school is likely to contribute to their own child's attainments.

Furthermore, by adopting a user perspective one can also begin to see gaps in the control mechanisms currently in place. The UK has a peculiarly centralized and bureaucratic public sector. Local authorities are weak, and subject to intense central scrutiny and control. Some important local services, such as benefits offices and the National Health Service, are central government hierarchies. As a result, individual citizens often have very few mechanisms for securing change in their local public services, and therefore have few incentives to scrutinize information about them. This state of affairs has led to the establishment of expert intermediaries, acting on behalf of local people, in the form in England and Wales of the Audit Commission. While the efforts of bodies such as this are often helpful in improving public services, their very existence betrays a lack of confidence in the ability of citizens to make sensible contributions to the shaping of local services.

It may be fanciful, but none the less instructive, to consider whether there are circumstances in which the panoply of outcome measurement becomes redundant because citizens take an active role in the public services they fund

(Etzioni, 1968). A more active citizenry may be able to gauge the satisfaction of stakeholders with services accurately, without recourse to outcome measures. Through its political actions it may then be able to insist that services are delivered efficiently. This would of course require mechanisms to be put in place to encourage citizens to take the necessary interest. The current obsession with performance measurement may therefore be a symptom of weaknesses in the existing democratic processes.

12.6 Conclusions

Much research on outcome tends to focus on a phenomenon of interest, then seeks to measure the phenomenon, and finally attempts to analyse the results. The implications of the discussion in this chapter are that the perspective should be shifted. As a preliminary, researchers should be asking themselves the following questions. Why is a measure of outcome needed? Who will use it? What actions can they take in response to reported outcome? What will be the impact on the user (and therefore on the service) of particular outcome measures? The proper framework for analysing these questions is a model of control, of the sort set out in Chapter 1. If any of the components of control – measurement, analysis or action – is seriously faulty, then reporting the outcome of activity is likely to lead to unexpected and possibly dysfunctional consequences (Smith, 1995). If, on the other hand, the measurement of outcome is viewed within a comprehensive model of control, then the result could be a substantial improvement in the effectiveness of the public services which are so essential to the proper functioning of society.

I therefore strongly believe that the search for better measurement practices should be continued with vigour. However, there is never likely to be an easy answer to the problem of evaluating outcome. It is important that those who use outcome measures should be made aware of their limitations, and should be encouraged to use them with discretion. Just because we cannot measure an outcome does not mean that it has no value. After all, the world would be a much poorer place without its scientific, artistic and cultural heritage, much of it arising from the activities of the state. Only a small proportion of that heritage might now be in place if a narrow view of measured outcome had been applied to the decisions taken by our forebears.

References

Etzioni, A. (1968) *The Active Society: a Theory of Societal and Political Processes*, New York: Free Press.

Smith, P. (1995) 'On the unintended consequences of publishing performance data in the public sector', *International Journal of Public Administration*, **18**, pp. 277–310.
Stewart, J. and Walsh, K. (1995) 'Performance measurement: when performance can never be finally defined', *Public Money and Management*, **14** (2).

Notes on Contributors

Rebecca Boden is a Senior Lecturer in the Department of Accounting and Finance, University of Sheffield. Her main interests include financial reporting and the self-employed, taxation, public sector accounting and the role of accountancy within public sector management. Since 1990 she has engaged in collaborative research with Anne Corden at the University of York looking at low-income self-employment, first with regard to family credit and currently in the area of child support. Previous publications with Anne Corden include *Measuring Low Incomes: Self-employment and Family Credit* (HMSO, 1994). She has also worked on women and taxation, the use of compliance cost-assessment techniques in public sector management, and the role of accountancy in the management of public sector services.

Laura Bouwknecht was a research student from the Department of Household and Consumer Studies, Wageningen Agricultural University, The Netherlands visiting the Department of Social Policy Work, University of York. She has now returned to The Netherlands.

Jonathan Bradshaw is Professor of Social Policy at the University of York. He is Head of the Department of Social Policy and Social Work, Director of the Institute for Research in the Social Sciences and Associate Director of the Social Policy Research Unit. He is co-director of the EU Observatory on National Family Policies. His main interests are in poverty and living standards, social security policy, family policy and demographic change and social policy. His current research includes comparative studies of social security arrangements, a comparative study of lone parents' labour supply and a national survey of fathers living apart from their children in the UK. He is Chair of North Yorkshire Welfare Benefits Unit.

Roy Carr-Hill is a Senior Research Fellow in the Centre for Health Economics, University of York. After degrees in mathematics and philosophy, training as a social worker, a Master's course in criminology in political theory, and a doctorate in penology, Roy's first academic appointment was to an interdisciplinary post at the University of Sussex in the School of Social Sciences. During that time, he also worked as a consultant with the Organization for Economic Cooperation and Development (OECD) to write *Indicators of the Performance of Educational Systems* published in 1972. He was subsequently appointed to the OECD as Administrator in the Social Indicator Development Programme based on Social Concerns agreed by the Council of Ministers, where he worked between 1974 and 1977 to produce criteria for the measurement of the quality of life and specific measures across a wide range of topics. Since that time he has retained an active interest in the area whilst working on education and health both in Europe and developing countries, publishing, for example, a book on *Social Conditions in Sub-Saharan Africa*. He has recently worked as a consultant for the Statistical Commission of the European Communities (Eurostat) as a preliminary to developing a system of social indicators across the countries of the EU; and is currently under contract to develop possible measures of 'social exclusion' for them.

Anne Corden is a Research Fellow in the Social Policy Research Unit at the University of York, where her work focuses on social security policy. Her main areas of interest include poverty and low incomes, the administration and delivery of benefits, means-testing and take-up, and financial support for carers. Since 1990 she has conducted collaborative work with co-author Rebecca Boden in a programme of research on low-income self-employment. Previous publications include *Measuring Low Incomes: Self-employment and Family Credit* 1994 (with Boden, R.) and *Changing Perspectives on Benefit Take-up*, (HMSO, 1995).

Huw Dixon was born in 1958, and studied PPE at Balliol College Oxford before doing his D.Phil at Nuffield College Oxford. In 1983 he became a lecturer at Birkbeck College London, and in 1987 a reader at Essex. In 1990 he obtained a chair at University College Swansea, before taking up a chair in York in 1992. He has published 42 journal articles and chapters in the area of imperfect competition at the microeconomic and the macroeconomic level. His current interests focus on the application of evolutionary ideas to economics.

A. J. Fowles worked in the Home Office Research Unit before moving to the University of York in 1977, where he is responsible for teaching courses on crime and the criminal justice system, youth policy and policy analysis in the Department of Social Policy and Social Work. He has written on prisoners' rights, mentally abnormal offenders, public expenditure on the criminal justice system, and on the development of analysis of 'total' institutions.

Hilary Holmes is a part-time research fellow in the Department of Social Policy and Social Work at the University of York. Her previous research includes work on the living standards of unemployed families and comparative research on child benefits and lone parents labour supply.

Meg Huby is a Senior Lecturer in the Development of Social Policy and Social Work at the University of York. From an original background in biology and mathematics she worked in research in politics, tropical rainforest ecology, health economics and overseas development before settling down to social policy in 1989. Her research on the DSS Social Fund was carried out at the Social Policy Research Unit and she now lectures in social security policy, research methods and social policy and the environment. Currently her main research interests are in water poverty and in HIV risk from illegal drug use.

Peter A. Kemp has been a Professor of Housing and Urban Studies at the University of Glasgow since January 1996. Prior to that he was the Joseph Rowntree Professor of Housing Policy, and founding Director of the Centre for Housing Policy, at the University of York. His research interests include housing benefit, privately rented housing, and the history of housing. He has also undertaken research on homelessness and the management of social rented housing.

John Lintott has been at South Bank University, London since 1986, where he is currently Senior Lecturer in Economics. Previously, he worked for the OECD's Social Indicator programme (1974–7), completed a Ph.D on National Accounting at the University of London (1982), and has taught both Economics and Statistics and Research Methods in a number of UK higher education institutions. His main research interests are social and economic statistics and ecological economics.

Andrew Nocon is a Research Fellow at the Social Policy Research Unit, University of York. He has carried out research on collaboration between health and local authorities, the impact for social services of GPs' assessments of older people, and the social support needs of physically and sensorily disabled people. He has a professional background in social work.

Hazel Qureshi is Assistant Director of the Social Policy Research Unit, University of York. Her research interests centre on the evaluation of community care services and the roles of family and professional carers. She has published widely in this area. Currently she is working on ways in which social services departments can develop regular and routine ways of assessing outcomes for service users and their carers.

Ana Rico is an Associate Professor of the Economics of Organizations in the Department of Business Administration at the Carlos III University of Madrid.

Her academic qualifications include a BSc in Sociology from the Universidad Complutense, Madrid, an MA in Social Sciences from the Instituto Juan March, Madrid, and an MSc in Health Economics from the University of York. Her PhD examined the impact of health care decentralization in Spain, and her principal research interest is now in the organization of health care services.

Peter Smith is Reader in Economics, Finance and Accountancy at the University of York. Previously he has worked as a management consultant to local and central government, and as an advisor to many other governmental organizations. His principal research interests are local government finance, health services resource allocation and public sector performance measurement.

John Suckling was born in Leeds in 1944 and was educated at the University College of Rhodesia and Nyasaland, LSE and Simon Fraser University (Vancouver). He is currently a Lecturer in the Department of Economics at the University of York. He has acted as consultant to the ILO, and was Visiting Professor at Lehigh University (Pennsylvania) in 1984. He has published on the labour managed firm, southern Africa and health economics.

Alan Williams is (part-time) Professor of Economics and Director of the Research Group on the Measurement and Valuation of Health at the Centre for Health Economics at the University of York. He had previously worked in HM Treasury Centre for Administrative Studies on the economic evaluation of a variety of public services, and served on the Royal Commission on the NHS, and on various research committees concerned with health and health care.

Index